BERLIN NOW

ise for *Berlin Now*

er Schneider makes the city come alive. He knows his stuff and shares it
utifully, elegantly, generously and informatively. Berlin has found its bard'
ten Breytenbach, author of *Notes from the Middle World*

nsightful. Schneider presents his collected musings about the city that has
'red and perplexed him since he was first seduced by West Berlin as a
man' *Booklist*, starred review

tening. Berlin resident Schneider unearths the city's charms and
... [to] reveal an authentic city that does not bother being more
'an beautiful' *Publishers Weekly*

The Wall Jumper

l' Ian McEwan

... creates, in very few words, the unreal reality of Berlin'
shdie

ABOUT THE AUTHOR

Peter Schneider was born in Lübeck, Germany, in 1940, and has lived in Berlin on and off since the 1960s, when he was a key spokesperson for its radical student movement. Renowned as a novelist and essayist, he is the author of more than twenty books, including the Penguin Modern Classic *The Wall Jumper*. He has taught at many universities, including Stanford, Princeton and Harvard, and written for many international newspapers, including *Der Spiegel*, *The New York Times*, *Le Monde* and *La Repubblica*.

Sophie Schlondorff is a translator, editor and writer. Originally from New York, she grew up bilingual in English and German and is fluent in French and Italian. She is a graduate of Yale University and has been living abroad for more than a decade, in Paris, Rome and Berlin.

BERLIN NOW

The Rise of the City and the Fall of the Wall

Peter Schneider

Translated from the German by Sophie Schlondorff

PENGUIN BOOKS

PENGUIN BOOKS

Published by the Penguin Group
Penguin Books Ltd, 80 Strand, London WC2R 0RL, England
Penguin Group (USA) Inc., 375 Hudson Street, New York, New York 10014, USA
Penguin Group (Canada), 90 Eglinton Avenue East, Suite 700, Toronto, Ontario, Canada M4P 2Y3
(a division of Pearson Penguin Canada Inc.)
Penguin Ireland, 25 St Stephen's Green, Dublin 2, Ireland
(a division of Penguin Books Ltd)
Penguin Group (Australia), 707 Collins Street, Melbourne, Victoria 3008, Australia
(a division of Pearson Australia Group Pty Ltd)
Penguin Books India Pvt Ltd, 11 Community Centre, Panchsheel Park, New Delhi – 110 017, India
Penguin Group (NZ), 67 Apollo Drive, Rosedale, Auckland 0632, New Zealand
(a division of Pearson New Zealand Ltd)
Penguin Books (South Africa) (Pty) Ltd, Block D, Rosebank Office Park,
181 Jan Smuts Avenue, Pa⋯

Penguin Books Ltd, Regi⋯

www.penguin.com

First published by Farrar,⋯
Published in Penguin Bo⋯
001

Copyright © Peter Schne⋯
Translation copyright © ⋯
All rights reserved

Portions of this book orig⋯
in Der Tagesspiegel, Der ⋯

Printed in Great Britain b⋯

ISBN: 978-0-241-97083-6

www.greenpenguin.co.uk

MIX
Paper from
responsible sources
FSC
www.fsc.org   FSC™ C018179

Penguin Books is committed to a sustainable
future for our business, our readers and our planet.
This book is made from Forest Stewardship
Council™ certified paper.

CONTENTS

BERLIN NOW

CINDERELLA BERLIN

It isn't all that easy to answer the question of why, for some time now, Berlin has been one of the most popular cities in the world. It's not on account of its beauty, for Berlin is not beautiful; Berlin is the Cinderella of European capitals.

Gazing out from a roof deck here, you won't see anything like the domes of Rome, the zinc roofs of Paris, or the architectural canyons of New York. There is nothing spectacular, in any way exciting—or even atrocious—about the view. No pool on the seventy-second floor, no palm garden at a dizzying height, no penthouse casino high above the rooftops promising an exhilarating plunge from the terrace to the gambler who has just suffered an unbearable loss. What unfolds before the viewer is a homogenous cityscape of four-to-six-story buildings whose red pitched roofs didn't originally come equipped with penthouses or sumptuous roof decks. It was only thirty years ago, not long before the fall of the Wall, that West Berliners discovered that life above the city's chestnut and linden trees was significantly better than life in their shadow. Tentatively, they began to carve windows and terraces into the roofs. This is where they now dwell, at a modest height, between the occasional hotel and office high-rise, whose architecture on the whole seems to have been inspired by a shoe box stood on its end. To the west, the Eiffel Tower's little brother, known as the Funkturm (Radio Tower), rises above the sea of buildings; to the east, the 1,207-foot-tall Fernsehturm (TV Tower) glimmers on the horizon, the afternoon sunlight etching a gleaming cross into its steel sphere—much to the ire of its communist builders, who erected the tower to prove the "victoriousness of socialism." Quick-witted Berliners christened the luminous cross "the Pope's revenge." The apparition proved as intractable as it was inexplicable—nothing could be done to get rid of it. It presaged the future: the end of the German Democratic Republic.

Those living in the new city center, Mitte, had to wait for Berlin's two halves to be reunified before converting their attics. Admittedly, they have the better view. They look out onto several metropolitan icons: the gilded dome of the reconstructed synagogue near Hackescher Markt and, beyond that, the Reichstag, its historical weight lightened by Sir Norman Foster's addition of a glass dome, and the restored horse-drawn chariot of the Brandenburg Gate, swept clean of the dust of the East German era. Even farther in the distance, Helmut Jahn's circus tent and the towers of Renzo Piano and Hans Kollhoff rise from what used to be Berlin's most prominent vacant lot, Potsdamer Platz.

Yet, to date, no urban climber has deemed any of these new high-rises worthy of scaling. No Philippe Petit has thought to stretch a cable between the office towers at Potsdamer Platz and to balance back and forth across it. A city in which a new, 389.8-foot-tall hotel (the Waldorf Astoria) sets a record for height is not exactly a magnet for extreme athletes. Compared to the skylines of Manhattan, Chicago, or even Frankfurt, Berlin's newly populated horizon still comes across as the silhouette of a provincial capital. In every other way as well, seen from above, Berlin lacks everything that makes a big city. It has no financial district like Manhattan or London, no venerable, centuries-old cathedral like Cologne or Paris, no notorious nightlife district like Hamburg. Even Berlin's "Eiffel Tower"—the aforementioned Radio Tower—is merely a modest copy of the Paris original.

A friend of mine from Rome, the writer Edoardo Albinati, told me about his first time in Berlin. In the 1990s, he got off a train at the Zoo station in former West Berlin and took a look around. What he saw was the bleak station square with its currency-exchange offices and snack bars, the war-damaged steeple of the Gedächtniskirche (Kaiser Wilhelm Memorial Church), the Bilka department store with its decorative façade—once considered bold—of crisscrossing diagonal parallel lines, the Zoo Palast movie house emblazoned with a painted poster of an American action film. Yet, no matter where he turned, no soothing arch, dome, steeple, or façade presented itself for his spoiled Italian eyes to rest on. The way the square turned his gaze back on himself was the only thing that struck him as noteworthy. A few walks around the city tempered his opinion somewhat, but it never gave way to a sense of well-being. Berlin, he confessed to me with a polite smile, was by far the ugliest capital he had ever seen.

Now, however, tens of thousands of Italians flock to Berlin every year, filling the streets of the northern metropolis with the melodious sounds of their language. On New Year's Eve, when temperatures are in the teens outside and the locals prefer to stay at home in front of the TV, hordes of Italian tourists swarm to the Brandenburg Gate to usher in the New Year with Berlin's famous fireworks—forbidden in Rome! And when natives of New York, Tel Aviv, or Rome ask me where I'm from and I allude to Berlin, their eyes instantly light up with curiosity, not to say enthusiasm. Without the slightest hesitation, they'll go on to tell me about their most recent or upcoming trip to Berlin—yet won't be able to tell me why they have fallen in love with this city of all places. They may bring up the ritual word "beautiful," but it doesn't really capture what it is that attracts them to the city. Mention the name of any other, far more beautiful European city and you won't get the same reaction.

If beauty isn't the point, then what is? When I ask any twentysomething, irrespective of nationality, the answer is obvious. Berlin is the only major city without a mandatory closing time, where you can eat and/or get wasted for ten to twenty euros, and where the S-Bahn will get you to any club, even at four in the morning. Is that it? Not entirely. Part of Berlin's appeal also seems to be its history—both the good and the atrocious: Berlin, "the world metropolis of the 1920s," home to an international bohemian crowd; Berlin, the "capital of the Third Reich," where the most egregious crimes of the last century were hatched; Berlin, "the Wall city," divided for twenty-eight years before finally being re-unified. Hardly any other city has experienced such extreme transformation in the last hundred years.

It is a truly astounding oversight that city officials failed to ensure that a thirty-yard section of the border area—including the watchtowers, dog runs, and mine-strewn "death strip" secured on the East Berlin side by a rear wall known as the *Hinterlandmauer*—was preserved for posterity. After all, the average tourist doesn't come to hear the Berlin Philharmonic play or to go to the Pergamon Museum—he wants to see the Wall. The Wall is quite simply Berlin's most famous monument—the German counterpart to the Statue of Liberty!

On the other hand, to be fair to the authorities, protecting even the tiniest section of the Wall in the wild days after November 9, 1989, would have been impossible. For weeks, tens of thousands of Berlin natives and visitors from around the world laid into the monstrosity with hammers and chisels. What would they have said if police had cordoned off a section of the Wall, under orders to protect it as a designated landmark? With what images and headlines would the international media have met such an attempt? Something along the lines of: EAST GERMAN BORDER TROOPS GIVE UP—WALL NOW GUARDED BY WEST BERLIN POLICE!

By now, Berlin's tourism managers have realized that monuments commemorating crimes are not the least of the city's attractions. Year after year, the Holocaust Memorial registers well over a million visitors; in 2011, 650,000 people gaped at the newly completed Berlin Wall Memorial on Bernauer Straße; that same year, 340,000 tourists chose to visit the Berlin-Hohenschönhausen Memorial (the special prison complex of the East German secret service), where they listened to former inmates describe what they had been forced to endure in Stasi prison cells and interrogations. Today, half of Berlin's tourists come from abroad, and their numbers continue to grow every year. Forecasts already predict that the city, which currently counts 25 million overnight visitors, could soon catch up with Paris (37 million overnight visitors), thus making it second only to London. Whether Berlin's tourism professionals like it or not, the dark episodes of the city's past are part of its appeal. We should consider ourselves lucky that the Führerbunker is no longer accessible, because if it were, rest assured it would have joined the ranks of Berlin's "tourist attractions"— certainly no later than after the release of *Downfall*, the film about Hitler's final days. Fortunately, the entrances to the 29,000-square-foot complex, which the Red Army tried in vain to demolish, were built over. Today, the site is identified by an inconspicuous information plaque, installed by the Berliner Unterwelten (Berlin Underworlds) association on June 8, 2006, the day before the start of the soccer World Cup.

To this day, the destruction of the old cityscape in the wake of two dictatorships still marks the architecture of Berlin—despite and because of so many fresh starts. Yet this defect does nothing to detract from the curiosity of visitors from around the world. What attracts them to Berlin seems to be precisely what they feel is missing in more beautiful cities: the weirdness, perpetual incompleteness, and outlandishness of Berlin—and the liveliness inherent in these qualities. Berlin was "condemned forever to becoming and never to being," the writer Karl Scheffler wrote in his 1910 polemic *Berlin, ein Stadtschicksal* (Berlin: Fate of a City). Scheffler described Berlin as an urban landscape "defined by a fundamental lack of organically developed structure."

While Scheffler may have identified Berlin's genetic code, he vastly underestimated its advantages. Imperfection, incompleteness—not to say ugliness—afford a sense of freedom that compact beauty never can. Young visitors to a beautiful, expensive, and perfectly restored city feel excluded. Looking around, it is clear to them: every space here is already occupied. Cinderella Berlin offers an inestimable advantage over these princess cities: it gives all newcomers the feeling that there is still room for them, that they can still make something of themselves here. It is this peculiarity that makes Berlin the capital of creative people from around the world today.

Twenty years ago, right after the fall of the Wall, I wrote a small series of articles for the German weekly *Der Spiegel* about Berlin and its impending reconstruction. I wanted to find out what city planners and architects had in mind for "my city." One of my most important sources at the time was a leading expert on Berlin: the publisher and journalist Wolf Jobst Siedler. I remember a walk we took together along the Kurfürstendamm in former West Berlin. At Lehniner Platz we turned onto Cicerostraße, a quiet side street off the Kurfürstendamm. The housing complex there, with its wavelike curved façades, had been built by the great architect Erich Mendelsohn in the 1920s. "There's no doubt," Siedler remarked, "that this is one of the most beautiful housing complexes in Berlin. But take a closer look. The entire complex is dead, a paradise for retirees, no matter how many young people may live here. There are no stores, no bars, no place for life outside the apartments. Only the tennis courts inside the complex provide any room to breathe."

As it happened, I knew exactly what Siedler was taking about. I had spent a good part of my Berlin life on those nine tennis courts, surrounded by tall poplar trees, just a five-minute walk from my apartment. In the extreme quiet of Mendelsohn's complex, the tennis players' serves rang out like shots fired in a civil war, provoking regular complaints from the residents. Not to mention the stridently performed arguments between players over whether a ball was out or had just managed to touch the line.

"In Berlin, you'll find you often have to choose between the beauty of a place and its liveliness," remarked Siedler, whose books conjure Berlin's forgotten and mistreated treasures with virtually unparalleled eloquence.

It's probably because of Berlin that this statement has stayed with me more than any other I heard during the course of my research. For beauty and liveliness rarely go hand in hand in this city.

But enough with the speculation and reminiscing. Instead, let me tell a story I just heard. My son and two of his friends recently moved into a cheap apartment on the top floor of a building in the Berlin-Neukölln district. Until recently, Neukölln, with the highest unemployment rate in Berlin (17 percent) and its predominantly Muslim population, was considered a doomed neighborhood. But my son and his friends put their money on Neukölln—because, in the meantime, young people from neighboring districts, who had inadvertently found themselves at the center of the city after the fall of the Wall and could no longer afford the rents, had moved there and opened Internet start-ups, fledgling galleries, even a few gourmet restaurants.

The uncle of one of my son's friends gave them a three-seater leather sofa for their new apartment. They were dead set on transporting the massive thing home that same day. But night had already fallen, and the moving-van rental places were all closed. So the three young men heaved the sofa out of the uncle's apartment and onto the street, carrying it three blocks on their heads to the nearest S-Bahn station. On the way, they paused by a fountain on a square, plopped down onto the sofa, returned the greetings of passersby, and indulged in a few swigs of schnapps from the bottle they'd brought along. Nobody stopped them when they carried the sofa up the stairs to the tracks of the turnstile-free S-Bahn station. When the train arrived and the automatic doors opened, ·

they shoved the couch into the car. Miraculously, it fit perfectly. The three young men sat down in their comfortable seats to enjoy the ride. Several passengers laughed, others offered to trade places with them, finally the entire car broke into applause: *"Das ist Berlin!"*—"That's Berlin!"—one of them shouted and everyone followed suit. *"Das ist Berlin!"* resounded throughout the car.

The hardest part of the operation came after the S-Bahn ride: the three friends had to carry the couch several blocks and up five flights of stairs to their apartment. They succeeded because they had to succeed. They almost broke down trying to navigate the mammoth sofa past the narrow landings, but they never once doubted that their endeavor would end in triumph. When they finally made it to the top, they set the behemoth down in their apartment, helped themselves to their well-stocked liquor cabinet, and toasted first to themselves, then to Berlin, before falling asleep on the couch.

THE GREAT AWAKENING

Images from the night of November 9 to 10, 1989, have gone down in the annals of history. For the first time, the world saw Germans relaxed, celebrating, and dancing, and celebrated with them. For a while, Hollywood's blond German clicking his heels together and shouting "At your orders, *Obersturmbannführer!*" disappeared into the archives. Less well known, photographed, and written about than the fall of the Wall, however, is what followed in the months and years after this historic date: the gradual coalescing of the city into one.

The opening of the Wall was like an awakening after a long sleep—for the eastern half of the divided city in particular. As though touched by a magic wand, the numb, giant body began to stir and, taking an enormous breath, burst out of the shackles of reinforced concrete, barbed wire, and iron bars that the communist regime had placed on it. The severed veins and limbs of the divided city fused back together with astonishing speed. Streets in West Berlin suddenly extended to the east again, though at first they had to coexist with the unfamiliar names of their recovered eastern halves. The sealed-off S- and U-Bahn stations at the border, which trains had rumbled through without stopping for twenty-eight years, were put back into service. Bridges, squares, and properties searched for and found their other halves. The chain-link fences in the canals, installed by the East German border police after the Wall was built to ensure that all underground escape routes were blocked, were cleared away. Even the water in the Spree River and in Berlin's canals and lakes suddenly seemed to flow more freely once the border buoys and armed police that had guarded them were gone. The sky, yes, even the sky over Berlin suddenly seemed bluer and less gray when it rained. Berlin's once famous air—which a resourceful entrepreneur had sold in cans in the 1920s—seemed easier to breathe again after November 10. It was an illusion, of course. Yet reality and illusion converged surprisingly quickly in the years that followed. In the 1980s, the air in Berlin had in fact reached almost Chinese levels of pollution as a result of East Germany's unfiltered factories and East Berlin's stoves, which were predominantly fueled by brown coal. After re-unification, East Germany's biggest polluters were shut down or equipped with filter systems. Suddenly, there was a hint of cocaine in the Berlin air.

Residents' reflexes failed to keep in step with the precipitous changes. I remember how, even years after the fall of the Wall, I still had trouble taking the new, direct routes to East Berlin. The inner compass I had developed while the city was divided automatically guided me and my car along detours to the transit points I had used during the years of the Wall. Again and again, much to my frustration, I would find myself taking the old detours. Nothing seemed more difficult to me than driving straight from west to east.

As for the obtuseness of my reflexes, it was only when I happened to see a made-for-TV movie on the Bavarian television network that I finally felt understood. The film captured the baffling behavior of deer on the Bavarian–Czech border. It showed how, in the 1990s, stags and deer continued to stop and turn around instinctively when they reached the border, even though it had long since been cleared of barbed wire. The strangest thing, according to the film's narrator, was that even young animals that had never encountered this fence displayed the same behavior as their parents. He wondered whether such learned reflexes are passed on from one generation to the next. Was it possible that the parents' experience of the border might continue to affect the next generation and maybe even the one after that?

Berlin has often been compared to New York—Berliners appreciate the comparison, New Yorkers consider it slightly presumptuous. It's obvious that the comparison can refer only to the energy of the two cities, not to their outward appearance. And as far as the Berlin lifestyle is concerned, it's more reminiscent of the Manhattan of twenty years ago—before Rudolph Giuliani came along.

There is another American city that has a lot in common with Berlin, though the comparison is not as flattering as the one to New York. This was brought home quite strikingly to visitors of the photography exhibit *The Ruins of Detroit*, held in Berlin in the spring of 2012. Massively enlarged prints of the photographs of the French photo artists Romain Meffre and Yves Marchand presented the dilapidated icons of the city of Detroit: the derelict main waiting room of Michigan Central Station; the sumptuous auditorium of the United Artists Theatre, cofounded by Charlie Chaplin; the abandoned factory workshop of a company that used to produce car bodies for Detroit's auto manufacturers; the magnificent interior of the National Theatre, where only adult films were still being shown when it was finally shut down for good in the 1970s. In the dust and rubble of these crumbling spaces you could sense and feel the dreams and will to power of the builders of Detroit, but also the sweat and longings of the thousands upon thousands of people who had worked there. Only the magnificently designed arched ceilings with their brightly colored arabesques had defied decay. The photographs showed a city—brought forth by the industrial era and once representative of the splendor and power of the United States—in the process of becoming mummified. Cities, the images announced, are far more vulnerable and ephemeral than people. In the span of a single human lifetime, they can transform beyond recognition—and more than just once, at that. Indeed, over the course of my years in Berlin, I have witnessed two or three versions of the city and I find it difficult to remember the "original" Berlin I arrived in by train from the West more than half a century ago.

But it was only the space in which they were exhibited that truly brought out the poetry in these images of Detroit. The exhibition was held inside a brick building at the Gleisdreieck (literally "railway triangle," the junction between three elevated train lines), in Berlin's first Kühlhaus, or refrigerated warehouse, where, for more than a hundred years, meat and produce had been stored. The companies that had kept their goods here had moved out during the last century, in the 1970s, abandoning the building to itself. The new operators, a cultural manager named Jochen Hahn and the general manager Cornelia Albrecht, had found investors to back their plan of turning the Kühlhaus into a sort of ice-breaking meeting point for the fledgling Berlin scene: a lounge downstairs, a gallery and a dance floor in the middle, and a theater upstairs. To this end, they had broken through several stories of the enormous building, formerly subdivided into numerous room-size cooling units, tearing down walls and ceilings until light, air, height, and breadth prevailed. In the vast hall created by these renovations, the photographic swansongs of old Detroit now hung. It was a congenial location for the exhibition: in the midst of the city of Berlin, just reawakened from a deep freeze, the ruins of an American pioneer city were on display. More and more young people crowded into the Kühlhaus, which until recently no one had even heard of. A DJ took over, bombarding the audience and photos with sound. It wasn't long before people began to dance, demonstrating their will to live in the midst of these melancholy images of Berlin's urban twin, Detroit.

Downstairs, back outside, there it was again, suddenly: the city I remembered. Across from the Kühlhaus, the glaring neon sign of a new hotel called the Mercure cut through the darkness. Its western face was a windowless firewall, every inch of which had been covered with spray paint. Themes typical of the mural graffiti of the 1980s were visible: a bare-breasted "nature girl" in the depths of a jungle with a big city skyline in the background and, reigning over it all a massive likeness of Karl Marx. A seedy parking lot spread out at the base of the firewall, bordered at its other end by another firewall. On the elevated tracks to the left an S-Bahn glided by. In the narrowly defined triangle above me—between the elevated railway, Mercure Hotel, and Kühlhaus—I could make out two infinitely distant pale stars in the January night sky. It had always seemed to me that the stars over Berlin were billions of miles farther away than above any other city. And never more so than in January.

The Kühlhaus is one of those new icons that draw young people from around the world to Berlin. It doesn't follow in the footsteps of the tourist attractions included in travel guides—Museum Island, the Berlin Philharmonic, the Brandenburg Gate. Nor does it take its cue from the lights of the once again glittering Friedrichstraße and Potsdamer Platz. When it comes to magnificent boulevards, every major city in Europe has something similar—or better—to offer. What's distinctive about Berlin are the warehouses and industrial ruins from which the city is recreating itself. There's no doubt: over the last fifteen years, some of the best architects in the world have built in Berlin and occasionally—though not always—constructed something great. But these buildings bear no real relation to the new dynamics of Berlin, to the city's severed soul. The landmarks of Berlin are old gasometers and water towers, deserted hospitals, disused airports, onetime docks, vacant train stations, abandoned CIA surveillance facilities and Stasi prisons, moldy bunker and tunnel complexes from two dictatorships, and warehouses of all kinds. This is where new life takes root. And, now as ever, the city's forgery-proof watermarks are thirty-yard-high windowless firewalls, buckling cobble-stone sidewalks, overgrown tracks, disused sky-high smokestacks with red aircraft warning lights flashing at the top at night, narrow courtyards with a single chestnut tree. No, Berlin neither wants to be, nor for the time being will it be, a proper capital. And maybe that's why Berlin is so popular.

But for how much longer? International investors, who make decisions based on helicopter flyovers or Google Maps and Street View, have long since discovered the new lairs and palaces of the creative set and added them to their must-have portfolios. It seems inevitable: ten to fifteen years from now, Berlin will be as expensive as New York or London. Bankers and hedge-fund managers will move into the gasometers, cooling and water towers, and warehouses that the pioneers of the new Berlin have made livable with the help of stolen planks and beams, used water joints and doorknobs, salvaged radiators, and tapped electric meters. The new owners will retrofit the abandoned lofts with marble bathtubs, safes, electronically controlled kitchens, private gyms, and swimming pools, and install helipads on the roofs. Then Berlin will become just as grand, expensive, and boring as most capitals of the western world are today. Berlin's mayors won't stand in the way of this development, because, like their colleagues in Manhattan and London, they will be blinded by the promise of high tax revenues. For now, Berlin is still considered an insider's tip for artists from around the globe. They arrive here from Manhattan, San Francisco, and Los Angeles, from Hong Kong, Tokyo, and Seoul. But as soon as only bankers, stockbrokers, and the international jet set can afford apartments and lofts in a city, the creative types move on. My guess for the mass exodus from Berlin ten to fifteen years from now? Sarajevo and Bucharest.

According to Berlin's only major city newspaper, *Der Tagesspiegel*, there are currently some 21,000 artists cavorting around the city—an underestimate, in my opinion. Half of them admit to being "professional artists." Yet what exactly does the adjective "professional" mean in this case? It means that the artists questioned primarily pursue their chosen artistic activity. But can they actually live on the income they earn from it? Any halfway curious Berliner knows a few artists, but not many know any who manage to earn a living from their work. Even so, the influx continues. In the wake of these artists, galleries and collectors are also flocking to the city. For some time now, they have no longer been fixated on the Scheunenviertel (literally, "barn district") around Hackescher Markt or in Prenzlauer Berg, where the first new galleries cropped up after the fall of the Wall. They have spawned new, rapidly changing neighborhoods in Berlin: near Checkpoint Charlie, around the Jannowitz Bridge, recently even West Berlin's old entertainment district, Potsdamer Straße. With four hundred gallery addresses, Berlin now boasts more than any other European city. Yet with estimated revenues of some 200 million euros (in 2010), the city can't compete with any of Europe's major art centers. Meanwhile, rents are rising sharply; over the last five years, Berlin has added 100,000 households, and the city will continue to grow. Just like Kreuzberg's long-established Turkish population, many recently arrived artists are already being forced out to more peripheral areas.

CLASH OF THE ARCHITECTS

Driving by Potsdamer Platz in the 1990s, those familiar with Berlin from before the fall of the Wall, who still carried the old image of the city in their heads, couldn't help but feel a sense of vertigo. It was as if the effects of the seismic tremor that had shaken the city in November 1989 were only now becoming visible. In a matter of weeks—in a matter of days, even—new buildings shot up in the wasteland formerly dominated by the Wall. A new city emerged from the scaffolding in the middle of the old city, and one could only guess what sounds and reflections it held in store, what life might play out against this backdrop someday. But hadn't this always been the hallmark of Berlin? Hadn't it always been a place of transit, a city with more of a past and a future than a present?

Berliners watched the radical reconstruction that began immediately with a sangfroid that could easily have been mistaken for numbness. One didn't sense much enthusiasm, but rather the surliness typical of soccer fans after their team has just lost. The debates about the city's future all too often took the form of political exorcisms. They lacked curiosity, playfulness, a sense of adventure. Instead, decisions with far-reaching consequences that one could have disagreed about gracefully were discussed using the exquisite means of personal suspicion and political vilification.

Among German intellectuals you can't have an argument about so much as a recipe without some worked-up gourmet detecting fascist ingredients in it.

And so Berlin's architecture debate also became bogged down in the quagmire of suspected fascism before it even really got under way. The question of whether one could or should build in the city center using light or heavy materials, glass or stone, *Zeilenbau* (a Bauhaus concept of linear blocks, usually oriented on a north–south axis), or perimeter blocks, became so weighed down with ideological ballast that the question of the quality of the actual designs was all but ignored. No sooner had the Berlin architect Hans Kollhoff publicly aired his doubts about the blessings of modernism and cast his vote in favor of a "stone city" than the former director of the German Architecture Museum in Frankfurt, Heinrich Klotz, detected "echoes of fascist architecture" in Kollhoff's plans. The American architect Daniel Libeskind had just begun building his spectacular Jewish Museum in Berlin. But when he saw his competitor Kollhoff's winning designs for Alexanderplatz, he was politely appalled and wrote: "I reject the idea that totalitarian planning can still be engaged in the late twentieth century." As a result of statements like these, the clash among architects in Berlin cropped up in the culture sections of international papers. Project sketches, floor plans, and models suddenly became as newsworthy as neo-Nazi arson attacks. Ridiculously facile dichotomies crystallized: glass, steel, and aluminum windows stood for plurality and democracy, while stone, perimeter blocks, and wooden moldings represented a reactionary attitude and monolithic social structures. As though light structures couldn't also be made of stone; as though glass and steel, by the very nature of their material, were immune to bulkiness and unimaginative designs. When it came to the architects, no one seemed to remember the rule that politicians should be judged not by their campaign promises but by their actions. People seemed to confuse the architects' declarations with their buildings. An opinion war that pitted "new historicism" against "second mod-ernism" broke out, with the protagonists on both sides jabbing at one another with rolled-up blueprints as though they were spears.

Nowhere was the battle for the soul of the city as fierce as in Berlin's new center. And this center was empty. It was a one-of-a-kind situation. A strip some 30 miles long and between 30 and 550 yards wide—whose western side, until 1989, had been home exclusively to mice and moles—cut straight through the capital. This wasteland, which until recently had marked the place where the two halves of Berlin ended, was now expected to become, over-night, the new heart of a world city.

Sky-high building cranes and bottomless construction pits became the new emblems of Berlin. It was only when they saw these pits that many Berliners realized that the city's center was built on sand and swampland—nothing but a thin layer of gritty earth separates the surface from the groundwater. Anyone drilling a few yards into the ground will hit water. In fact, the foundations of medium-tall town houses and commercial buildings were al-ready being built in the water centuries ago. Time and again, in their efforts to renovate surviving large-scale buildings or to re-build vanished ones—during the renovations of the Deutsche Oper and the reconstruction of the Berlin Schloss, for example—construction workers have unearthed sixty-five-foot-long wooden piles that were driven into the earth below groundwater level. Ap-parently, the center of Berlin was built on pilings—like Venice, except that in Berlin you couldn't see the water aboveground. No, this definitely was not ideal ground to put up the skyscrapers that many hoped to see in the recovered city center. Older East Berliners were reminded of something the East German architect Hermann Henselmann reputedly said. Henselmann had designed but not built Berlin's TV Tower. He reportedly admitted that he never went to the top because he wasn't convinced the tower wouldn't—at that very moment, just when he was up there—lean to the side.

The many lakes surrounding the city were now joined by

huge water-filled construction pits. Divers were the heroes of these new construction sites. Their job was to install base plates and walls in the water so the groundwater constantly seeping in could be pumped out and foundations for the new high-rises laid. Floating construction cranes maneuvered above the prone divers, supplying them with the necessary parts.

Volker Hassemer, the senator for urban development at the time, together with Manfred Gentz, who was in charge of managing the Daimler project at Potsdamer Platz, hit upon the idea of maximizing the entertainment potential of these enormous new construction sites. Along the edges of the most impressive ones, three- and four-story kiosks and info boxes shot up, from which locals and tourists could watch the works in progress. The idea was an astounding success. Visiting construction sites in Berlin soon became more popular than going to the theater, a museum, or a concert.

POTSDAMER PLATZ

The most contested construction site was Potsdamer Platz.

This square, which had been the busiest intersection in Europe in the 1920s, had turned into Berlin's biggest urban wasteland during the Cold War. Any building that had managed to survive the bombings of World War II reasonably intact had subsequently been torn down. On August 21, 1961, along the line that had been painted on the asphalt to mark the border between the three western sectors and the Soviet sector since August 1948, the Wall went up. Under the pretext of needing to protect the western border against the alleged daily threat of invasion by "imperialist forces," East German authorities tore down almost all of the remaining buildings located within their territory; they destroyed houses on Ebertstraße and Stresemannstraße, as well as what remained of the Wertheim department store. Erich Mendelsohn's Columbushaus (Columbus House), and the Haus Vaterland (Fatherland House), both of which had still been in use during the East German era, had already burned down after being set on fire during the workers' uprising of June 17, 1953.

Yet the authorities in West Berlin were no better; with their postwar dreams of creating a "car-friendly city," they had razed the ruins of the Vox-Haus, Prince Albrecht Palace, Museum of

Ethnology, and Anhalter train station. As a result, Potsdamer Platz had become a building cemetery of sorts, without tombstones. Only older Berliners could still conjure up the ghosts of these former buildings in their minds' eyes.

Until the early 1990s, the square was dominated by the one structure that had replaced the vanished buildings: the Berlin Wall. On the western side of the almost five-hundred-yard-wide desert at the center of the city, a platform surrounded by snack bars and souvenir stands had been put up, from which curious bystanders could observe the Wall. There they stood, looking directly into the binoculars of the border police at their guard posts, who in turn stared straight back into the tourists' own.

Only one building had survived the demolition mania: Weinhaus Huth, a "wine house" built in the early twentieth century by the wine dealer Willy Huth on a lot purchased by his grandfather. To support the load of his wine stock, Willy Huth had had it built with a steel-frame construction, a technique that was new at the time. Thanks to this provision, as well as to sheer luck, the building had survived the bombings and artillery fire of World War II with minimal damage; yet even the modern steel-frame construction had not been able to protect the building's supplies from the thirst of the invading Soviet troops. For decades, the Weinhaus—together with the remains of the bombed-out Hotel Esplanade—sat like a prehistoric boulder on the otherwise desolate Potsdamer Platz.

Whenever I drove from Charlottenburg toward Kreuzberg and saw the building standing there, I'd inevitably shake my head in disbelief. The image could have been from a Western shot in Arizona: a lone building in the middle of a desert, rising up like a mirage before the eyes of a thirsty cowboy after a long ride—and its name, at least, delivered what it seemed to promise: a good drink. Except that this particular forsaken building happened to be located at the center of a major city. It was a fixed star in a barren wasteland, a preposterous beacon. Who lived behind those glowing windows, who held down the fort in this far-flung outpost in the former city center, to the west of the Wall, the construction of which had relegated the building to the edge of the world?

Books and articles about the Weinhaus tell us that Willy Huth continued to run a pub there for a long time after the Wall went up. He couldn't bring himself to sell the family legacy, though by now its iron girders were rusted and its wine storage spaces filled with rubble. He set up his office in the corner of a wood-paneled hall, which in the 1920s had been a well-attended ballroom. Here, once a month, he would collect rent from his tenants. Occasionally he could also be seen on the roof of the building, looking out over the empty square where the world's first traffic lights had once controlled the flow of traffic. Maybe he saw the vanished buildings in whose midst he had grown up: the beer halls, Potsdamer Platz train station, Haus Vaterland, and the Rheingold next door; the newspaper boys, shoe polishers, and flower sellers; maybe he heard the trams, motorized cabs, the crush of the crowds that used to fill the old ballroom in Weinhaus Huth. But these were sights and sounds that he alone could see and hear.

It was said that in the years immediately after the Wall went up a lone trombonist would sometimes play a mournful melody, heard only by the border police and tenants of Weinhaus Huth. No one knew who this strange horn player was. But when his solos stopped, they were missed.

One of Huth's former cellar masters got into trouble because of one of the wine dealers associated with the Weinhaus. Apparently, this wine dealer had been a spy for the CIA in East Germany, and Huth's cellar master had assisted him in his activities. The man was sentenced to five years in prison, but was granted a pardon and had to serve only five months.

Willy Huth died shortly after his ninetieth birthday party at Weinhaus Huth. It was the wine, one obituary claimed, that had kept him and his wife so young.

The West Berlin authorities were at a loss as to what to do with the building. In 1967, Willy Huth's widow had sold it and the attached property to the West Berlin Tiergarten district for a pittance. The bureaucrats of the Social Democratic Party decided to use the building as public housing. But instead of the families with multiple children they had anticipated, it was mostly loners, masters of the art of living, painters, and castaways, with their preference for unorthodox living arrangements, who moved in. And, after all, what was a family supposed to do with an apartment located in the middle of an enormous, undeveloped plot divided by a wall? There were no bakeries nearby, let alone supermarkets; no schools, no kindergartens; the closest bus stop was a ten-minute walk away. The U-Bahn trains thundering underground through the sealed-off Potsdamer Platz ghost station every few minutes made an earth-shattering noise.

The tenants who lived in the building in the 1980s were treated to novel sights and sounds several times a year. Potsdamer Platz became the preferred location of politicians and presidents from around the world for visiting and making public appearances. Watching from their balconies or through open windows, the tenants of Weinhaus Huth enjoyed the best seats in the house.

The writer Inka Bach had grown up in East Berlin and fled from East Germany with her family in 1972. In the summer of 1989, after several extended stays in New York and Paris, she moved into Haus Huth with her newborn son. And so the girl from East Germany unexpectedly found herself at the juncture of East and West Berlin.

The father of her child, an architect from West Berlin, lived in an apartment on the third floor of Haus Huth. An 800-square-foot loft with a small bedroom, it was hardly ideal for a young family, which soon grew to include Inka's second child, a daughter. While there was a huge amount of space outside for playing, there were few other children. Getting to the supermarket or bus stop was inconvenient. Sure, Inka was living in the old heart of the former capital and had what seemed at the time to be an "unobstructable view"; there was no more central location than this in all of Berlin. But life in this center, forsaken by god and man, reminded her not so much of her beloved Paris or Manhattan as of the outskirts of a provincial American city. She had to take her car just to buy a carton of milk or a pencil.

But there were unique advantages as well. Inka never had any trouble finding a parking spot for her minivan directly in front of the building, and the police didn't give out tickets anywhere in the greater vicinity of Weinhaus Huth. At 2.50 deutsche marks per square meter, the rent was a dream. And while she may have needed a car to pick up day-to-day essentials, the Berlin Philharmonic, Martin-Gropius-Bau, and New National Gallery were all within walking distance. As far as the view from the apartment was concerned, even on the third floor she could feel like she was on the fortieth floor of a Manhattan skyscraper. Her curved bay windows offered a unique view of both Berlin half-cities.

The building's other occupants weren't exactly the sort of tenants the Tiergarten district office had hoped for. The renter next door, a gay dermatologist from Munich, had a weakness for old Berlin brass doorknobs, a few of which could still be found in the meticulously constructed turn-of-the-century building, recently renovated by the Tiergarten district office. This neighbor unscrewed the doorknobs from the doors of the empty apartments and attached them to those in his apartment. No one in the building was able to make sense of this eccentric habit of their isolated fellow tenant from the German south. At some point, he was found dead in his apartment, having shot himself. His apartment was overflowing with Nazi emblems and relics—a collection that apparently had little or nothing to do with the mentally disturbed man's convictions.

An actress from East Germany, who was trying her hand at

the esoteric arts after abandoning a career in theater, lived on the fifth floor—supposedly she was a close friend of the East German dissident and civil rights activist Bärbel Bohley. Far Eastern scents and meditation music wafted into the stairwell from her apartment. Sometimes Inka would get a massage from this neighbor. The woman's name later showed up on a list of informers for East Germany's state security service. From that point on, Inka stopped availing herself of the mystic's services. She would baffle her friends by telling them that she had been "in the hands of the Stasi" twice a week.

Another longtime tenant of Haus Huth had planted a garden on the overgrown street in front of the building. The garden took up a section of Potsdamer Straße that no one had driven on for decades but that had once been a main artery of the traffic hub of Berlin. Rumor had it that the writer Theodor Fontane had lived not far from this garden. The old lady spent half the day uprooting weeds that sprouted from the famous old street and tending to her plants. When her work was done, she would sunbathe on a deck chair. She never imagined that her little garden had become the focus of a global corporation that wanted to build on this very spot.

But the idyllic state of affairs on the Potsdamer Platz wasteland changed—even before the fall of the Wall. The rabbits that had been moving freely back and forth between East and West for years were now joined by new border crossers: in the summer of 1989, Poles started showing up by the Landwehr Canal and near Potsdamer Platz on weekends, bringing souvenirs with them: tools, chinaware, a painting on wood of the Madonna with child. West Berliners, used to dealing with Turkish salespeople, discovered that it's impossible to haggle with Poles. You either paid the asking price or went your way empty-handed. It remained a mystery how these inexperienced vendors from the neighboring eastern state managed to get into West Berlin. Arriving Saturday morning, they were gone again by Sunday night.

Then the Wall came down. For months, Inka heard the hammering of the "Wall woodpeckers" hacking away at the monstrosity day and night. After the rabbits and the Poles, the "city Indians" arrived with their tents and corrals of wagons, laying siege to Potsdamer Platz. It was Inka's son who alerted her to the new possibilities after the fall of the Wall. Inka had always taken her children with her on her daily walks to the Gropius-Bau and the New National Gallery, which the city's culture buffs could reach only by bus or taxi. Where other kids demanded the "playground," for Inka's children the word was "Gropius-Bau." At one point, her son, an enthusiastic walker, discovered a kindergarten on the eastern side of the Wall. "We go look at girls?" he asked his mother. Inka valiantly enrolled him in the kindergarten, which was still being run by a staff from the state she had fled. But Inka was familiar with kindergarten teachers from East Berlin; she spoke their language and trusted her ability to influence them. Besides, it was clear to her that her spectacular view from the third floor would not remain "unobstructable." Her family's days in Haus Huth were numbered.

Shortly before the fall of the Wall, Edzard Reuter, the CEO of the Daimler Group at the time, bought fifteen thousand acres to the southwest of Potsdamer Platz from the West Berlin Senate. The sale, which was made at a time when hardly anyone believed in an imminent end to the divided state of Germany, let alone in the dissolution of the Soviet Union, was a bold—a prophetic— investment. Indeed, it was driven more by a political vision than by commercial interests. Edzard Reuter, who was the son of West Berlin's legendary first mayor, Ernst Reuter, wanted to build not only a new Daimler headquarters here but a whole new urban area, which would—at some distant point in the future—be connected to East Berlin. Rarely has the CEO of a major group been so right about a decision that many of his business colleagues greeted with smirks. Reuter himself was surprised by how quickly his bet paid off. The plot of land, which he bought for 93 million deutsche marks, is now one of the most valuable properties in Berlin.

As an unwelcome "dowry," Reuter had also inherited Weinhaus Huth, which the city had just spent 3 million deutsche marks renovating. The building stood in the way of every possible overall design for the area, but happened to be part of it. Moreover, in November 1979, the Tiergarten district office designated Weinhaus Huth a landmark, "one of the last examples of modern commercial architecture from the Kaiser era." Yet neither Edzard Reuter nor his architect, Renzo Piano, whose design had won the competition for the Daimler property, suspected at the time just how many headaches the building would cause them.

For the new owner-builders, Haus Huth's landmark status meant one thing above all: enormous costs and the task of integrating into their plans a relatively unexceptional turn-of-the-century Berlin commercial building, which wasn't exactly on a par with the Coliseum or Hadrian's Villa outside of Rome. The building stood on marshy ground and needed to be "underpinned," to use the construction term. Because the architects feared that a 130-foot-deep construction pit being dug nearby might cause the building to sink or even collapse, they decided to place "the gem" on a framework of pilings anchored 60 feet into the ground. There was something touching about this 50 million euro measure: here was the owner-builder Daimler making an effort that the Italians won't even make to safeguard the ruins of Pompeii in order to preserve a wine merchant's building with nothing exceptional about it beyond the fact that it had survived World War II and all the demolition that followed.

The tenants, including Inka Bach, who had held down the fort in Haus Huth until the last possible moment, were given generous financial settlements to move out. Inka Bach is reticent about the amount, but it was probably equivalent to the proceeds of a bestseller. And why not? Why should an automotive group be the only one to benefit from the miraculous fall of the Wall—why not also a few smart tenants?

From the moment construction began, however, Daimler faced strong headwinds from both East and West. Doomsday prophets, of whom there has never been a shortage in Berlin, predicted that the construction lake would deprive the surrounding areas of groundwater; the trees in the neighboring Tierpark would die of thirst. These prophecies were coupled with more valid concerns expressed by the engineers. There was reason to fear that one of the internal partitions in the construction pit in front of Haus Huth would buckle, flooding the S-Bahn tunnels behind it with water from the pit. This risk was averted at great cost. There were other difficulties, on the other hand, that could not be prevented by technical means.

From the start, the Daimler project was "the most hated construction project in Berlin," reports Manfred Gentz, whom Daimler had put in charge of it. Daimler was categorically rejected as an owner-builder at Potsdamer Platz not just by the media-savvy guild of architects in East and West Berlin, but also by the population of East Berlin, bolstered by a swelling chorus from the city's West. How, they asked, can we allow an entire area of the city to be developed by an automotive group from Stuttgart, which might well decide to lock the gates to "its section of the city" at night? And what's the rush anyway? Why does the area have to be developed in just four years? Why not let the city grow there organically over the next twenty to thirty years? And does the entire plot really have to be covered with buildings? Couldn't part of it be set aside for the generations to come?

The situation reminded some of a warning from a 1960s best-seller by the psychoanalyst Alexander Mitscherlich. In a popular book titled *Die Unwirtlichkeit unserer Städte: Anstiftung zum Unfrieden* (The Inhospitality of Our Cities: A Deliberate Provocation), he cautioned against producing cities like cars. The good man never could have imagined that an automotive group would give birth to an entire section of Berlin. Yet this was precisely what was now planned for Potsdamer Platz. A city produced by an automotive group?

Manfred Gentz made up his mind to turn "the most hated construction project in Berlin into its most popular" by opening it to the public. The idea was to involve the famously curious Berliners in the project by turning them into a permanent audience for the "tower-building" performance. Haus Huth, Gentz decided, was a fitting location for this kind of dialogue.

From that point on, Gentz regularly invited the press and West Berlin glitterati to the new operational headquarters. Weather permitting, guests would stand around on the roof of Haus Huth—glass of champagne in one hand, crab appetizer in the other—listening to the architects explain the construction in progress, peering, every now and then, over the edge at the brown construction-pit lake below with a slight shudder. Eventually, tricks from the magic box of event culture were added to further sweeten the deal. Rock climbers were hired to rappel down the walls of the unfinished high-rises; poets from around the world recited their texts in the middle of the incomplete structures; bands performed on the most improbable makeshift stages. Truth be told, all that was missing was an appearance by the Berlin experimental punk band Einstürzende Neubauten, which, presumably because of its name—literally, Collapsing New Buildings—was never invited.

Manfred Gentz recounts how Daimler's big guns in Stuttgart watched nervously as the Berlin project—which was also a source of contention back at headquarters—appeared to transform a construction site into an amusement park of sorts on weekends. The board of directors worried not only about potentially undermining the respectability of the world-famous brand but also about the cost of the events and the safety of the audience and artists. A single fatal accident would have ruined public perception of the construction site. In response to these detractors, Gentz argued that winning the public's acceptance of the Daimler project was just as important as finishing the work on time and on budget.

Gentz's strategy paid off. Month after month, the show-site cast its spell over an ever-larger number of Berliners.

On several occasions, I was among the guests invited to the roof of Haus Huth. Attending one of these Daimler press conferences meant being witness to a strange spectacle at the entrance, before you even got in. Cheerful and festively dressed guests searched in vain for an opening in the chain-link fence surrounding the area. Ladies in high heels and evening gowns asked for directions from construction workers, who had to take off their hardhats to hear them. Nodding in thanks, the guests headed off in the direction indicated, lifting their expensive coats and dresses, but unable to prevent their steps across the building boards from splattering mud, which flecked the ladies' white calves and their escorts' dress pants. Some took an elevator, others the stairs, the entire party hurrying up toward the asphalt rooftop, which was secured with nothing but a makeshift rope barrier. Up there, you would run into other party guests, already holding glasses of champagne in their hands. Several people danced to the sounds of a German New Orleans band. But there was almost always a stiff wind blowing—the barely 130-foot-tall building was the tallest point far and wide—so most guests were busy pulling up their coat collars and clutching their expensive hats to their heads. Once, a gust of wind snatched up an elegant lady's straw hat. She was too late in grabbing its brim, and the updraft whirled it about in a spectacular dance before it finally sailed toward the muddy groundwater-lake below. Delighted, the guests followed the hat's aerial display, leaning out over the rope barrier as their partners held on to them, emitting a collective *ooh* and *aah* when it finally landed on the water. But that wasn't the end of the performance. A swimming crane immediately made a beeline for the hat. A diver, invisible until then and apparently summoned by the crane operator, briefly surfaced in the muddy lake, fished the hat out of the water with his black rubber-sheathed hand, and set it on the edge of the floating crane base before diving back down into his element. He probably didn't even hear the enthusiastic applause from the roof.

At one of these rooftop press conferences, I met Renzo Piano, the world-famous Italian architect. Since I speak Italian, we quickly struck up a conversation—a conversation that continues to this day. I studied Piano's designs, he read my books about Berlin—in the hopes of discovering something about the city's soul through them. Before coming to Berlin, he would usually give me a ring. His calls came from New York, London, Japan, and Australia. Once in Berlin, he would treat me to dinner at a sinfully expensive restaurant, where we would pick up right where we had left off. I, in turn, went to visit him in his studios in Genoa and Paris and learned about his other projects. Our conversations developed into a long friendship, on the strength of which I can now say that Piano is one of the most modest and curious people I know. And, when it comes to friendship, he is as uncomplicated and straightforward as a farmer from the Abruzzi.

After visiting Centre Pompidou, an example of Piano's early work, designed together with his friend Richard Rogers, the writer Italo Calvino coined the expression *intelligenza leggera*, or "light intelligence." I asked Piano whether *intelligenza leggera* could hold its own even in the northern light of the Prussian capital—under the influence of gray sandstone and red brick, and with a German client like Daimler, which aimed to control every possible contingency: a constant noise level of twenty-eight decibels, an average temperature of sixty-four degrees Fahrenheit in the shopping mall—in short, life subjugated by standards.

Piano admitted he was nervous about the project at Potsdamer Platz. It wasn't the usual *horror vacui*, or aversion to empty spaces, that set in before every large construction project. And it wasn't even the scope of the undertaking that he was worried about. He remembered how he felt the first time he had stepped onto the wasteland in the heart of the city—a place, as he put it, "saturated with history. You can sense the ghosts of the past at every turn, but ghosts are all that you encounter—there's nothing you can see or touch."

Initially, he was stumped by the task of creating urban life from this tabula rasa. He felt like a mathematician who had been asked to solve an equation with not just one, two, or three unknown variables, but twenty. Except for Haus Huth and the remains of the Hotel Esplanade, there were no reference points—no ensemble that might have provided inspiration or acted as a springboard. He would have liked to be able to integrate at least a section of the Wall into his designs, but the Wall had also disappeared without a trace. Wasn't this hasty disposal just another bout of the very same cleaning-up mania that had compelled German postwar planners to erase all structural traces of the prewar era?

He didn't believe in the advantages of a tabula rasa, Piano said. "A city is a text with many pages, and every page counts. Too many pages are missing from Berlin's urban history."

He had begun his work at Potsdamer Platz with the vision of a piazza with water flowing around it, the city's streets radiating outward in a starlike formation. "You always start with emptiness, not fullness. It's the voids in a city that determine its structure." At the same time, a few icons had served as points of reference for his designs, because they offered context either as existing solitary structures or even as mere ghosts of buildings. The theater he built pays homage to Hans Scharoun's State Library, across from which it stands. The entrance tower to "his section of the city," the Debis office high-rise, is meant to evoke a Mies van der Rohe skyscraper that was never built. Piano was inspired by the desire— technically all but impossible at the time—to counteract gravity. As executed, his designs resulted in a barely 330-foot-tall glass-and-steel battle-ax hurled into the sands of Brandenburg. Piano likes the fact that the facing tower, designed by Hans Kollhoff, is at odds with his own building in every way. As a counterpoint to Piano's tossed ax, Kollhoff built a classic high-rise, thoroughly elegant in its own way, out of dark red, burned-looking brick reminiscent of New York buildings from the 1920s. "A fortress, of course, a *castello*," Piano remarked with an amiable smile. Glass and steel versus stone—why not play them off against each other?

What Piano missed most in Berlin was the energy he referred to in plain Italian as *passione eroica*—heroic passion. Lorenzo de' Medici, the Renaissance dreamer and statesman, experienced precisely such a magical moment. He gathered the best minds of his generation around him and, in just a few short decades, succeeded in establishing the incomparable Florence. To build a marvelous city like Florence, Piano said, you need a great deal of power, a great deal of money, but more than anything you need passion and a willingness to play hard.

What worried him was the incredible speed at which new urban entities arise. In his view, the constant and worldwide revolutionizing of construction materials, computer-programmed building techniques, and new transport routes had resulted in an unprecedented acceleration of construction processes and endless possibilities. This material revolution, Piano said, virtually precluded the biological growth of cities: "This is the first time in history that you can produce an entire urban area in five to ten years. It's like giving birth to a baby two months after it was conceived. You have no idea who is going to breathe life into the new neighborhood. It has to work right away. So you take advantage of tried-and-true attractions that generate some semblance of hustle and bustle: a shopping mall, cinema, casino, theater, public square, fountains. You create a space not for life with its unpredictable, biological rhythms, but for virtual life. This kind of awakening by bombardment scares me sometimes."

Can't something be left unfinished, I asked, some small part of the construction area set aside for the ideas and revisions of future generations?

The financial constraints of a large-scale project like this are despotic, Piano replied. They don't allow for leaving openings. It would be expecting too much of him as an architect to leave untouched any part of an area he had been hired to develop.

At that moment, a little boy's defiance flashed in the eyes of the Genovese architect, who had grown up with the city's most famous son, Christopher Columbus, as his role model.

"If you're an explorer, you cut the anchor cable and set sail— you'd be crazy and a wimp not to. Columbus had no idea where he'd end up, either, when he set out for the West Indies."

The Daimler project at Potsdamer Platz was one of the very few major projects in Berlin that was completed exactly on time and on budget. The first of several big celebrations took place at the end of October 1996, to mark the topping out of a twenty-two-story high-rise. Manfred Gentz and his colleagues had come up with something special for the occasion. Their plan was for Daniel Barenboim, the musical director of the Deutsche Oper, to conduct an unusual ballet: nineteen construction cranes would move their massive steel arms in rhythm to Beethoven's "Ode to Joy" as conducted by the maestro. No one in Gentz's team really believed that the world-famous conductor would agree to it. But to everyone's surprise, he did.

The night before the "premiere," Manfred Gentz tells me, he stopped by the construction site one last time. He was puzzled to find that it was brightly lit. All of the cranes had their lights on and were going through motions that made no sense in the context of normal construction-site operations. Unrelated to any sensible task, their arms moved about in the night, like gigantic insects practicing how to fly. It was some time before Gentz grasped what this nocturnal spectacle was about. Apparently the crane operators had arranged to meet for a final dress rehearsal, possibly to the accompaniment of portable radios they had brought along.

The next day, Daniel Barenboim conducted the "Ode to Joy" from Beethoven's Ninth Symphony. Waving his left hand in the direction of the first and second violinists—the nearby cranes—then his right toward the steel monsters farther away—the horns and percussionists—he called everyone up for the tutti. The crane operators did their best to follow the conductor's vigorous gestures, which they could barely make out from the enormous height of their operating cabins. The Golden Gospel Singers, who had been flown in for the event, belted out the all-too-familiar repertory piece into the vastness of the construction site, independent of the maestro's cues and oblivious to the iron arms that swayed about high above them.

Due to the delayed mechanical transmission from the crane operator's levers, Manfred Gentz notes with a smile, the swiveling of the cranes "wasn't always" perfectly in sync.

It was a crazy time, an incredible time. Every few months the reawakened city would surprise its residents and visitors with yet another new, unheard-of construction "happening." Shortly before the concert of the cranes, on the other side of Potsdamer Platz, dominated by the Sony Center, the so-called Kaisersaal had been relocated.

The Kaisersaal was more or less all that was left of the legendary Hotel Esplanade after World War II. The neobaroque-style hall owed its name to the last German kaiser, Wilhelm II, who had used it to host his "gentlemen's evenings." In keeping with the misogynistic tradition of Frederick the Great, women were not welcome on these nights. The kaiser's blue-blooded friends would play chess and cards before ending the evening by telling aristocratic men's jokes.

In the 1920s, after the abdication of the kaiser, the hall had served as a ballroom. Here, Barnabás von Géczy had played for the afternoon tea dance; before leaving for Hollywood, Billy Wilder had earned a reputation as a gigolo, working for five deutsche marks and a free meal. He taught dolled-up ladies aged twenty to fifty how to dance the Charleston; his friend Margerie looked after their male escorts. From four-thirty to seven, dancers were required to wear dark suits; from nine-thirty to one in the morning, tuxes. Wilder kept his celluloid dickey and paper cuffs lily-white with the help of an eraser. Greta Garbo and Charlie Chaplin, ridiculed as a "Jewish clown" by the National Socialist newspaper *Völkischer Beobachter*, stayed at the Esplanade. In this same hotel, in 1944, conspirators in the July plot against Hitler waited for the code word "Valkyrie."

Following an air raid, out of the Hotel Esplanade's total of 400 rooms and 240 bathrooms only the Kaisersaal, imperial toilets, and reading room survived intact. Until the end of the 1980s, sheep grazed behind the hotel ruins. During the years of the Wall, the Kaisersaal alone succeeded in carving out some semblance of an afterlife for itself—as an event venue and film set. Scenes for movies including *Cabaret*, *Breakthrough*, *Wings of Desire*, and *Marianne and Juliane* were filmed here.

The Kaisersaal never would have survived the construction work at Potsdamer Platz had it not been designated a landmark after the opening of the Wall. Just like Weinhaus Huth, it suddenly seemed indispensable—due simply to the fact that it had remained standing. These retroactively ennobled Berlin monuments are hardly going to inspire anyone to fall to his or her knees in devotion. Even so, the landmark preservationists deserve a word of thanks. Because that's just how it is in Berlin: after the destruction of the war and the architectural crimes committed afterward, you had to learn to appreciate the chance survival of even the merely average and banal.

Originally, the architects of the Sony Center had wanted to tear down the Kaisersaal. When they drew up their plans, they simply overlooked the protected landmark. Now, they unexpectedly found themselves faced with the task of integrating the bulky isolated island into their designs. The oversight apparently ended up costing the group a total of 75 million deutsche marks. The

Kaisersaal couldn't just stay where it was since it stood directly in the way of the new Potsdamer Straße, so the decision was made to relocate it. The unusual undertaking required the development of special technology. The plan was to raise the colossus some eight feet and place it on an air cushion of sorts with the help of hydraulic levers. It would then be shifted a few feet south, where it would take a sharp turn right before floating 250 feet west. A viewing platform was set up to allow curious onlookers to watch.

The film director Wim Wenders gave the signal for the operation to start. The hall rose up hydraulically, shuddered southward, canted, and came to a groaning standstill in the air. But it refused to make the planned turn to the right. Thanks to the ingenuity of German engineers—East German engineers, this time, for the technique had been developed by the Bauakademie (Academy of Architecture) of the German Democratic Republic—and after several false starts and new attempts, the maneuver succeeded at last. The two-story monster finally made the turn and moved to the designated spot, where it was welcomed with thunderous applause.

After this grandiose spectacle, however, it turned out that the operation to relocate the Kaisersaal inspired much more powerful emotions than the relocated hall itself. When the first guests entered the renovated Kaisersaal, a subtle sense of disappointment was palpable. Had this room, with its faux pomp and restored façade ornamentation, really been worth so much money and effort? Never mind. It had, in any event, survived both the war and construction.

Back to the Daimler project on the other side of Potsdamer Platz. The opening ceremony took place on October 2, 1998—on the eve of the anniversary of German reunification. The only noteworthy thing about the lackluster speech given by Daimler's new CEO Jürgen Schrempp was the fact that he didn't so much as mention his predecessor, Edzard Reuter, who had acquired the property before the fall of the Wall. Apparently Schrempp couldn't bring himself to share credit with his predecessor for the success of inaugurating the new city section. The dignitaries' speeches were followed by a ceremonial procession of all the construction vehicles, in which 250 musicians and a thousand construction workers participated. The tail end of the parade was made up of a convoy of all the cleaning vehicles. One crew that had played a decisive role in making the celebration a success, however, was missing. In the days and nights before the celebration, an employee of Renzo Piano's told me, hundreds of sanitation workers had cleaned the construction dust from the new city section. These cleaners, who came from all corners of Europe and spoke a dozen different languages, washed thousands of windows and mopped hundreds of hallways, leaving not so much as a single speck on the streets and squares. This major cleaning operation, my source confessed, had been the grandest and most beautiful spectacle he had ever seen. But on the day of the celebration itself, these helpers, who had not been invited, were asleep in the barracks of the companies from which Daimler had subcontracted them. Others dozed in trains that carried them back to their respective countries of origin.

And where was the project's prophetic inventor, Edzard Reuter, during this celebration? A Daimler insider told me that Jürgen Schrempp had disinvited Reuter, who had already been asked to join as guest of honor. Deeply hurt, Reuter steered clear of the event.

From the moment Jürgen Schrempp took over as CEO, he broke off all contact with his predecessor. The insider told me he thought Schrempp was never able to forgive Reuter for having failed to brief him, before a shareholders' meeting in 1995, about a profit warning that was due to be issued. But the falling-out may also have simply been the result of the cultural distance between the two men. Schrempp, a former car mechanic from Freiburg in Baden-Württemberg, had risen to the head of the group under

Reuter's aegis. With his chummy manner—Schrempp reputedly had a virtually irresistible ability to turn superiors into close friends—he had won even the trust of this rather reserved Berlin intellectual and mayor's son. Reuter then found himself at a loss when Schrempp suddenly wanted nothing more to do with him and asked him not to attend the christening of Reuter's own brainchild.

Nothing was apparently done to repair the rift. From that point on, I was told, before accepting any invitation, both men would find out if the other planned on going—and decline if the other had accepted.

In the world of CEOs, differences and skirmishes of this kind can play a determining role in the history of an entire company, or even—as in this case—of an entire urban area. During his years in office, Schrempp made a determined effort to rid himself of the neighborhood that had been inspired by his predecessor.

In late 2012, I visited Manfred Gentz, whom I had met at the start of the construction works and grown to appreciate, at his office in Haus Huth. (By this point, the prefix "Wein" had been eliminated from the word "Haus.") The immaculately renovated building sits like a museum piece from the Gründerzeit—the period of rapid industrial expansion and economic growth in Germany at the end of the nineteenth century—between Renzo Piano's high-rises with their yellow screen cladding. When I rang the buzzer, a voice answered, asking who was there and what I wanted. In the hallway, after passing through an automatic door, I found myself in front of a brand-new elevator. Without my glasses, I couldn't make out the numbers engraved on the bronze-plated buttons and initially rode up to the wrong floor.

This building, where I had witnessed so much hullabaloo, seemed quiet now, downright forlorn—as did Manfred Gentz, who had directed the giant Potsdamer Platz project. I asked him how it was possible that the Daimler project had been sold just a few years after being completed. He had always considered the

sale a mistake, Gentz replied with a barely audible trace of melancholy in his voice. The decision had been related primarily to
changes in the capital market. The new evaluation criteria had
pushed companies to reduce their required operating capital as
much as possible so they could report higher returns; the more
capital was tied up, the smaller the returns.

Daimler had invested some 2 billion deutsche marks in the
Potsdamer Platz project. Inevitably, there were big write-offs on
the investment during the first few years; it was only after ten to
fifteen years that the group broke even and began to make a profit.
Jürgen Schrempp had never made a secret of his aversion to Berlin and to the Daimler project in the city. Investment bankers
kept at him with their philosophy of reducing tied-up capital
and convinced him it was essential to get rid of Potsdamer Platz
as quickly as possible. But it was only in 2008, when rents and
real-estate prices in Berlin were completely depressed, that it
was finally sold to a real-estate fund of the Swedish banking
group SEB.

Gentz, who had been against the sale and was not involved in
the negotiations, would or could not reveal the proceeds. Yet he
didn't contradict me when I suggested that it had occurred at the
worst possible moment imaginable. Haus Huth, where the Daimler group's Berlin representatives had their own headquarters, had
also been sold. Renting the building is probably more expensive
than the cost of depreciation would have been if Daimler had
held on to it. As Gentz saw me out, he allowed himself a little
laugh as he remarked that, after years of creating and supervising
the Daimler project at Potsdamer Platz, he was now a guest in his
own house.

There is an epilogue to the story of the two CEOs who started
off as friends and later became enemies that I owe it to the reader
to tell. Reuter and his diversification strategy had cost the Daimler group several billion deutsche marks in losses. But Schrempp,
who held this against him, was responsible for causing the group

a far greater loss. He banked on a new ideology that clouded the thinking of many CEOs at the time: if you aren't one of the world's top two or three groups in the industry, you're doomed. The year the Daimler project at Potsdamer Platz was inaugurated, Schrempp celebrated another event, this time one that he himself had initiated: the merger of Daimler and Chrysler. The man in charge of the merger called the association, which many experts had explicitly warned against, a "marriage made in heaven." After the glamorous failure of this marriage, as well as the failures of subsequent unions also initiated by Schrempp, the value of Daimler stock fell to 24 percent of its original value. This did not, however, prevent the global strategist Schrempp from profiting during its decline. The day after he left the company, the price of the group's stock rebounded vigorously. Had Schrempp sold his options at that time, he would have reaped a substantial profit on options he had acquired when shares were at their lowest. In 2007, their value was estimated at 50 million euros.

There aren't many professions where the person responsible for a disaster can walk away with profits of this magnitude.

In the meantime, the Sony Center, which was initially sold to Morgan Stanley, had also changed hands again. In 2010, it was acquired by a Korean pension fund for 573 million euros. No one is talking about a profit. The displaced-at-great-expense Kaisersaal serves as a café, gourmet restaurant, and lounge for special events—more than anything, it lives on the fame of how it got to its new location. It sits at the edge of Helmut Jahn's plaza like a befuddled temple. It still seems to be asking itself: How did I end up here; what in the world am I doing here?

I don't consider Potsdamer Platz a masterpiece of modern urban architecture. Too many disparate demands, interests, and mentalities acted as midwives to the project. The prescribed pace and the pressure to adhere to standards guaranteeing immediate

public success—casino, shopping mall, fountains—produced an
aesthetic of the lowest common denominator.

In fact, two very distinct sections have emerged on the former wasteland in the middle of Berlin. In contrast to Renzo Piano's rather conventional, entirely Italian ocher-tinged area, the
Nuremberg-born American architect Helmut Jahn put up a spectacular circus tent. What these two sections, both established by
major corporate groups, have in common is the fact that they
have absolutely nothing to do with the old Potsdamer Platz. Not
with the Potsdamer Platz of the 1920s, not with the Potsdamer
Platz of the postwar years, not with the desert that reigned here
during the years of the Wall. Piano's section, with its yellow screen
cladding, attempts to deliver a Mediterranean message of lightness and transience in Prussian Berlin. Helmut Jahn's tent op-
poses this with the noise and festive atmosphere of a soccer stadium,
albeit not a very well-attended one. Instead of being ringed with
bleachers, Jahn's arena is surrounded by apartments, which, like
box seats at a stadium, overlook the field below—though, in this
case, nothing much really happens there. Unfortunately, those
who find themselves down in the arena itself are obliged to pull
up their collars: the tent's seven openings ensure that it is reliably
drafty almost everywhere.

Even so, Potsdamer Platz has become a popular success. Berliners couldn't care less about the acquisitions and sales of the corporate groups that built it and then tried to pawn it off on the rest
of the world. They've already embraced it. Most of them probably
aren't even aware that it is a one-of-a-kind meeting point between
East and West Berliners: the only place in the center of Berlin
where locals meet as strangers, as nonnatives. Because no one
can claim to have called this former wasteland and no-man's-land
home anytime in the last six decades.

Besides, in the bitter cold of February, when Angelina Jolie
and Nina Hoss, Brad Pitt and Bruno Ganz, George Clooney and
Volker Schlöndorff, Wim Wenders and Udo Lindenberg step out

onto the red carpet in front of Renzo Piano's movie theater for the Berlin Film Festival, every criticism is forgotten anyway.

What was it that my city guide Wolf Jobst Siedler had said? "You'll find you often have to decide what matters more to you: the beauty of a place or its liveliness!"

A beauty Potsdamer Platz is not. But it's definitely lively!

BERLIN SCHLOSS VERSUS PALACE OF THE REPUBLIC

The revamping of Potsdamer Platz, as complicated as it was, was nothing compared to the task of appropriating the recovered old city center. Potsdamer Platz had been virtually empty; the *horror vacui* evoked by Renzo Piano had reigned there. In the center, on the other hand, a landmark that symbolized the power of old East Germany, the Palast der Republik (Palace of the Republic) wrestled with the ghost of the vanished city Schloss—the palace of the Hohenzollern kings.

For city planners and architects, designing the center represented a unique challenge. No other capital in the world offered a similar opportunity to resuscitate an enormous area at the heart of the city.

Immediately after the fall of the Wall, strange—even downright absurd—propositions had been considered. The Green Party in Berlin favored an idea that its members always suggest whenever a gap appears: along the stretch where the Wall had stood, they wanted to develop a green space for cyclists, joggers, and stroller-pushing mothers and fathers. An enormous farmers' market was also under discussion, possibly directly connected to an amusement park with a Ferris wheel of the kind often found on the fringes of other cities. Implementing these ideas would have been like turning Ground Zero in New York into a park rather than putting up a new skyscraper.

Star architects in Berlin, including Hans Kollhoff and Josef Paul Kleihues, warmed to the idea of rebuilding the Hohenzollern's old Schloss; in their opinion, modern architects were incapable of adequately filling such an enormous area in the middle of the city. In the view of the senator for urban development at the time, Volker Hassemer, it was clear that urban development was a lost art. Modern architects rarely still study the subject, since most city centers tend to suffer from a shortage rather than an excess of undeveloped areas. The opposite was true in Berlin. Most of the city's structural icons had been wiped out by World War II and by the tabula-rasa ideology that held sway on both sides of the city in the postwar years. There was no choice but to come up with new ways of thinking and planning. What, Hassemer asked, would be the contemporary equivalent of the classic icons—churches, domes, royal palaces, piazzas—used by city planners in past centuries to convey a city's soul?

In the dispute over the future of the city center, there was much talk of an initiative: the Förderverein Berliner Schloss e.V. (Association for the Berlin Schloss, Inc.). This foundation was campaigning to rebuild the former city palace of the Prussian kings. (After World War II, the East German government had demolished the façades of the Schloss, which had survived the war almost entirely intact.) This plan, however, would require attending to one "minor detail": the Palace of the Republic would have to go. Based on designs by the East German architect Heinz Graffunder, the Palace of the Republic had been built between 1973 and 1976 on part of the grounds formerly occupied by the city Schloss.

When they got wind of these plans, alarmed East Berliners rallied round the Palace of the Republic as though it were the last remaining relic of their identity. How dare those "Wessis," who had done nothing but stand by and watch during the revolution of 1989! Wasn't it enough that they had "liquidated" former East German companies—or, more accurately, left them to the mercy of greedy receivers from the West—without them now having to

raze an icon of East German history as well? Was this supposed
to be the result of reunification: the resurrection of the city Schloss
along with the ill-fated tradition of the Prussian kings and the
infamous "Prussian virtues" of love of the fatherland, uncondi-
tional execution of one's duties, discipline and obedience to the
point of death—virtues that had ultimately helped the Nazis
build concentration camps? *NIE WIEDER PREUSSEN!*—"Prussia,
never again!"—appeared on walls and posters around the Palace
of the Republic. It sounded like an echo of the cry *"Nie wieder
Deutschland!"*—"Germany, never again!"—that, in turn, West
Berlin leftists and members of the radical leftist *Autonome* movement had spray-painted and stridently hollered after the opening
of the Wall.

The city divided into two factions: Schloss against Palace,
Palace against Schloss. East Berliners, who had never really warmed
up to the Palace of the Republic, suddenly fell in love with it and
claimed that they couldn't live without it. Signatures were gathered, vigils organized, rumors of an imminent self-immolation
circulated.

The participation of West Berliners in the debate was sub-
dued. How were they supposed to get excited about the reconstruction of a royal palace most of them had never even seen?
Politicians and academically trained Schloss-lovers increasingly
hounded these undecided Berliners, telling them that the vanished palace was the most important legacy of the Renaissance
and baroque in Berlin and that it was being vilified unfairly as a
symbol of Prussian values, the monarchy, and fascism.

The longer the debate raged, the more blurred the lines became. The opposing positions on the Schloss no longer conformed
to the old divisions: East against West and vice versa. The guard-
ians of the grail of modernism among Berlin's architects adopted
an anti-Prussian stance. "All the misery in the world," one statement by West Berlin architects proclaimed, could be traced back
to Prussianism and the Prussian kings' bulky Schloss in the heart

of the city. By the same token, influential proponents of the Schloss's reconstruction suddenly cropped up in East Berlin.

Truth be told, both buildings had very little to do with the passions that flared up in their name. The Prussian soldier-kings hadn't been fond of the Schloss and had avoided it; Adolf Hitler had never set foot in it. Yet the Hohenzollern Schloss had survived the Allied bombings surprisingly well. It had been gutted by fire, but its façades and walls, along with its interior courtyards, had remained largely intact. In 1950, to the outrage of many East Berliners, the East German government had demolished the ruins. "Once the Schloss is gone," decreed Otto Grotewohl, the East German prime minister at the time, "no one will crow for it anymore!" Only the former so called Lustgartenportal, or "Gateway to the Pleasure Garden," from whose balcony Karl Liebknecht had declared the revolution—in vain!—on November 9, 1918, had been saved from destruction and integrated into the State Council Building of the fledgling German Democratic Republic ten years later.

Yet, for its part, the Palace of the Republic didn't exactly embody the myth of a socialist state power close to the people either. Over the years, East Berliners had grown used to "Honecker's lamp shop," as they called the extravagantly lit building. It was the only parliamentary building in the world that housed not just the People's Chamber, the already impotent former East German Parliament, but also a first-class bowling alley, countless restaurants, a disco, and expansive dance floors. But the president of the Bundestag, the East German–born Wolfgang Thierse, poked holes in the nostalgia of the professed admirers of the Palace of the Republic. The truth was, he explained, that it had been a venue exclusively for communist bigwigs during the years of the German Democratic Republic. If any normal citizens had ever even set foot in the building, more likely than not they had been visitors from the West carrying foreign currency.

The dispute came to a head when the new city government—

reunified Berlin's first—decided to tear down the Palace of the Republic. At first glance, there was nothing suspicious about this decision: an inspection of the building had detected an excessive amount of asbestos. A total of five thousand tons of sprayed asbestos had been used to fireproof the building—far more than was usual for a structure this size anywhere else in the world. No sooner were the findings of the building inspection made public than the sympathy of the Palace's supporters in East Berlin, which until then had been rather noncommittal, transformed into staunch determination to protect it.

The building's defenders saw the report as a cheap trick on the part of the new city government. How much asbestos, they demanded to know, was there in the important buildings of West Berlin? Wasn't the International Congress Center (ICC) near the Radio Tower in West Berlin also contaminated? Why should the Palace of the Republic be torn down and not the ICC? Supporters of the Palace of the Republic considered the claim that the ICC was not nearly as polluted with asbestos pure propaganda. And not without good reason, as soon became clear. Removing the asbestos from and renovating the ICC is estimated to cost some 320 million euros—far more than the total for completely refurbishing the Palace of the Republic.

An Old Testament–like logic of retribution seemed to be developing: an eye for an eye, a tooth for a tooth—you take my Palace, I'll tear down your congress center.

While the dispute failed to prevent the demolition, it did delay it. The asbestos was removed from the Palace of the Republic at a cost of some 45 million euros and five years of work. All that remained was an impressive dark scaffolding of steel girders, which rose up in the middle of the city like the skeleton of a prehistoric dinosaur. It stood its ground for five years. And, as seems to happen in Berlin whenever something clashes completely with its surroundings, the skeleton found a place in the hearts of more and more Berliners, and the creative types came flocking. The steel framework became a temporary home to "survival artists" from around the world. On its roof, a Norwegian artist placed a twenty-foot-high neon sign whose letters spelled out the word ZWEIFEL, or "doubt." The ruins' fame spread around the globe, ensuring that the same debates that had taken place locally were repeated at the international level. While city planners and architectural firms argued about what the building could be used for, the gutted Palace of the Republic served as a stage for rock musicians, artists without galleries, and experimental theater performances. To many people it seemed as though it had never been more beautiful than in its current, most extreme pared-down state.

In January 2006, the Bundestag put an end to these creative goings-on. Rejecting 180 (!) petitions for the preservation of the Palace of the Republic, it decided in favor of its complete demolition. The building's deeply disappointed devotees had no choice but to bid the Palace of the Republic a final adieu, floating around in inflatable rafts on its now-flooded ground floor.

In this situation, one man's commitment changed the entire game. Talent, according to one definition, is the ability to be in the right place at the right time. Wilhelm von Boddien possessed this talent. In the summer of 1961, shortly before completing high school, this young man from near Hamburg found himself somewhat by chance in the city whose fate he would shape decisively. Because he owned a moped—a rarity for a student in those days—his class had sent him to Berlin to report on the divided city for a school newspaper. He drove the 170 miles to Berlin on his moped, where he unexpectedly became an eyewitness to a world event. On August 13, on Bernauer Straße, he saw workers of East Germany's operational task forces unrolling barbed wire and laying cement bricks one on top of another. He witnessed the desperate last-minute attempts by residents to flee to the West. He saw young newlyweds, who had just barely managed to escape, waving to their parents who remained in the East; a member of the "VoPo," or Volkspolizei, the People's Police of East Germany, kept them from approaching one another by even just a few feet. A woman jumping from the second floor into a safety net of the West Berlin fire department made a lasting impression on von Boddien. He was fascinated by the Berliners' anger and sharp wit, and by the cold, automatonlike resolve with which the People's Police carried out their orders. Without knowing it, the young man who had arrived in Berlin by moped had found his life's theme.

In October 1961, von Boddien traveled to East Berlin—on board a train this time. Back then, non-Berliners holding a West German passport could enter East Germany with a visa, which West Berliners were not allowed to do until the first transit agreement of 1964, unless they declared residency in West Germany. After getting off the train at the Friedrichstraße station in East Berlin, von Boddien strolled aimlessly through the nearby streets, past stores with their meager displays. Along the way, he encountered almost no other pedestrians. The police presence, on the other hand, was impossible to miss. The city seemed frozen, still in shock from the recent building of the Wall. Seemingly by chance, von Boddien found himself on the once magnificent boulevard Unter den Linden and then on Marx-Engels-Platz, where an enormous platform caught his eye. From this platform, the East German powers-that-be watched military parades on May Day and other political holidays, and waved to the Young Pioneers brandishing their little flags. Von Boddien found himself wondering how the vast empty area between the State Council Building and Karl-Liebknecht-Straße had once looked—before World War II. The square couldn't possibly have been as empty and barren then as it stretched out before him now. Trying his luck, he approached an older man walking by and asked him what buildings had stood here twenty, thirty years before.

"Well, the Schloss," he answered with a broad Berlin accent, "but they blew that up ten years ago!"

"Who, the Russians?" von Boddien inquired.

Scowling at his clueless young interlocutor, the old man glanced around warily to see if anyone was listening to their exchange before quickly walking away.

Wilhelm von Boddien couldn't stop thinking about the man's specification "ten years ago." If that date was correct, then the destruction of the Schloss—at the time, he didn't even really know which palace was at issue—and its complete leveling to make way for parade grounds must have happened after the war.

No sooner was von Boddien back in Hamburg than he began to investigate the history of the Berlin Schloss. He hunted down illustrated volumes in libraries to get an idea of what the vanished building had looked like. He didn't find much aside from a few black-and-white photographs and two or three newspaper articles. But the high school graduate refused to give up. Somehow he felt as though, like Heinrich Schliemann before him, he had stumbled on the traces of a buried Troy. He dedicated four pages of his school newspaper to the Schloss.

Von Boddien forged ahead with his research for years; he wanted to know everything there was to know about the vanished Berlin Schloss. At the end of the 1970s, he happened upon a significant archive of materials concerning the building, kept in the Charlottenburg Palace. There, he got to know a small group of scholars who were compiling extensive documentation—a monograph—about the Schloss. They included the architectural historian Goerd Peschken and the art historian Liselotte Wiesinger, who became his mentors. The former supervisor of the Berlin Schloss, Margarete Kühn, also worked with the group. Goerd Peschken's study of the demolished Schloss was only finally published in 1982, but von Boddien had the opportunity to pore over Peschken's and his coauthors' documents years before it came out. He soon became so familiar with the gigantic building—whose surface area had been equivalent to three soccer fields—that he could "walk around" the art-historically significant rooms, halls, stairwells, floors, and interior courtyards of the palace in his mind without ever losing his way. No matter where he entered the virtual Schloss and which path he followed, he always knew exactly where he was. He became, as one architectural critic for the weekly *Die Zeit* later scoffed, the "palace ghost"—in fact, he was more like a ghost without a palace, who had yet to bring into existence the home he was so eager to haunt. Not that the young man seriously believed that the Schloss would be resurrected back then, decades before the fall of the Wall. Still, he was convinced that the history of the Schloss had not come to an end with its razing, that it still had a role to play in the future of the city.

The fall of the Wall gave wings to von Boddien's lonely hopes. Two well-known columnists from the West now spoke out in favor of rebuilding the Schloss. The first was the editor of the culture section of the *Frankfurter Allgemeine Zeitung,* Joachim Fest. In a seminal article published in the paper on November 30, 1990, he argued that the demolition of the Schloss had created a symbol of the victory of socialism and a "red square for submissive gestures." Reconstructing the Schloss would in turn be a visible manifestation of the failure of the "totalitarian model of society."

The second, more influential, article took a longer view and called for the Schloss to be rebuilt from an urban-historical perspective. It was written by Wolf Jobst Siedler, the previously mentioned publisher and journalist. Siedler pointed out that, unlike other European cities, Berlin had not come into being *before* the Schloss, but only with and after it. In reality, the Schloss, established in 1443 and subsequently constantly expanded upon, had been the founding act of the city; it was only when the Schloss was built that the former twin cities Berlin and Cölln, with their population of six thousand at the time, grew into the city of Berlin around it. In other words, Berlin hadn't even existed before the Schloss and thus couldn't exist without it. "The Schloss wasn't located in Berlin," Siedler wrote, getting to the heart of his argument, "Berlin *was* the Schloss."

For Wolfgang von Boddien and his associates, these two articles became the prelude to their momentous enterprise. Heartened, in 1992 they founded the Förderverein Berliner Schloss e.V. and began to promote the idea of rebuilding the Schloss, initially through rather clumsy means. Standing on Marx-Engels-Platz, von Boddien and his friends handed out postcards with a black-and-white photograph of the Schloss to both invited journalists and harried passersby who were preoccupied with a thousand other things. The culture sections of various papers lost little time in mocking the endeavor. A journalist from a left-leaning daily claimed to know why von Boddien wanted to rebuild the Schloss: his name was Wilhelm and he aspired to become Wilhelm III, and in order to do so he needed a palace. It wasn't easy to keep up good spirits in this climate.

The turning point came thanks to an idea that occurred to the Berlin art dealer Bernd Schultz. "Those who refuse to listen must see," von Boddien remembered Schultz decreeing, and by that he meant nothing less than a one-to-one simulation of the north and west faces of the Schloss—in other words, the part of the façade that had caught the eye of every pedestrian and driver approaching the palace from the Brandenburg Gate before 1943. The idea of reproducing the imposing façade as a painting and mounting it on scaffolding seemed as insane as it was unaffordable, yet Wilhelm von Boddien felt like he was in his element. The media immediately began to protest: How dare one rebuild the "most Prussian of Prussian palaces"—the very palace from whose balcony Kaiser Wilhelm II had declared World War I?

A few days later, von Boddien happened to take a trip to Paris. While there, not far from Place de la Concorde, he caught sight of the Church of the Madeleine, which was under restoration. The famous templclike façade had been painted to actual scale on the tarpaulin that covered the scaffolding in front of the portico. Taking a closer look, von Boddien jotted down the name and telephone number indicated—that of the Parisian painter of large-scale works, Catherine Feff. Standing before this perfect simulation of the façade of the Madeleine, he knew immediately whom he would commission to reproduce the Berlin Schloss.

With the help of his friends, von Boddien was able to drum up enthusiasm among donors for this unusual undertaking. According to the estimate, the scaffolding and gigantic painting on more than 100,000 square feet of canvas, along with the necessary information posters, would cost many millions of euros. But von Boddien and his backers braved the risk—and ultimately made out well, even financially. Under the direction of Catherine Feff, fifty Parisian art students set to work in an abandoned Renault workshop. Their task was not simply to copy the façade but to reproduce the play of light and shadow on its surface through trompe l'oeil—literally, "trick the eye"—a tried-and-true technique used in Italy and France since the baroque era. In fact, the French artists really did succeed in giving a three-dimensional quality to their colossal painting of the Berlin Schloss.

Determining the color of the façade proved to be tricky. It was impossible to deduce the original shade of the plasterwork from the surviving black-and-white photographs; at best, the paintings of the palace by baroque artists might be of help. But was the coloring in these paintings authentic? The mystery was solved thanks to the former supervisor of the Schloss, Margarete Kühn, who had salvaged a piece of early-eighteenth-century plaster from the ruins of the Charlottenburg Palace and guarded it like a relic. It was of the same ocher tone, fashionable in the baroque era, as the plasterwork of all the important Prussian palaces.

The completed canvases were mounted on scaffolding with shock chords to absorb the wind pressure, resulting, practically overnight, in the illusion of a resurrection. It was a crazy dream come true for Wilhelm von Boddien—and not just for him. Any-one driving by the Berlin State Opera and Humboldt University in the spring of 1993 saw, at the next left bend in the road, the ghostly presence of a baroque palace that had been demolished forty-three years earlier, fluttering slightly as though preparing to take flight. It was a sight that made both pedestrians and driv-ers seeing the apparition for the first time pinch themselves. Were they dreaming? The baroque façade of the vanished Schloss, last decorated by Andreas Schlüter and Johann Fried-rich Eosander von Göthe, rose up on the right side of the street, making the TV Tower behind it look shabby in comparison. The effect of the faux façade was especially powerful and ro-mantic at night, in the light of the half-moon, billowing out-ward or curving inward depending on the direction of the wind. Even notorious Prussian-haters had to admit: the Schloss was not quite as ugly as they had imagined during the long period of its absence. In any event, its western façade looked signifi-cantly better than a great deal of what modern architects had built between Potsdamer Platz and the city center after German reunification.

I, too, succumbed to the magic of these canvases. I was espe-cially in thrall to its ocher hue, familiar to me from Italy and so rarely seen in Berlin. Wasn't it proof that this color had also once been at home under Prussian skies, that it could glow here as well? Of course the artful trompe l'oeil also contributed to the overall idealization. Thanks to its canvas alter ego, which reacted to every gust of wind, the bombastic Schloss gained a lightness the original had never had. Anyone who has ever admired the playful Hohenstaufen palaces in southern Germany and Austria couldn't fail to see that magnitude and ostentation had prevailed over beauty in the Hohenzollern Schloss. Newer Berliners like me, who had never seen the original nor witnessed its demolition, secretly wished that the Schloss would remain just as it was now—a beautiful trick of the eye.

The simulation was a spectacular success. All of a sudden, hundreds of thousands of Berliners from both East and West discovered their love of the vanished Prussian palace. Thanks to his surprise coup, Wilhelm von Boddien was able to extend the "Schloss show" twice—as a consolation and elixir against the impending gray days of winter, and to continue to draw tourists to Berlin the following spring and summer. The mayor at the time, Eberhard Diepgen, who had supported the Schloss plans from the start, pushed through the extension. The set piece remained on view for a total of fifteen months (until September 1994), and von Boddien was able to watch with satisfaction as his bold venture paid off. Polls showed that there was a clear shift in opinion in favor of rebuilding the Schloss.

In 2003, the German Bundestag voted with a two-thirds majority to rebuild the Schloss and allocated 600 million euros of federal funds to the venture.

Wilhelm von Boddien had reached his goal. He had come close to abandoning the whole endeavor only once, in the fall of 2008, when the lawyers of two anti-Schloss parties charged him with suspicion of "embezzlement" and "money laundering." The reasons given were, among other things, an anonymous donation of 750,000 euros from Switzerland and the supposed embezzlement of donations. WHERE DID ALL THOSE MILLIONS GO? the press headlined. The dispute over the preservation of the Palace of the Republic and the rebuilding of the Schloss had stirred up deep emotions; the more obvious it became that the pro-Schloss party had won, the lower the punches thrown to thwart it became. Von Boddien was close to giving up on his life's dream. He had reached the limit of his willingness to suffer for the Schloss, he explained, the moment his and his family's good reputation were dragged through the mud. His friends talked him out of his doubts. If he gave up now, he would only confirm that there was some truth to the defamatory accusations. In late 2008, the district attorney's office suspended the proceedings. The final word in the matter was that the investigation had failed to establish reasonable suspicion of wrongdoing.

So the Schloss was going to be rebuilt—fine. But what should be done with this new old colossus in the middle of the city? How could one fill—what spirit would occupy—the 590-by-394-foot palace? For a long time, a mixed use was considered—the Schloss should be open to both commercial and cultural occupants. Trade fair organizers, museums, and galleries expressed interest; an enormous underground parking lot was planned in place of the imperial cellar to facilitate financing of the project. In the end, a simple idea won out. In the spirit of Alexander von Humboldt, the city's most famous son, it was decided that the Schloss should become a meeting place for the cultures of the world. It will serve the same intellectual and humanistic traditions that had already found a safe haven in the old Hohenzollern palace. There, in the royal tearoom, the scientific explorer and polymath Alexander von Humboldt had told the Prussian king's aristocratic and learned guests about his world travels; in the palace archives, he had stored some of his ethnological and botanical collections. Now the Humboldt Forum is taking shape in the new Schloss. The Ethnological Museum and the Museum of Asian Art of the Foundation of Prussian Cultural Heritage, Humboldt University's history of science department, and the Regional Library of Berlin all plan to house their valuable collections here. The idea is to turn Berlin into a global center for art and culture. The Humboldt Forum is intended to become a place where all of the world's civilizations can present themselves and enter into dialogue with one another—in keeping with Humboldt's statement that "the most dangerous worldview is the worldview of those who have not viewed the world."

What can already be seen now of these noble plans in the "Humboldt Box" next to the construction site seems rather anemic. So far, the project lacks the urgency, passion, and madness that motivated Alexander von Humboldt's research. It's not easy to incorporate Humboldt's inner conflict between his universalistic desire for knowledge and his fragile relationship to his self and his body into the concept of this gigantic circus. A letter written by the twenty-year-old Humboldt contains this astonishing sentence: "Serious activities, but especially the study of nature, will keep me away from sensuality!" But this enormous cultural project is only just getting under way. Let's hope that convincing, inspiring content for the expensive shell will be found in time for the Humboldt Forum's opening in 2018. The resurrected Schloss could—must—become the beating heart of the new city.

Ground was broken in June 2012. In the foundations of the former Schloss, workers came across three thousand pine and oak pilings, which had been remarkably well preserved in the swampy, hermetically sealed subsoil for three hundred years. The Schloss had been built on these pilings laid over with a wood-beam grid, and they now had to be pulled out with a special crane, one by one like teeth, in order to make room for the new foundation.

The discovery of this strange treasure immediately incited greed. It brought to light the fact that an especially strict law applies to treasure hunters in Berlin, entirely irrespective of what they find. If they come across something valuable in the ground, it automatically belongs to the state—with the result that private parties in Berlin almost never report found items. Yet to whom in fact does the treasure of the three-hundred-year-old pilings belong? "The wood automatically becomes the property of the company charged with the digging and shaft work," deemed the director of the Berlin Schloss–Humboldt Forum Foundation, which happens to be the owner-builder, in an article published in *Der Tagesspiegel* on November 9, 2012. Except that, unfortunately, said foundation subcontracted the job of pulling out and exploiting the pilings to another company, which is now making its own claims to the "wooden treasure."

First, the pilings need to be desanded and dried. But then

what? Should they be used, as Thomas Loy suggested in the same piece in *Der Tagesspiegel*, to make flooring for the Schloss or furnishings with a "Hohenzollern Schloss" proof of origin? Or to outfit a room in the Humboldt Forum, as Wilhelm von Boddien has in mind? Or maybe even to make violins and cellos, as experts claim the wood will turn a glowing amber color once it is treated?

No one believes that the projected budget of 590 million euros will suffice to build the Schloss. Its anticipated completion in 2018 also seems all too optimistic in light of the fate met by other large-scale ventures in Berlin. When in doubt, experienced Berliners simply double the cost of every large-scale project and extend the expected completion date by three years.

Notwithstanding such contingencies, for the now seventy-year-old Schloss fanatic Wilhelm von Boddien the dream that has defined his life has almost come true. Perhaps he won't live to see the roof built. But in his lifetime he will at least be able to haunt the rooms, halls, and courtyards of the new Schloss, which until now he has only been able to wander through in his mind. Von Boddien has earned the right to sit back and put his feet up. The man who almost single-handedly rescued the vanished Schloss from oblivion would prefer to stay in the background from now on. In any case, at the opening ceremony of the Humboldt Forum, he plans to sit all the way in the back—in the twenty-seventh row or so, he says.

It goes without saying that the disputes surrounding the Schloss aren't over just because construction has begun. In February 2013, the former German chancellor Helmut Schmidt spoke up: "I would not rebuild it," he said. "It's a Prussian palace, after all, and there is no reason to resurrect the Prussians . . . But I find it especially odd that Berlin doesn't want to pay for the Schloss, and that instead the federal government is expected to pitch in yet again . . . The grandiosity with which other people's money is spent in Berlin is phenomenal!"

In the face of this harsh criticism from the Hamburg native Schmidt, even anti-Schloss Berliners rallied around the project. And this is doubtless how it will go until the Humboldt Forum is completed. But when it finally opens one day, you can be sure that almost no one who was against it will miss attending the opening ceremony.

WEST BERLIN

The name West Berlin refers to a city that no longer exists. With "Where Are We Now?," his new song about the time he spent in West Berlin, David Bowie—who lived on Hauptstraße in the Schöneberg district in the 1970s—has unleashed a veritable wave of nostalgia. The strange life people led during the years of the Wall has become an object of memory and invocation. Magazine covers now feature headlines like WEST BERLIN IS BACK, and books have titles such as *The Half-City That Is No More*—as though West Berlin were a sunken island, when in reality this section of the city still exists and has changed a lot less physically than East Berlin has.

A Polish couple, Danka and Anatol Gotfryd, offered me their unusual perspective on life and the atmosphere in the old West Berlin. They came to the half-city back in the 1950s. In his moving book *Der Himmel in den Pfützen: Ein Leben zwischen Galizien und dem Kurfürstendamm* (The Sky in the Puddles: A Life Between Galicia and the Kurfürstendamm), Anatol Gotfryd describes how he survived being deported to the Belzec extermination camp as a ten-year-old boy. An engineer managed to saw through and bend back the iron bars across the window of the freight car in which they were being transported. Several of Gotfryd's fellow passengers—adults condemned to the same fate—helped the boy through the bars, ejecting him from the moving train. He made his way to Lemberg on foot, where he found temporary shelter in a small guesthouse run by an anonymous woman.

Sixteen years later, newly wed, Anatol and Danka arrived in West Berlin.

On a Sunday morning in 1958, their train pulled into the Ostbahnhof station. From there, they took a taxi to the Kurfürstendamm in West Berlin. Anatol remembers how much he enjoyed the Berlin air. Whenever he took a deep breath in the Upper Silesian city of Katowice, where he had lived with his parents after the war, he had always felt as though he were sucking on a piece of brown coal. He found it easy to breathe in West Berlin. Maybe he managed to avoid the brown-coal dust blown over from the furnaces in East Berlin; maybe he simply refused to acknowledge it. Danka remembers the same feeling but gives it another name. Sorry, she says, but there's no other word for it: what she breathed and felt at the time was freedom. A feeling of elation in her heart and entire body that probably no one who hasn't lived under a dictatorship can imagine. The Kaufhaus des Westens (KaDeWe) department store sparkled in the sun. They marveled at the thousands of shoes, dresses, and suits, necklaces and earrings, the abundance of fruits and meat. But because of their scant resources, the Gotfryds were only able to admire these wonderful displays.

As a result, they were all the more mystified when, immediately after their arrival, they met people who raved about the blessings of socialism. These people wanted to make it clear to their Polish acquaintances how good they had had it in Poland, how superior real socialism was. Apparently they couldn't imagine that the works of Marx, Lenin, and Lukács, which they had appropriated for themselves through their own independent study, had been tedious required reading for their Polish guests. In an attempt to lighten the conversation, Anatol Gotfryd would tell the story of a speech given by a Polish Communist Party official. This man had attempted to convince his assembled comrades that someday—thanks to socialism's productivity—it would be necessary to work only on Wednesday. Someone in the audience had stood up and asked, "Every Wednesday?" The Gotfryds' genial laughter failed to infect their hosts.

They felt no less alienated several years later when they saw demonstrators parading along the Kurfürstendamm, their speeches and slogans replete with mentions of "social change"—a "revolution," even. For the love of god, what kind of social change, the Gotfryds asked themselves—we only just left behind precisely such "change"! Even years later, they had only one thing left to say of the insurgents: hopeless!

At first, they muddled through by working—for two deutsche marks an hour—as substitute dentists. The dental practices where they worked were usually located in West Berlin's poor neighborhoods. Anatol Gotfryd remembers one in Neukölln. There, he had to treat some one hundred patients a day, including Turkish immigrants. These patients would wait in the long bench-lined hallway in front of the packed waiting room. The walls were covered with paneling to prevent the plaster from crumbling from the thousands and thousands of backs constantly rubbing against them. A black-and-white television set that was always on hung from the ceiling of the waiting room, suspended from a clothesline. The treatment room was strewn with fancy Persian dental bridges, which lingered in the clinic until people could write them off on their taxes and take them home. A lab produced the false teeth so quickly, based on just one dental cast, that patients were often unable to close their mouths after inserting them.

In their search for permanent jobs, the Gotfryds encountered the usual difficulties immigrants face. In order to get a residence permit, you had to have a work permit, but you could only get a work permit if you had a residence permit. Both papers were necessary to become licensed as a dentist. In an attempt to reduce the waiting time, the Gotfryds enrolled as guest students at the university clinic's Department for Dental Medicine. Their aim was to work toward a doctoral degree. A helpful colleague recommended that they try doing so through the Americans; as far as he knew, the U.S. Army in Berlin was looking for dentists. And you didn't need a permit to work there.

Anatol's experience when the Gotfryds went to register at the headquarters on Clayallee was surprising. The recruitment officer, a colonel, apparently wasn't the least bit interested in Anatol's professional exams or his letters of recommendation. He wanted to test the candidate's technical skills, wanted to see how adept he was at practical work. In the "theoretical" part of the exam, the colonel asked him to turn a piece of wire into a paper clip—a test the examinee successfully accomplished in seconds. For the practical test, the colonel brought in a GI with a hellishly impacted wisdom tooth. To the colonel's surprise, Anatol also mastered this challenge in next to no time. When he told the colonel afterward that the operation had been no problem for him, the officer gave him a rather surly look. Anatol explained that, in the state outpatient clinic in Katowice, he had been responsible for pulling teeth for a year and a half, seven hours a day. After this dental boot camp, nobody could best him at this particular operation. The colonel gave Anatol a resounding slap on the back and hired him on the spot.

The Gotfryds were impressed by their employer's emphatic emphasis on their doctors' practical skills. Every day in the American dental practice, with the help of a point system, a "skillfulness score" was posted, which the dentists could consult to see how well they were doing. Efficiency and ergonomics—that was what mattered to the Americans. The dentist pair from Poland quickly grasped that they were in an unaccustomed position of power. They had both been hired at the rank of lieutenant. As a result, they no longer had to settle for giving their patients nonbinding advice that was usually ignored. They could now downright order them to brush their teeth a certain way. Later, when the Gotfryds ran what may have been the most successful private dental practice in West Berlin, their recommendations for dental care always retained a mild trace of the commanding tone they had learned with the Americans.

Being hired to work in the U.S. hospital was the beginning of a life of luxury for the two dentists. Every morning, they would find freshly washed and starched lab coats in their lockers, along with two elegant coats for their walk to the cafeteria. A young man, whose job it was to anticipate their every wish, was put at their disposal. If they asked him to pick up some coffee and a piece of cake in the afternoon, he would show up with an entire enormous cake. The leftovers were simply thrown in the trash. The cafeteria food was also served in oversize American portions. But the Gotfryds enjoyed other privileges as well. As employees of the U.S. Army, they could send their assistant to go shopping at PX stores. Members of the U.S. Army could buy duty-free goods not only from everywhere in Europe but also from the Far East: rugs, vases, furniture, grandfather clocks, and porcelain from every corner of the world. American officers could even have their extra-long gas-guzzlers shipped to Berlin from the United States entirely at the Army's expense.

The dollar-to-DM exchange rate at the time was one to four. "Suddenly, we were rich," Danka says. There was a party at the Harnack House every weekend—it was the most sought-after social address of the time. During the week, the Gotfryds were often invited to officers' apartments. Despite the official ban on fraternization, the Americans liked to surround themselves with guests from Berlin; in any event, they didn't have a problem with dentists who worked for the Army. For Danka, these visits were a revelation of the American lifestyle. The American facilities in Berlin-Dahlem had been newly built according to American standards. No sooner did you open the door to an apartment from the stairwell than you found yourself not in the long hallway typical of Berlin apartments but directly in the living room. The moment you crossed the threshold, you were in the middle of the apartment. There, the Gotfryds found themselves surrounded by teak furniture—anyone with a reputation to uphold who could afford it had teak furniture at the time—and they admired the brand-new beds and couches from Scandinavia, which were almost as wide and luxurious as those in Hollywood movies.

The two dentists from Poland had landed in the midst of Berlin's Americans; they felt like they had won the lottery. They went to the Café du Lac or the Maison de France—always accompanied by Americans. "As an Allied power," Anatol Gotfryd explains, "the Americans were the kings of the city, but they didn't act like occupiers. That was their great charm as an occupying power."

Naturally, the Gotfryds didn't let the chance to go to East Berlin with an American acquaintance escape them. They were waved through at Checkpoint Charlie: East German officials were not allowed to control Allied vehicles. Alongside a uniformed representative of the occupying power, they attended the Deutsche Oper. "But sitting in the middle of thousands of locals in an enormous auditorium in the GDR," Anatol remembers, "was not the same as sitting in the back of a Buick with U.S. Army plates. We were scared!" "No, you were scared," Danka corrects him. In any event, scared or not, they both enjoyed the generally excellent performances.

About a year after Anatol started working for the U.S. Army, Professor Ewald Harndt, the director of the Dental Clinic of the Free University of Berlin, offered him an assistantship. At the same time, the colonel proposed that the Gotfryds work as dentists on an aircraft carrier with six thousand soldiers—with a view to earning American citizenship and retirement after twenty years of service. Anatol chose the university dental clinic. What tipped the scales was the fact that he didn't know how to swim, his wife claims, laughing. Anatol argues that there were other reasons—namely, the fact that the position in the dental clinic would give him civil servant status. In any event, he accepted the assistantship, while his wife continued to work for the U.S. Army in Berlin. At Harndt's instigation, he became naturalized virtually overnight so he could take the oath on the German constitution.

I asked Anatol Gotfryd whether his German or American superiors knew that he was Jewish and had only barely managed to escape the Belzec extermination camp. He replied that he hadn't exactly walked around Berlin at the time with a banner proclaiming, "I'm a Jew!" On the other hand, he never hesitated to admit to his Jewish identity if the conversation happened to turn to his background. The Americans were only interested in his skills as a dentist—something he experienced as a blessing. And he had hinted at his heritage only once to the always friendly and helpful director of the university dental clinic. The latter had responded with just one sentence, saying that he was self-conscious when dealing with Jews. The subject never came up between them again. Over the years, their professional relationship developed into a friendship.

Other colleagues also found out about Anatol's Jewish identity. This was awkward, he remembers: they were all at a loss for words, and he could sense they felt guilty toward him. They would overwhelm him with information about where this or that colleague of theirs had "served" on which part of the Polish or Russian front. He felt like he existed in some sort of protected space—like wild game that could no longer be hunted. Once, however, a colleague had revealed his mentality with the most exquisite candor: "When we SS struck, not much survived in our wake." Anatol had had to take a deep breath before responding: "I can confirm that. I witnessed the efficiency of the SS when they struck, from another perspective—during the Warsaw Uprising." Sometimes memories would flash through his mind entirely unprompted, catapulting him out of the present. Invited to a private event, he found himself surrounded by guests, most of whom were wearing boots. The sight of so many boots caused him to panic for a moment—even though it was just a party for a riding club.

The fall of the Wall reawakened old fears. He worried about the imminent withdrawal of the Allied troops from Berlin, especially after hearing the tipsy occupants of a passing convoy of cars yelling xenophobic and anti-Semitic slurs in the days after November 9. But the Gotfryds were quick to forget irritations like these. They had been in Germany for a long time and felt they were in the very best of hands in their rapidly growing circle of friends.

The American invitations were then followed by invitations to the homes of their German colleagues—a different culture, at least in the early years, Danka notes with an ironic twinkle in her eye. She remembers one strange evening. The apartment of the German dentist's family hosting the party was also filled with teak furniture. But unlike in the American homes, here curtains had been drawn across every single one of the windows. A few bottles of wine and some pretzel sticks were set out on the table. After waiting for dinner for what seemed like a long enough time, Anatol valiantly asked if he might possibly have a sandwich. Upon which the guests were served potato salad with pieces of sausage.

In 1962, the U.S. Army decided to reserve for its members a privilege that until then all Americans in the city had enjoyed: free treatment in the Army's hospitals. The colonel advised Danka, "You should open a practice now, right away. Everyone knows you and will come to you."

It was good advice. With a loan of ten thousand deutsche marks, the Gotfryds opened a practice on Lehniner Platz. Sausages and sauerkraut were served at the opening party. As it turned out, their first patients really were exclusively American. But before long German private patients also started showing up, because they had heard that Americans went there. At the time, Anatol points out, Germans were convinced that anything American was technically superior—which was, in fact, the case.

Thanks to their experience and connections, the Gotfryds had access to the latest materials and studies in American dental medicine. Theirs was also the first practice in Berlin with an exorbitantly expensive "Made in U.S.A." reclining dentist's chair. The chair had originally been designed for pilots and contributed significantly to the legend surrounding the practice. The new approach was referred to as "Dental medicine on reclining patients."

The practice attracted various social circles, from which it drew its deep-pocketed regular customers: artists connected to the Academy of the Arts; actors and directors from the Schaubühne theater across the way, who invited the Gotfryds to their premieres and recommended the practice to their colleagues; fellowship recipients of the city's programs for foreign artists. By the time the practice closed at the beginning of the new millennium, entire casts of plays and throngs of writers and artists had reclined in the Gotfryds' famous chair to have their teeth repaired. Since many artists paid their dental bills with paintings, and thanks to the Gotfryds' virtually impeccable taste in art, today they are the proud owners of an exquisite collection of artworks from the second half of the twentieth century.

In the summer of 1962, the same year that the Gotfryds opened their private practice, I boarded a train in Freiburg, arriving in the Prussian metropolis the following day. It was the farthest distance you could travel within West Germany—some five hundred miles. I wanted to go to Berlin for the same reason that most students of my generation chose this city: studying in the "front city" counted as a sort of voluntary military service—if you studied in West Berlin, you were exempt from serving in the Bundeswehr. Outside, under the station's elevated platforms, my first impression of the city came into focus. I liked the bleak avenue of amusements with its sausage stands and minicasinos and the Bilka department store with its crumbling façade. I especially liked the double-decker buses. Boarding one that went down the Kurfürstendamm, I climbed to the upper level. At Olivaer Platz, I got off and sat down in a café on Xantener Straße. It was the only café in the sun that had set a few tables out onto the sidewalk. All I noticed were the artfully presented mounds of ice cream, not the old women sitting alone at the neighboring tables, who would become my landladies in the coming years. At the kiosk across the way, in the course of fifteen minutes, I saw two women from behind that I would have liked to see from the front. It was a good street, I decided; this was where I'd live.

My room in a huge classic Berlin apartment looked out onto my first Berlin courtyard and cost eighty deutsche marks a month. In my memory, it's empty except for a black brass bed with gilded spheres on the bedposts. I liked the room because it had high ceilings and because the sun would shine onto the two decorative spheres at the head of the bed in the morning, from eight-thirty until quarter to noon. When the sun started to arrive an hour later or not at all, I knew that another season had begun.

During my first few weeks there, a gurgling creaking and groaning woke me up at five one morning. It sounded like the hoarse whistling and wheezing of a sick old person upstairs or next door. I sat up in my bed; it took a moment to be sure I wasn't dreaming; then I put my ear against the wall. The sounds seemed to be coming from above. I followed them up into the attic. When I opened the moldering wooden door, my eyes fell on hundreds of pigeons celebrating the arrival of morning with their cooing.

Ever since, pigeons in Berlin have reminded me of death and decay. I saw them fluttering around the attic in pestilent conglomerations, shoveled into piles after a visit from the exterminator, hitting the ground in the courtyard whenever the invisible mad marksman from a window across the way managed to hit another one of his targets. The dead bird would lie there for days, until someone finally picked it up gingerly and tossed it in the garbage. The cooing of pigeons and my landlady's weightless step in the hallway are among my earliest memories of Berlin. Every night when I came home, I had to make my way past her and her mentally disabled son's legs. The two of them would sit far apart from each other in the large *Berliner Zimmer*, the vestibule-cum-living-room typical of old Berlin apartments, the landlady busy with some sewing, her son staring fixedly at his mother. He sat on a red velvet pillow right by the door that led from this room to the hallway to my room. He would sit there all day long, in shorts in the summer, his pale legs blocking my way.

I later lived in other rooms with other landladies, but it was a long time before I managed to shake the feeling of inhabiting a stillness that seemed to aspire to death. The pigeons and war widows in Berlin were my first muses. Without entirely realizing it, I spent my first years in Berlin in the company of these old, lonely women, whose husbands had fallen, died, or simply gone away in the war. I rarely spoke with them, and whenever I did the silence afterward was unbearable.

Another odd thing about West Berlin was the enormous number of dogs. There seemed to be more dogs than children in the city. Apparently the owners of these dogs thought it was perfectly okay for their darlings to do their business in the middle of the sidewalk. Both—owners and dogs alike—would react aggressively if a passerby lectured them about it. Some owners would play innocent. Hurrying on a few steps when their four-legged friends relieved themselves, they would suddenly stop as if on a whim and piously raise their eyes to the sky until the dog finished his business. Incensed citizens would regularly spearhead initiatives to combat dog waste, demanding fines. There were debates of dubious value, some of which were even broadcast on television. These would feature extremely upset owners with a poodle or pug in their arms and tears in their eyes, fighting for their dogs' right to express themselves freely and unimpeded everywhere in the city. A right that no one actually wanted to deprive them of—obviously it was only the subsequent removal of the animals' bequests that was at issue. But the advocates of cleaner sidewalks failed to prevail; the canine lobby was more powerful. In my mind, nothing was more emblematic of West Berlin than an unsuspecting tourist stepping on something soft, examining the sole of his shoe, and cursing as he scraped it against the curb. Experienced West Berliners behaved differently. Like mushroom hunters, they were conditioned to notice the little brown piles. If they did happen to step into one, they would just walk on resolutely, as though nothing had happened.

Inevitably, I regularly experienced bouts of nostalgia. It was only being in this Prussian city that I realized how good the food and how friendly the conversational tone had been in Freiburg. If you asked a local there for directions, he would launch into an elaborate answer in his Baden dialect and sometimes even accompany you to the street in question. Berliners felt inconvenienced when approached and made it clear that, in principle, they were not available to supply information. Those that deigned to do so liked to couple their response with a reproach: *Don't have a map on you, eh?* The worst was when, unbeknownst to you, you were actually already on the street you were looking for. Then the person you had asked would point to the street sign in the distance and bark: *Don'tcha have eyes in your head? It says so right up there!*

But no one reacted worse to being asked something than West Berlin bus drivers. Either they would immediately point to a sign indicating that passengers were prohibited from talking to the driver, or they would answer in a tone that made you fear for your eardrums. An acquaintance from southern Germany told me that he had sent the Berlin Transport Authority a letter of complaint about the yelling bus drivers. Months later, he received a reply: *Out of consideration for the city's many senior citizens, drivers are required to express themselves especially loudly and clearly.* He definitely hadn't expected the agency to go so far as to justify its employees' behavior as being a matter of courtesy.

The pleasure some Berliners took in catching their fellow human beings making a mistake was also mysterious to me. What drove the superintendent to watch from his window to see if I touched another vehicle's bumper when I parked my VW? Would he write down my plate number if I did? Sometimes I'd shout it out to him to make it easier for him to report me. And what motivated the group of pedestrians waiting for the light to turn green at an intersection with hardly any traffic to shout "It's red!" at the one sinner who dared cross the street before the light had changed? What passion impelled the driver of the still-distant car who caught sight of this pedestrian to suddenly floor it and speed toward him? The only human right Berlin drivers seemed willing to risk their lives for was the right of way.

Inscrutable signs were affixed in building hallways: IN THE INTEREST OF ALL TENANTS, CHILDREN AND TENANTS ARE PROHIBITED FROM PLAYING AND SINGING IN THE COURTYARD, HALLWAYS, AND STAIRS! In a train car, I read the warning: IT IS FORBIDDEN TO LEAN OUT OF THE WINDOW WHEN THE TRAIN IS IN MOTION. How much more reasonable the French and Italian versions were: IT IS DANGEROUS TO LEAN OUT OF THE WINDOW WHEN THE TRAIN IS IN MOTION. Outside a housing office, I saw the declaration: NO ACCOMMODATIONS SERVICES FOR STUDENTS OR FOREIGNERS! The craziest notice I discovered—identical word for word in West and East Berlin—was in old elevators: IT IS FORBIDDEN TO TRANSPORT PEOPLE IN ELEVATORS IN WHICH THE TRANSPORT OF PEOPLE IS FORBIDDEN.

But more important matters soon diverted my attention from quirks like these. The stresses and charms of living in West Berlin were a result of its exceptional geographic and political situation. Even though West Berlin was located at the farthest end of the western world, those of us who lived there felt like we were at the heart of conflicts of world-historical importance. I had missed the Wall being built, but its consequences were palpable every day. The defining event for me was the fate of Peter Fechter. On August 17, 1962, while attempting to flee, Fechter was shot and critically wounded by border police near Checkpoint Charlie. He was just a few yards away from reaching West Berlin territory. East German border guards, their weapons unlocked, watched for nearly an hour as he bled to death. Soldiers of the U.S. Army trained their loaded weapons on the same section of the border. West Berlin residents watched the drama in disbelief, urging the American officer on duty to help the dying fugitive. He wasn't sure what to do. He later said that when he called for guidance, the U.S. commander of Berlin at the time, Major General Albert Watson II, replied: "Lieutenant, you have your orders. Stand fast. Do nothing!"

For me and many of my fellow students, the mortal agony of Peter Fechter, who kept crying out for help, became a test of our as-yet-untested political conscience: Who among us would have been willing to risk his life to pull the dying man onto West Berlin territory? The arguments for and against it provoked heated debates. Several students actually did go on to put their lives and freedom on the line by smuggling willing East German citizens into the West; when, just a few years later, the new left came to see anticommunism as a deadly sin, they had a hard time admitting to their earlier heroic deeds.

In the final weeks before August 13, 1961, tens of thousands of people had managed to flee from East Germany. One of them, who made it to the West via S-Bahn two days before the Wall was built, became my first great love. In West Berlin, she quickly found other young women who shared her fate. Whenever these three friends went out—with me as their only escort—I got a sense of the completely different world in which they had grown up. Wearing summer dresses and flats, they sauntered along the Kurfürstendamm, trying out their effect on the West Berlin Casanovas. They attracted droves of admirers but were unimpressed by their conceited carryings-on and, above all, by their clueless-ness. The women's confidence and the delight they took in mocking these suitors sent the latter running. Whenever the three friends spent time together, they would tell one another stories from their schooldays, sing FDJ (Freie Deutsche Jugend, or Free German Youth) songs, mimic the empty catchphrases and proclamations of the party bigwigs, and dissolve into cheerful laughter. I noticed in particular that they didn't have the same hatred of Germany and of all things German that was de rigueur in West Berlin's intellectual circles—I loathed German folk songs, even German pop music. In their eyes, the enemy wasn't our parents' generation and their Nazi past but the party of bigwigs that had established a second German dictatorship after the war. I often found myself feeling irritated and also a bit envious of how uninhibited these three East German refugees in West Berlin were about being German.

The student movement of 1968 changed everyday culture and people's attitude in the city from the ground up. In England and the United States, the revolt of hair and nails, hoarse voices, and secondhand clothes had preceded the political outburst against the Vietnam War. The revolt of 1968—which, in Berlin, was actually the revolt of 1967—reprised all that. In the collective ferment of those years, thousands of people discovered their desire for another life. Never since have I found out so much so quickly from so many people about their personal hopes and fears. Gays admitted to being gay for the first time, women claimed that it was their men and not capitalism that were preventing their emancipation. Stutterers asserted their right to speak in front of crowds a thousand strong. A star of the German commune Kommune 1 managed to turn his personal difficulty reaching orgasm into the entire movement's problem.

A false myth claims that the Sixty-Eighters were anti-American. There's no doubt that the protest against the Vietnam War was the springboard for the movement. But, in the early flyers and speeches at least, an effort was made to distinguish between the U.S. government and the "American people." And, in fact, the protest against the Vietnam War had begun in the United States and spread from there to Western Europe. The key concept of "civil unrest" and every single related form of protest—teach-ins, love-ins, sit-ins—also came from America. Ditto for the typical outfits of the time, every element of which—from jeans and khakis, T-shirts and parkas to sneakers—the Sixty-Eighters bought at the PX store near the Free University. Among Berlin clubs, the International, which was frequented primarily by GIs, as well as by some conscientious objectors, was an insider's tip. None of us listened to German pop music; we listened to Bob Dylan, Joan Baez, and the Rolling Stones. And the Sixty-Eighters accounted for the second-largest group of listeners—right after the GIs—of AFN, the American Forces Network. Of course this didn't stop the rebels from burning American flags and even, in the heat of protest, shouting out genuinely anti-American chants such as "USA-SA-SS," evoking the Nazi storm troopers and paramilitary. But the much talked about anti-Americanism of the Sixty-Eighters was at worst the result of a love-hate relationship. Unlike in East Germany at the time, where people were taught to condemn U.S. imperialism starting in kindergarten, in West Berlin the impulse didn't have legs. The rebellious youth of the 1960s was probably the most Americanized segment of Berlin's population at the time.

But the student movement also caused a second rift in the already divided city—a rift within West Berlin. The half-city split into two camps: a minority of rebelling young people, and an anticommunist majority, whose mouthpiece was the tabloid press owned by the media mogul Axel Springer. In the spirit of the motto "My city, right or wrong," many Berliners were deaf to the protests against the Vietnam War. To these Berliners, burning American flags and slogans such as "Hey hey hey, LBJ, how many kids did you kill today?"—chanted on the occasion of a visit by the American president Lyndon B. Johnson—seemed sacrilegious. For the older ones among them, the Berlin airlift and the building of the Wall were still fresh in their minds. Weren't the "riot mongers" and "Mao followers" on the streets in the process of alienating the locked-in city's most important protector? The rebels, for their part, were too high on their successes and on the revolutionary delirium increasingly taking on a life of its own to try to meet the other side halfway.

In 1980, I spent six months on a lecture tour in Latin America. When I got back to Berlin, I saw the Wall, which had been remodeled in the meantime, through a stranger's eyes. Yes, I thought to myself, this is the most absurd and well-known structure in the world. Yet, at the same time, we know next to nothing about what it does to the people who live in its shadow. When I began research for my book *The Wall Jumper*, I met with skepticism from almost every friend I told about the project. Wasn't I encroaching on the territory of the anticommunist press baron Axel Springer? After all, an unchallenged tenet of the left claimed that the division of the country was simply the price Germans had to pay for the crimes of the Third Reich. Not that anyone had ever asked the East Germans, who after all paid this price entirely on their own, if they were okay with this settling of German guilt. Anyone who dared touch the Wall, this supposed consequence of Hitler's war, was suspected of being a Cold Warrior, not to say a revisionist and revanchist.

So it hardly required any special talent or prophetic ability to identify the longstanding "wall in the mind" that I described in *The Wall Jumper*. All it took was curiosity. But curiosity was in short supply in that hysterical period of the Cold War and pervasive us-versus-them mentality. A reviewer for the paper *Die Welt* (part of the Springer Group) observed at the time that it was astonishing that an avowed leftist of all people should have written this book; the book, he concluded, was decidedly smarter than its author.

By the mid-1980s, it felt like history had abandoned West Berlin; it only made its presence felt in the barely acknowledged headlines on newsstands. The great collective passions had run out of steam, the policy of détente was making quiet, tenacious progress, the enemy camps in West Berlin were once again moving toward each other. Sure, some areas of the city were still smoldering. In Kreuzberg, young people occupied empty buildings, provisionally repairing them and asserting their claim to live there free of charge as they saw fit. Everyone was talking about bands with strange names like Einstürzende Neubauten (Collapsing New Buildings) and Die tödliche Doris (The Deadly Doris), and about new and not-so-new clubs like Risiko, Sound, Dschungel, and SO36. A wild art scene ran riot in Berlin's nooks and crannies, generating paintings that conveyed a sense of life as exalted as it was suicidal. But what these at times brilliant, at times amateurish forms of expression all shared was a self-celebratory tendency and an inclination to seal themselves off from the outside world. They were internal insurgencies, limited to the entrails, completely lacking in the impulse to change society—an impulse that, in light of the failure of the proclaimed "revolution" of the Sixty-Eighters, was scorned with good reason. Somehow and without noticing it, West Berlin had become the world capital of minorities: masters of the art of living and the unemployed, gays and lesbians, political sects and esoteric types, Turks, Poles, Italians, and Russians. And somewhere in the midst of these groups, the three Allied powers and Berlin city government had also found their place as minorities of a different kind. "Keine Macht für niemand"—"No power for nobody"—the legendary band Ton, Steine, Scherben (Clay, Stones, Shards) had sung. In those eerily calm years, this slogan seemed to describe the state of affairs in the half-city. West Berlin dozed; it had become a comfortable biotope protected by generous subsidies and a wall. The name given to the western half-city by East Germany's ruling party wasn't far off the mark: "Independent political entity West Berlin."

From 1984, a duo of Christian Democratic Union (CDU) politicians, Eberhard Diepgen and Klaus-Rüdiger Landowsky, dominated politics in West Berlin. Activists of the student movement knew the pair as members of the dueling fraternity Saravia, a formerly progressive, nationally oriented student organization that had grown increasingly reactionary over the course of its more than 160 years of existence and was characterized by a strong team spirit. During the years of the revolt, the student movement had driven Diepgen and Landowsky from their positions in the Free University's student council. In the early 1980s, the old enmities had blown over. At some point, everyone came together again in the same fancy bars: political leaders from dueling fraternities and erstwhile rebels, construction magnates and subsidy swindlers, hairstylists and fashion designers, theater directors and actors— and the author of these lines. All of us sat, albeit never at the same table, at Fofi on Fasanenstraße, in the Paris Bar on Kantstraße, and at Ciao on the Kurfürstendamm. And sometimes, when they recognized me, my old enemies from the dueling fraternities would wave to me benevolently—we knew each other and it was clear who had won. I actually wouldn't mind, I'd think to myself after three glasses of wine, if this unhealthy but cozy idyll lasted for another thousand years.

Shortly after the fall of the Wall, I ran into Klaus-Rüdiger Landowsky at a reception for a major weekly at the Brandenburg Gate. We both held glasses of wine in our hands, and I pulled him aside to an alcove. I'd been wanting to ask him a question since the immemorial days of the 1960s, I told him. How was it possible, I asked, that neither he nor Diepgen had so much as a trace of a scar on their faces, despite having been members of a dueling fraternity? Landowsky laughed. At the time, the Saravia fraternity exempted talented speakers from its code of conduct. Ah, if only we'd known that then, I thought. We would have massacred you!

Over the course of my years in West Berlin, I regularly met colleagues in East Berlin who had remained communists at heart. I asked myself what in the world drove them to remain loyal to a state that had banished so many of their colleagues and had even threatened them personally—as well as their "solidarity criticism"—with censorship, professional debarment, and prison.

What was the source of this strange loyalty to their tormentors? Was it the conviction that, in the end, the German Democratic Republic really was the better—the only—antifascist state on German territory? Or had this state in fact spoiled them?

In any event, after the fall of the Wall it became clear that many of them experienced this epochal event as a historical catastrophe—as a personal insult, even. Instead of joining in celebrating their liberation, they acted anguished and aggrieved. It was not they who had made a mistake, but history—just like in 1933. They would rather recommend that Germans in East Germany participate in a new socialist experiment called "Dritter Weg" ("Third Way") than entertain the possibility that maybe they had been wrong to believe in the superiority of communism. The loyalty many East German intellectuals showed to the failed experiment remains a distinctly German phenomenon—nothing comparable was seen in any other country of the former Eastern Bloc.

No less astonishing is the fact that, even among left-leaning writers in West Berlin and West Germany, only a few welcomed the storm of freedom that swept across Central and Eastern Europe. They loved the East Germans as long as they shouted, "Wir sind das Volk!"—"We are the people!" When demonstrators in Leipzig changed this chant to "Wir sind *ein* Volk"—"We are *one* people!"—their sympathy waned. I'm afraid that to this day Germany's senior intellectuals still haven't completely recovered from the shock of the fact that history ignored their warnings against reunification.

On November 9, 1989, a demonstration to preserve the Wall was held on Kurfürstendamm, organized by one member of this group, a satirist by the name of Wiglaf Droste. Two thousand West Berliners participated.

A "WESSI" ATTEMPTS TO FIND BERLIN'S SOUL

Until the Wall came down, it felt to me and many of my contemporaries as if West Berlin was the center of the city. East Berlin as I remembered it was above all gray and packed with *Plattenbauten*, prefabricated concrete housing. Big-city pizzazz, and shop windows and façades that reflected it—if they existed anywhere in Berlin—could be found in the western half city: on the Kurfürstendamm and its side streets, on Tauentzienstraße with the KaDeWe, and on Savignyplatz—and maybe also in the area around Nollendorfplatz. To us West Berliners, the unlovely Breitscheidplatz, with the Europa Center and its ice-skating rink, cabaret, boutiques, and pedestrian bridge over the Tauentzienstraße, was the modern heart of the West city—a small constructed piece of America. It was only when I traveled to Italy and France that I noticed that West Berlin completely lacked the sort of great public squares and big-city architectural ensembles that visitors to Florence, Rome, Lyon, and Paris encounter at every turn.

So it came as a shock to us when we discovered after the fall of the Wall that the new sign for MITTE—literally "center"—pointed unequivocally east. Little by little, we discovered that

Berlin's historic center really did lie on the other side of the former Wall, and that everything Berlin had to offer in terms of magnificent buildings, venerable churches, and urban squares was located in the eastern part of the city. Indeed, Berlin's most beautiful surviving square, the Gendarmenmarkt, which Karl Friedrich Schinkel enlivened with the addition of his new Schauspielhaus (theater) between the French and German cathedrals, is the only urban ensemble in Berlin that can reasonably compete with similar European models. (Though in fact the square only became worthy of admiration in 1987, after the East German government salvaged the ruins of Schinkel's theater and refashioned it into a concert hall, on the occasion of the 750th anniversary of Berlin.) West Berlin hadn't even been home to the spectacular, early-twentieth-century buildings that had established Berlin's reputation as the capital of modernism. Instead, most of these iconic buildings—which by then survived only in photo albums— had been located close to where the city was later divided, near Potsdamer Platz. It had been there, on this now vacant plot, that Berlin had developed its new face as a world city in the early twentieth century.

In the fall of 2012, I saw an exhibition at the Gemäldegalerie: "Karl Friedrich Schinkel: History and Poetry." In his short forty years of life, Schinkel created some of the most influential buildings in the heart of Berlin, subsequently largely destroyed, including the aforementioned Schauspielhaus on the Gendarmenmarkt, Neue Wache (New Guardhouse), Friedrichswerder Church, and Bauakademie (Academy of Architecture). But Schinkel's well-known buildings were nowhere near as surprising as those he imagined in copperplate engravings and gouaches but never built. In these, the universal artist runs riot, confidently drawing on the wealth of available Greek and Roman models. One charming design, which Schinkel drew after a trip to Rome, shows a hall for the Marienburg Castle in Prussia, with columns whose capitals grow into the ceiling like tropical mushrooms, taking up so much space that they barely leave any room for royal ceremonies. No Prussian aristocrat, let alone the king, would have awarded Schinkel a contract for this design. What impressed me most was Schinkel's attempt to convey his predilection for Mediterranean architecture through the only cisalpine building form he apparently liked: the two-towered gothic cathedral. His etchings and gouaches frequently show Italianate medieval cities with a towering gothic cathedral under stormy skies. Where does this cathedral stand—where is this city, north or south of the Alps? Schinkel's expertly etched designs, in which he attempts to wed Italian gardens and villas on the Mediterranean to gothic cathedrals discreetly hidden by trees, were never built. A Mediterranean bay and Italian light were nowhere to be found under Prussian skies; a gothic cathedral nowhere on Italian shores. But Schinkel refused to be deterred: he wanted to bring to Germany what he liked about Italy.

What luck, I thought to myself, that this young genius had adopted the German classicists' veneration of antiquity rather than furthering the tradition of German manor houses. A collection of stone statues of heroes and princes I had seen in a so-called lapidarium on the Hallesches Ufer in the 1980s suddenly sprang to my mind. At the time, the lapidarium had served as a provisional sanctuary for all the hero figures of Prussian-German history that had been damaged or had fallen into disfavor: massive crusaders, ironclad warriors with enormous calves, hefty Prussian princes, kings, and kaisers—there were no women. The first time I encountered this petrified community, I was glad that these charmless forefathers had been banished to an out-of-the-way depository.

Later, I heard that the lithic occupants of the lapidarium on the Hallesches Ufer had been moved. Specifically, to a Renaissance fortress called the Spandau Citadel—"more than just a fortress," according to its promotional brochure. The epithet "Renaissance" attached to this stronghold, built between 1559 and

1594 on the site of a former fortress, is a bit of a stretch. It is certainly accurate as far as the building's origins are concerned: the citadel was in fact built during the Renaissance—at a time when Italian city-states such as Milan, Genoa, Venice, and Florence, and groundbreaking artists including Leonardo da Vinci, Titian, and Donatello were turning the medieval worldview on its head. However, this revolution reached Germany only a hundred years later. Consequently, what the exhibition in the citadel showcases are the advances made in the art of war and in its cast-iron instruments during the Renaissance. Generations of cannons are on display; there is little evidence, on the other hand, of the spirit and atmosphere of renewal of the Renaissance.

Then, in a fenced-off area, I rediscovered them all: the warriors and princes from the lapidarium. Exhibit labels informed me that they had been "a gift" from Kaiser Wilhelm I to the Berliners. At the time, the sculptures—starting with the twelfth-century crusader Albert the Bear and continuing up through Kaiser Wilhelm I himself—had stood on what was known as the Siegesallee, or Victory Avenue. In 1938, they had been forced to make way for the north–south axis Albrecht Speer had planned for *Hauptstadt Germania* (Capital of Germania) and to settle for the neighboring Sternallee instead. In 1947, at the behest of the Allies, Berlin's municipal authorities decided to do away with the statues, which by that point had been heavily damaged. Some were buried in the garden of the war-wrecked Charlottenburg Palace. In the 1950s, at the request of the Berlin Senate, they were unearthed and transferred to the lapidarium, where I had seen them, crammed tightly together—the invalids of history.

Now, thanks to the distance of the years as well as the greater physical distance between them, I examined these statues with greater curiosity and patience. There was Albert the Bear in chain mail, the archetypal German knight, a cross in his raised left hand, gazing off into the distance, probably in the direction of the city he aims to conquer, Jerusalem. On closer inspection, I noticed how lovingly and perfectly his chain mail had been rendered; the statue of this German knight suddenly struck me as vulnerable, delicate almost. Behind the fence, at a considerable distance from Albert, the Brandenburg-Prussian ancestral line was assembled: clunky male figures with helmets or crowns, looking off into the distance, some still headless or legless, others with their feet in chain-mail socks reminiscent of crocodile feet. The closer the ancestral line moved toward the baroque era, the more buoyant and amusing the figures became. A long-haired prince in knee breeches, out and about with a plumed hat, is rather amusing reproduced in marble. And then I discovered the sole woman among them: Queen Luise, whose eyes, unlike those of the men, are cast chastely to the ground. When I happened upon her here, set slightly apart from the row of men at the far end of the fence, I knew next to nothing about her; still, her bowed figure in the midst of all these dignitaries moved me. But the most expressive sculpture is probably Friedrich Drake's representation of Friedrich Wilhelm III, the art-minded ruler who so generously awarded contracts to Friedrich Karl Schinkel.

Once they are restored, these statues won't be set up around the city again, as this imperial "gift to the citizens" was originally supposed to be. Instead, they will take their place in a yet-to-be-refurbished barracks of the Citadel. A wise compromise: anyone who wishes to see the former Brandenburg-Prussian rulers can visit them there, yet they will no longer define the cityscape of the now democratic Berlin.

Populations have the right to continue to develop their moral values and sense of beauty. Not all periods of the past deserve to be given the same prominence in a city. That which is dark, pompous, tasteless, or was created in the spirit of dictatorship, should be preserved—but in the city's basements rather than aboveground. Not every office building from the Nazi era or East German *Plattenbau* needs to be designated a landmark. Nor does every tacky remnant of the imperial era. Reunified Berlin needs to re-create itself and choose its own vision of its democratically determined future. After all, in reality, choices are being made whenever a historical building is reconstructed. Take the Hohenzollern Schloss: Which phase of the palace's more than four-centuries-long construction history do we want to resurrect—the Renaissance palace of the margraves, the baroque palace of the prince-electors, or the royal palace, which, as it happens, was supposed to include a dome, according to one of Schinkel's designs? Which elements of the façade decorations do we want to reconstruct? Choices like these inevitably involve political and aesthetic censoring, which is determined by the tastes and values of the present—and by the limits of the available budget.

BERLIN: EMERGENCE OF A NEW METROPOLIS

The distinctive face of Berlin that is still apparent today emerged in the second half of the nineteenth century, during a time of rapid industrialization. From 1850 to 1871, the city's population doubled to 800,000. Thirty years later, there were already 2 million people living and working in Berlin. It was during this period that the residential building model of the Gründerzeit, which still characterizes the cityscape today, became widespread: five or six stories with a basement below; commercial and gastronomic spaces on the ground floor of the front building, the owner and administrator on the second floor, civil servants and white-collar workers above them, and retirees and workers in the rear building. Yet this combination of residential and commercial spaces originally advanced by the engineer and government building officer James Hobrecht failed to keep pace with the city's vigorous growth, and his specifications were quickly overhauled to meet the demands of big industry. Already at the time, builders were forbidden to build past the *Traufhöhe*, or eaves height, of seventy-two feet, which continued to frustrate world-famous architects a hundred years later, after the opening of the Wall. When it came to depth, however, nineteenth-century builders had complete freedom. Consequently, they added up to six or seven inner court-yards beyond the first one—after all, they had to create homes for hundreds of thousands of workers and professionals as quickly as possible. In working-class neighborhoods especially, this resulted in the creation of those apartment buildings, infamous to this day, that have passages leading from one barrackslike extension to another. According to the building inspection regulations, the inner courtyards had to meet just one requirement: they had to be at least 17.5 feet wide so a fire hose could be turned around in them. Light, air, and an unobstructed view didn't count for much in the emergent Prussian metropolis. Hobrecht, the inventor of the new perimeter block development, later complained about these prisonlike inner courtyards: "Four times as much space would hardly be enough if we wished to maintain a sufficient quantity and quality of sun, light, and air for our back rooms."

In vain. The interests of the builders and industrialists proved more powerful. What resulted were the inner courtyards I described in *The Wall Jumper* in 1983:

> In the center of the city, the apartment buildings are massed like fortresses. For the most part they are built in squares enclosing an inner courtyard, each with a chestnut tree in the middle. When the top of one of these chestnuts begins to move gently, residents can assume that a force six to eight gale is sweeping along the streets outside.

Already in the early 1930s, the British writer Christopher Isherwood had noticed the sad sight of Berlin's inner courtyards. Looking for his friend Arthur Norris, who has disappeared, the narrator sets out for the neighborhood in which Olga—a dominatrix of whose services the boot fetishist Arthur has availed himself regularly—lives:

> I found the house without difficulty and passed under the archway into the court. The courtyard was narrow and

deep, like a coffin standing on the end. The head of the coffin rested on the earth, for the house fronts inclined slightly inwards. They were held apart by huge timber baulks, spanning the gap, high up, against the grey square of sky. Down here, at the bottom where the rays of the sun could never penetrate, there was a deep twilight, like the light in a mountain gorge. On the three sides of the court were windows; on the fourth, an immense bank wall, about eighty feet high, whose plaster surface had swollen into blisters and burst, leaving raw, sooty scars. At the foot of this ghastly precipice stood a queer little hut, probably an outdoor lavatory. Beside it was a broken hand-cart with only one wheel, and a printed notice, now almost illegible, stating the hours at which the habitants of the tenement were allowed to beat their carpets.

This specialty of Berlin described by Isherwood can still be seen today, albeit minus the huge wooden beams holding apart the listing inner walls: in Kreuzberg, Wedding, and Neukölln, but also in Berlin's center, at Hackescher Markt.

Yet this was also the period when, mostly during the two decades from 1890 to 1910, the lavish bourgeois apartments with 11.5-foot-high ceilings and the large walk-through room known as the *Berliner Zimmer*—which aficionados of apartments like these are hard-pressed to find almost anywhere else in Germany—were built. Families that had achieved prosperity during the imperial era lived in these six- to eight-room apartments in the front building, with its elaborately decorated façade. The personnel lived in the rear building, in apartments that had the same high ceilings as the front building and were equipped partly with parquet, partly with floorboards. In the hallway of my rear-building apartment on a street parallel to the Kurfürstendamm, a Hammacher & Paetzold K.G. device still hangs on the wall, with little windows that would signal to the service staff in which of the front-building rooms their services were desired. To this day, the surviving apartment buildings from the Gründerzeit, most of which are in Charlottenburg, are among the city's most stately. After flirting rather briefly with the blessings of Bauhaus and modernism, what little remained of Berlin's bourgeoisie and its solvent intellectuals opted for these Gründerzeit apartments, most of which had been extensively renovated by then. In the 1970s and 1980s, tenants of these apartments still had to defend themselves if they decided to strip crudely painted wooden doors, replace perfunctory hardware-store doorknobs with classic Berlin brass doorknobs, and freshen up—often by their own efforts—the ceiling stucco with gold or red paint instead of just whitewashing it. "I never realized what a petit bourgeois you were," those who upheld these traditions would be told. Today, many of their former critics go to viewings of these renovated old apartments, with their high ceilings, double doors, and wide stripped cornices, discreetly inquiring into how much it costs to rent or buy them.

But Berlin's rise as the industrial metropolis of the continent also spawned an astounding new species of building that forever changed the face of the city. Willing to pay handsomely for their modern production facilities, the industrial barons hired the most renowned architects of their day. Many of the city's great industrial facilities were built by the pioneers of modernism. The AEG building designed by Peter Behrens became a precursor to industrial buildings of the future around the world. Glass, steel, and brick became symbols of the new age. To this day, Emil Fahrenkamp's Shell-Haus office building—later owned by BEWAG and GASAG (Berlin's electric and gas companies), and, since 2000, by the commercial real estate company Viterra Gewerbeimmobilien GmbH—continues to impress drivers heading along the Landwehr Canal from Kreuzberg to Charlottenburg with its seemingly vertically surging waves of glass and travertine. Architects drew on the vocabulary of these large industrial buildings for ideas for the new housing complexes they were hired to build for the masses. The same "modular construction" used for industrial facilities was now also expected to serve as the basis for the mass production of affordable housing in satellite cities. Industry produced huge quantities of the prefabricated structural components for this new style: flat roofs, walls, balconies, doors, windows, kitchens.

The flat roof and cube-model for future buildings was born. With his essay "From Bauhaus to Our House," Tom Wolfe penned what remains to this day one of the fiercest and wittiest critiques of the modernist revolution and its ideology of liberation—a gorgeously written polemic by an outsider that still infuriates the Salafists of the architectural trade today.

> Under socialism the client was the worker. Alas, the poor devil was only just now rising up out of the ooze. In the meantime, the architect, the artist, and the intellectual would arrange his life for him. To use Stalin's phrase, they would be the engineers of his soul. In his apartment blocks in Berlin for employees of the Siemens factory, the soul engineer Gropius decided that the workers should be spared high ceilings and wide hallways, too, along with all of the various outmoded objects and decorations. High ceilings and wide hallways and "spaciousness" in all forms were merely more bourgeois grandiosity, expressed in voids rather than solids. Seven-foot ceilings and thirty-six-inch-wide hallways were about right for . . . re-creating the world.

In his own furor, however, Tom Wolfe overlooked the fact that it was the Nazis who had anticipated his critique—without the slightest trace of humor yet with all the more rage as a result—and who had put a temporary end to the influence of Bauhaus in Berlin. The pioneers of the new building style were banished and relocated their projects to the United States, Australia, and Brazil.

In the German capital, Hitler's city planners embraced Bavarian-Austrian towns as their model—when they weren't busy coming up with megalomaniacal designs for the new world capital.

One tragicomic memorial to the Nazis' attempt to make themselves at home in the Prussian metropolis is the woodland residential estate Krumme Lanke, originally known as the *SS-Kameradschaftssiedlung*, or "SS Camaraderie Colony"—a name that, for obvious reasons, it no longer bears today. "It has been my wish for a long time now," SS leader Heinrich Himmler had decreed, "to create a gated settlement for the three main departments of the SS that offers members of the SS adequate and healthy living space, which is especially suited to promoting the advancement of family. In order to provide a special place for the cultivation of the community spirit of the SS, the plan is to cluster the settlement around a row of buildings devoted to the social activities of the SS."

The complex, with its six hundred residential units, which were intended to provide single-family homes for the higher ranks of the SS and semidetached and row houses for its lower ranks, was built between 1937 and 1939. The "community buildings" Himmler had envisioned for hosting SS social gatherings never made it past the drawing board. Thanks to Berlin's landmarks preservation commission, it's still possible to marvel at—and live in—this residential estate commissioned by SS leader Heinrich Himmler in its original form. Today, the Krumme Lanke woodland estate is among Berlin's most coveted housing complexes. Of the old street signs, carved out of wood at Himmler's request— DIENSTWEG ("Service Lane"), TREUEPFAD ("Loyalty Path"), STAFFELWEG ("Squadron Lane"), BRAUTPFAD ("Bride's Path"), SIEGSTRASSE ("Victory Street"), and AHNENZEILE ("Ancestral Row")—only innocuous names such as IM KINDERLAND ("In the Land of Children") and HIMMELSSTEIG ("Path to the Sky") remain. Yet the complex still exudes the spirit of its builders. Located near the U-Bahn stations Onkel Toms Hütte and Krumme

Lanke, the estate expresses the premodern desire to live in the woods—in the middle of a major city, shielded from the noise of the streets, highways, and S-Bahn.

The narrow, one-to-two-story houses with their small muntin windows, shutters painted red and green, and steep roofs are essentially a structural declaration of war against modernism. Roofs like these make sense in the countryside of Bavaria, the Black Forest, and Austria, where they ensure that accumulated piles of snow slide off in winter. But they seem silly in the flat sandbox that is Berlin, where snow almost never sticks on the ground for long. In fact, the entire complex was modeled on a prize-winning Munich design. The Nazis considered flat roofs a Jewish-Bolshevik aberration. In the Nazi iconography, family homes built in the so-called *Heimatstil,* or "home-style," with their steep roofs and wood-framed dormers, promised safety, coziness, and communion with nature.

When I visited the complex on a weekday afternoon in August 2012, all that was left of the originally planned community spirit was a strange stillness and faux gemütlichkeit. A retiree in a bathing suit, presumably having just gone for his daily swim at the nearby lake Krumme Lanke, trotted toward me and said hello. In the front and back gardens of the houses, I saw many children's swings, kiddie pools, Ping-Pong tables—but no children. Maybe these gardens were used only on weekends, by the tenants' grandchildren. A quiet rustling moved the tops of the soaring pine trees. In the distance, I could make out an undertone of the traffic on Berlin's AVUS highway and Argentinische Allee—like a reminder of the city.

Most of the lanes were accessible only on foot. I had trouble imagining the huge flat-screen TVs no doubt installed within the confines of these narrow walls and low ceilings—let alone sound systems capable of blasting rock music from one end of a semidetached house to the other, or even across the entire estate. Impossible to fathom how the wide SUVs parked in front of the houses had managed to get there across the paths strewn with pine needles. Only the sky-high pine trees themselves, which cast their shadows across the idyll, were irrefutable and unquestionable. Hadn't the original occupants of the estate missed their Austrian and Bavarian oak and fir trees? The estate's many pine trees must have seemed foreign to them.

CITY WEST VERSUS CAPITAL CITY (EAST) AND VICE VERSA

It was inevitable that war-ravaged Berlin would become a place for architects and city planners to experiment. It would be diffi-cult to imagine a bigger playground for radical innovators and architect-philosophers with the confidence to rethink and put up entire neighborhoods in next to no time. Consequently, unlike almost any other city, Berlin has also become an unwitting open-air museum for the deeds and misdeeds of the pioneers of the ar-chitectural profession.

According to a grim Berlin bon mot, the city was destroyed twice—once by the Allied bombers, the second time by the de-molition mania of Berlin's city planners. And the second wave of destruction may well have been more thorough than the first. This cutting quip doesn't distinguish between West and East Berlin—and rightfully so. Despite their opposing social systems, the eastern and western half-cities espoused building philoso-phies that were actually similar to an astonishing degree. On both sides, planners banked on radical rebuilding from scratch, wide-ranging demolition, and an extensive highway system for a "car-friendly city." And while those on one side dreamed of a modern "world city," with Los Angeles in mind, those on the other looked to Moscow as their model, striving to turn the old heart of the city into the heart of their nation, with vast parade grounds and new public buildings. In designing this "worker-friendly" capital, they visited the Soviet metropolis for guidance and inspiration. In Berlin, the dense and narrow layout of the streets of the old city near the Schloss, where the imperial era's higher civil servants as well as its intellectual elite—publishers, writers, architects, lawyers—had lived, stood in the way of East Berlin's city planners. Reminiscent of the reviled Prussian tradition, it would have to be razed.

City planners in the West didn't lag behind their eastern colleagues by much. They leveled the area between what is now Breitscheidplatz and Potsdamer Platz, which had become *the* place for American modernism in Berlin after World War I. It was here that Berlin's bohemian crowd had socialized in local salons, office buildings, cafés, and hotspots, including the Café Größenwahn, Romanisches Café (where the avant-garde of the 1920s rubbed elbows), Haus Vaterland, and other famous meeting places on whose remains the Europa Center now stands. This entire neighborhood, which was home to the cultural and moneyed elite of the 1920s for which the city is famous to this day, was modernized—"modernized" meaning the same thing in the West as in the East: bulldozed. An absurd saying used in the architecture department of West Berlin's Academy of the Arts captured this philosophy of eradication: "The stucco on the façades is the dust in people's heads." So get rid of it. In the 1960s, Wolf Jobst Siedler was thrown out of West Berlin's Academy of the Arts because his book *Die gemordete Stadt: Abgesang auf Putte und Straße, Platz und Baum* (The Murdered City: Swan Song to Putti, Streets, Squares, and Trees) bemoaned the loss of Berlin's bourgeois villas with their elaborately ornamental wrought-iron fences.

In reality, the plans for the eradication carried out after World War II dated back to the 1920s. "Trepidation and veneration of the old," decreed Berlin's social-democratic director of urban development in 1929, "makes us weak, paralyzes, and kills . . . We want to live as Frederick the Great let Berlin live through his buildings, breaking up the old in order to replace it with the new." Solutions like these fell on sympathetic ears in the social democracy of the 1920s and were taken up again by the Social Democratic Party of Germany (SPD), which governed West Berlin after the war. "We are tearing down the old city and building new working-class towns on the outskirts," Willy Brandt explained after being reelected as governing mayor in 1963.

When it came to removing the stucco from the façades, Willy Brandt's director of city planning, Rolf Schwedler, was significantly more successful than his East Berlin colleagues. In the East, many of the disintegrating façades with stucco figures, which hadn't been repaired since before 1945, survived—the administration quite simply lacked the means to remove them. As a result, significantly more balcony-buttressing virgins, their breasts amputated by the teeth of time, and crippled knights endured in Prenzlauer Berg and Friedrichshain than in West Berlin. After reunification, the East Berlin façades, along with their stucco figures, were spruced up, filling West Berliners with envy today.

"Take a look at the public squares in West Berlin," Hans Stimmann, a staunch social democrat and acting director of city planning after reunification, challenged me. "Every last one of the most hideous squares and streets in West Berlin bears the name of a commendable SPD leader: Ernst-Reuter-Platz, Breitscheidplatz, Willy-Brandt-Straße, Paul-Löbe-Allee, Walther-Schreiber-Platz . . . Just look at the party affiliation of the man after whom the square is named, and you'll know it turned out badly."

Indeed, it really was the SPD that, with its philosophy of eradication and highway building, shaped the architectonic history of West Berlin for a good three decades. To this day, it remains a mystery how an entire generation of architects on both sides of the Wall could have surrendered to an ideology of progress rooted in the obliteration of prewar buildings. Apparently architects are no less susceptible to the ideology of an era than political parties or sects. With a sort of Maoist zeal, they were convinced that the flat roof and shoe box placed upright on its side were the *ur*-formula of progressive construction, discovered at long last.

Notwithstanding their shared obsession with progress, planners in East and West Berlin approached the construction of new buildings in their respective half-cities like armies engaged in fierce trench warfare. Whatever was built in the center—in other words, near the Wall—also had a Cold War mandate to satisfy. The West German publisher Axel Springer made a spectacular debut. As he himself admitted, the decision to build his media empire's high-rise Berlin headquarters right by the Wall in the 1960s was a political statement. From the roof of this shimmering golden solitaire, an electronic ticker tape broadcast news from the Free World in huge letters. To limit the reach of this subversive influence from the West, the East German government in turn put up a row of residential high-rises on Leipziger Straße, blocking the view of the Springer Group's building. It's surprising they didn't put the balconies on the back of the buildings. In the 1980s, a rumor spread in East Germany that the Rolling Stones were planning a concert for the country's youth on the roof of the Springer building. No one knows who started the rumor or how it spread. Whatever its origins, the result was that hundreds of thousands of young people flocked to the capital from all over East Germany to watch the event of the century from Leipziger Straße. East German security forces intercepted fans arriving by train and blocked off access to Leipziger Straße. The writer Ulrich Plenzdorf gave a charming fictional account of this event-that-never-happened from the point of view of a speech-impaired young man in his story "kein runter kein fern" ("no down no far").

Yet this construction competition was hardly restricted to the immediate vicinity of the Wall. Taking their cue from the sound trucks that bombarded tenants with contradictory messages to the left and right of the Wall in the early 1960s, ambitious new buildings went up in subsequent decades to broadcast the advantages of the respective systems that built them. Naturally, the sinfully expensive Westin Grand Hotel (formerly the Interhotel Grand Hotel Berlin) on Friedrichstraße, which Erich Honecker built during the final years of the East German regime, was meant to fly in the face of West Berlin's luxury hotels, which were rather modest at the time; the Palace of the Republic was seen as a socialist answer to the Centre Pompidou; East Berlin's TV Tower eclipsed West Berlin's Radio Tower and even the Eiffel Tower; and, even if the Wall hadn't come down, Edzard Reuter probably still would have erected a western global group's glittering conglomerate directly across from the East Berlin apartment buildings near the border. We really only have luck to thank for the fact that nothing ever came of West Berlin's city planners' insane plans to build an airport for business travelers near the Zoo station.

LOVE (AND SEX) IN BERLIN

When I told my grown children that I was planning to write a new book about Berlin, they looked at me with indulgent skepticism. They didn't say what they were thinking, but it wasn't difficult to guess their reservations: Go for it, if your target group is the fifty-plus generation, but how can you expect to write about the things that really matter to twenty- and thirtysomethings—the bunker and tunnel parties and clubs that open only after midnight and where, once you manage to pass muster in the bouncer's eyes, you stay the entire weekend until Monday or Tuesday afternoon?

This much is certain: the vast majority of young Berlin tourists and newcomers don't come to Berlin to visit Museum Island or to take advantage of the extensive cultural offerings on which the bankrupt city spends 750 million euros every year. They're drawn to Berlin because of its reputation for turning into a unique-in-the-world nightspot at the end of the day, offering opportunities for wild parties, drugs, and every form of sex, conventional or less so. While the city's "cultural offerings," in the broadest sense of the term, may also include countless small theaters, music cafés, cabarets, informal exhibitions, and poetry festivals, almost all of these usually short-lived gathering places for young audiences exist outside the official cultural sector.

Only 5 to 10 percent of the city's culture budget flows to the alternative scene.

The situation wasn't all that different in the legendary 1920s. The international bohemian crowd and artistic avant-garde to which Berlin still partly owes its status as a world metropolis hardly created this reputation from nothing. Today, we associate the Golden Twenties with the poet Bertolt Brecht and his musician friends Kurt Weill and Hanns Eisler, the theatrical visionary Erwin Piscator, the writers Frank Wedekind and Alfred Döblin, the journalists Joseph Roth and Alfred Kerr, the painters Otto Dix, Max Beckmann, and George Grosz, and the pioneering filmmakers Fritz Lang and Friedrich Wilhelm Murnau. But these are merely the names we remember. All these personalities built their works of art, later canonized as masterpieces, on the foundation of a largely forgotten, highly politicized mass culture of street theaters, variety shows, cabarets, cafés, bars, and nightclubs, whose performances were considered low art at the time. Without this popular entertainment and protest culture as a basis, now-famous trailblazers of modernism like Bertolt Brecht and Max Beckmann would have been unthinkable. Moreover, the 1920s weren't golden. They were years of mass unemployment and a growing gap between rich and poor, years of social disintegration that led to the global economic crisis of 1929 and ultimately to the triumphant barbarism of the Nazis.

A well-known star at the time was Claire Waldoff. Born in Gelsenkirchen in North Rhine–Westphalia, Waldoff originally wanted to become a doctor, but as the daughter of innkeepers with sixteen children she never had a chance to study. So she decided to become an actress, and after one engagement in a provincial theater she left for Berlin. There, it was not long before she met Olga von Roeder, who came from an American family of actors and, like many curious women at the time, had somehow found her way to Berlin. Olga, whom Waldoff affectionately referred to as "Olly," became the cabaret artist's life partner, and together the two women enlivened Berlin's lesbian scene.

Claire Waldoff became famous overnight for her appearance in an "Eton boy" outfit—the black school uniform worn by students of that college—in the theater Roland von Berlin on Potsdamer Straße. From then on, she sang sassy ballads and songs in the Berlin dialect, and all of Berlin sang along with her— or like her. Her songs stood out more for their humor and firm grasp of Everyman's life than for their poetic brilliance. She lambasted men—"Oh gawd, how stupid men are"—and made fun of women who turned to plastic surgery—"I ain't letting no doctor touch my breasts / Because of Emil's dirty desire." She sang about the modest pleasures of Berlin's *Laubenpieper* (allotment gardeners)—the city's ordinary people, many of whom had a little garden house near the S-Bahn tracks. "What does a Berliner need to be happy? / An arbor, a fence, and a garden patch." Her trademarks were a shirtwaist, necktie, and red-dyed bob. Claire Waldoff smoked and cursed onstage, appearing in operettas and musical revues, once even alongside Marlene Dietrich, an unknown at the time. The names of the clubs, cafés, and theaters in which Waldoff performed reveal just how international the entertainment scene was in those years: the Scala vaudeville, Chat Noir club, and Café Dorian Gray.

But the city's greatest tourist magnet was mass prostitution. What Venice had been in the eighteenth century and Paris in the nineteenth, Berlin became in the twentieth century: an El Dorado for sex-addicted tourists. But unlike Paris, which earned the epithet the "City of Love," Berlin stood for something more raw—for fast, cheap sex, and love in all its aberrations. Arguably no one depicted vulgar and loveless sex as crassly as George Grosz in his caricatures and paintings. Here, half-dressed ladies meet with randy soldiers and politicians in pursuit of stale pleasures under the cynical eyes of death. Ernest Hemingway, who visited Berlin in the early 1920s, reported in a piece published on December 15, 1923, in the *Toronto Star Weekly*: "Berlin is a vulgar, ugly, sullenly dissipated city. After the war it plunged into an orgy that the Germans called the death dance." Paris, where Hemingway was based as a European correspondent at the time, offered the "most highly civilized and amusing" nightlife in Europe, whereas Berlin's was "the most sordid, desperate, and vicious." Instead of champagne like in Paris, in Berlin you were constantly being offered cocaine, which waiters served openly on trays.

Already by the early 1920s, the city had become a mecca for sexual minorities and adventurers. Vaudevilles and cabarets shot up in the city's west in particular; the first clubs for homosexuals and lesbians emerged in proletarian neighborhoods such as Wedding, Kreuzberg, and Neukölln. "The club was in the north, in the proletarian part of Berlin, where the more tomboyish girls went in their 'Sunday best'—in other words, in a tuxedo with a necktie and the like," Annette Eick recounts on the website www .lesbengeschichte.de. "I already felt the need to be with women. In this club, I met a woman, Ditt, who looked a little like Marlene Dietrich. I really liked her type, even if she was a bit vulgar. She had enormous sex appeal, was very attractive. She seduced me. She gave me Swedish punch to drink, I was drunk and came home too late." Another meeting point in the flourishing lesbian scene was the previously mentioned Dorian Gray on Bülowstraße, where, among others, the readers and staff of the magazine *Frauenliebe* would meet. Another icon of those years was the nude dancer Anita Berber, who is buried in Neukölln. The Eldorado, where she performed at the time, is now a grocery store called Speisekammer des Eldorado—"The Pantry of Eldorado"— which sells organic food.

In his novels *Mr Norris Changes Trains* and *Goodbye to Berlin*, which were the basis for the worldwide hit *Cabaret*, the British writer and reporter Christopher Isherwood described the key ingredients of what made Berlin so fascinating at the time. The Troika bar is a meeting place for gays, aristocrats, bankers, and fledgling dreamers who know no taboos and are willing to do whatever it takes to make it as singers. Isherwood himself remains ever the proper English gentleman, watching with curiosity from a distance and refusing to get involved—even with Sally, with whom he is in love. He limits himself to observing and reporting. Yet the global influence of his descriptions of pre-Nazi Berlin was doubtless also bolstered by his at once discreetly British yet at the same time explicit allusions to "cruel sex" and "barbarous Berlin"—for example, his observations, characterized in equal measure by fascination and condoning disgust, about the boot fetishist Arthur Norris and the gay Baron von Pregnitz's sex parties in his country villa in Mecklenburg:

> The largest room in the villa was a gymnasium fitted with the most modern apparatus, for the Baron made a hobby of his figure. He tortured himself daily on an electric horse, a rowing-machine, and a rotating massage belt. It was very hot and we all bathed, even Arthur. He wore a rubber swimming-cap, carefully adjusted in the privacy of his bedroom. The house was full of handsome young men with superbly developed brown bodies, which they smeared in oil and baked for hours in the sun . . . Most of them spoke with the broadest Berlin accents. They wrestled and boxed on the beach and did somersault dives from the spring-board into the lake. The Baron joined in everything and often got severely handled. With good-humoured brutality the boys played practical jokes on him, which smashed his spare monocles and might easily have broken his neck. He bore it all with his heroic frozen smile.

With the fragile figure of the young Sally Bowles, Isherwood created an unforgettable testament to the fleeting "life in the moment" in the nocturnal swamp of Berlin.

But the lost, libidinous nineteen-year-old Sally was hardly a solitary blossom in the Berlin of those years.

At the time, the city had developed a scene, probably unique in Europe, of gay haunts, women's clubs, S&M bars, brothels, and jazz clubs—some of which, as it turned out, outlived the Nazi era. These locales are the source of energy, the engine room, as it were, over which the enchantingly shameless child Sally acts out her dissolute lifestyle and her musical balancing acts. But they also comprise the basic melody of the lasting fascination of Isherwood's books around the world to this day. What would his stories be without the eccentric news dealer Mr. Norris, who seeks relief through his visits to Olga and her whip; without the astoundingly unprejudiced landlady Fraeulein Schroeder, who rents rooms not just to Isherwood but to red-light workers as well, and who always knows where to send a girl for an abortion? What would Isherwood's books be without this shameless and morally corrupt—this "brutal"—Berlin?

The city owes this reputation not only to night owls from around the world but also to unflinching researchers. Magnus Hirschfeld founded his later world-famous Institute for Sexual Science in Berlin and fought against the hegemony of the "heterosexual norm." Jewish and non-Jewish doctors opened outreach clinics for better contraception and for the proletarian youth. According to the sex researcher Dagmar Herzog, Berlin in the 1920s was "the most liberal place in the world."

Rereading Isherwood's books, I noticed that almost all the venues he refers to were located in the western districts of Charlottenburg and Schöneberg. The centers of nightlife he and his heroes frequented were on Tauentzienstraße, Motzstraße, Potsdamer Straße, Bülowstraße, and Nollendorfplatz. In the 1920s, Berlin's bohemian crowd migrated away from the center, heading to the city's west—which should serve as a warning to those who claim today that Charlottenburg's only future after the Wall is as a paradise for retirees. This much is true: walking across the

Kurfürstendamm or along its side streets at midnight on a weekday today, you feel like you've inadvertently landed in a medium-size city in southern Germany, or even in the East Berlin of the 1980s. A kind of voluntary closing time seems to rule over West Berlin's nightlife. Wandering by, you see stacked tables and waiters shooing away the one remaining customer at the bar. The streets are empty, the sidewalks abandoned by midnight, except for a few retirees walking their dogs.

I remember how, in the 1990s, the owners of my favorite restaurants in West Berlin complained that many of their regular customers were drifting to the new trendy restaurants in Mitte, while there was no sign of a reverse influx of customers from East Berlin. Some lowered their prices and added traditionally East Berlin items such as borscht or *Broiler* (the East German term for roast chicken) to their French- and Italian-influenced menus. But nothing helped; their restaurants remained half-empty. East Berliners simply didn't show the same curiosity for West Berlin's food culture as the traitors from the West who all suddenly wanted to eat in the East. It should be said in the East Berliners' defense that, by then, Charlottenburg was no longer "the West" to them so much as a suburb. After one quick visit once the Wall fell, they preferred to stay home—in the center of the new capital.

But Berlin's dynamics are as volatile as the stock market. It won't be long before the new trendy restaurants, clubs, and bars in the former East will become too expensive once and for all, and a new exodus to the West will begin.

There is a common misconception that the terror unleashed by the Nazis also brought Berlin's nightlife into line. The Nazis considered Berlin not just a bastion of communists and socialists but also a city of vice. Yet they never fully succeeded in bringing this aspect of the city—which they found fascinating and repulsive in equal measure—under their control. Jazz clubs and bars for gays, lesbians, and transvestites survived in Berlin until the end of the Third Reich. Impertinent, sometimes openly antifascist sketches and songs were performed in the vaudevilles and cabarets. Experienced bouncers guarded the entrances to these establishments and would signal to the performers and musicians whenever a customer they suspected of being a Nazi came in. The artists would shift gears immediately, often in midact, performing innocent, catchy tunes from the operetta repertoire.

One of the most well-known bordellos was Salon Kitty on the fourth floor of a villa at Giesebrechtstraße 11. The head of the Gestapo, Reinhard Heydrich, personally founded the establishment and made sure that every bedroom was bugged. Under orders from the Gestapo, "man-crazy girls" loyal to the regime were expected to coax antiregime statements out of prominent Nazi customers and foreign diplomats during sex. Despite these excellent arrangements, the secret-service returns were low. Those charged with listening to the recordings only registered crude or bizarre sexual requests and animal sounds. Apparently the clients all knew that they were being bugged in this high-class bordello, which only made them surrender to their desires with all the more abandon. By the end of the failed operation, even Salon Kitty's founders and snoops—including the foreign minister of the Reich, Joachim von Ribbentrop, and Salon Kitty's own inventor—had taken to frequenting the brothel to recover from their exhausting daily grind.

After the war, Kitty Schmidt's daughter and grandson carried on the business on the ground floor, in the guise of a boarding-house, but low revenues finally forced it to close. In the early 1990s, the brothel was turned into an asylum-seekers' home—welfare-state subsidies promised to bring in more than the payments of straying flaneurs from the Kurfürstendamm. But the asylum-seekers' home was shut down as well, due to protests from the neighborhood's now well-to-do inhabitants—lawyers, accountants, architects, and doctors. Numerous films and books—and above all the legend of Salon Kitty, which continues to spread around the world—have kept the Nazi brothel alive in people's memories. To this day, tourists from around the globe still ring the bell of the 3,660-square-foot apartment on the fourth floor, despite the fact that it was renovated and remodeled years ago; they all want to check off "Salon Kitty" on their itineraries.

Salon Kitty, which was founded by the Gestapo and ultimately catered above all to its founders, is a conspicuous example of the Nazis' failed attempt to control Berlin's nightlife. There is no doubt that Berlin was the capital of the Third Reich: it was here that World War II was planned and decided, and many other crimes concocted—the burning of the Reichstag, the detention of social democrats and communists and their deportation to concentration camps, the persecution of Berlin's 170,000 Jews, Kristallnacht, and the Holocaust. And hundreds of thousands of Berliners participated in the ignominious Nazi celebrations held in Berlin after the successful campaign in France. But the Nazis never succeeded in completely dominating Berlin culturally the way they did their secret capital of Munich. There were simply too many social-democratic and communist resistance cells and antifascist-leaning citizens in the city who refused to succumb to the collective madness and provided shelter to Jews and the politically persecuted. This is exemplified by a scene in a tram captured by the writer Ursula von Kardorff in her *Diary of a Nightmare: Berlin, 1942–1945.* Getting up to give his seat to a woman marked with a yellow Star of David, a worker on the tram says: "Sit yerself down, ya old shootin' star!" When a party member objects, reminding the proletarian gentleman of his duties as a German, the worker retorts: "What I do with my ass is my business." Von Kardorff's one-sentence commentary on the scene: "I think the common people behave more decently than the so-called educated or semi-educated."

There were also some prostitutes among those who helped the roughly fifteen hundred Jews who were successfully hidden in Berlin. When, in the 1950s, the Berlin Senate honored them, the social-democratic senator of the interior seemed ill at ease shaking the hands of these quiet heroines, by now well advanced in their years.

The image of Berlin in the 1920s that lives on in collective memory was decisively shaped by Christopher Isherwood's Berlin books and the global success of the film based on them, *Cabaret*. Unfortunately, Vladimir Nabokov's Berlin books, which describe the same period from a very different perspective—that of a Russian immigrant—haven't enjoyed the same good fortune. Berlin's largest group of immigrants by far in the 1920s has been as good as erased from the city's memory. Until the currency reform of 1923, some 250,000 to 360,000 Russians stayed or settled in Berlin. Unlike the Russians who came after the fall of the Wall, the great majority of these immigrants belonged to the economic, military, and intellectual elites that were expelled—or no longer saw a future for themselves at home—after the victory of the Bolsheviks. Many of them got stuck in Berlin on their way to the city of their dreams, Paris. In those days, as today, Berlin was significantly cheaper than other European cities. It was closer to Moscow and Saint Petersburg than London, Paris, and Rome—and the refugees benefitted from the inflation in Germany.

The Russian immigrants didn't linger in the proletarian vicinity of the Ostbahnhof station where they arrived—nor did they stay in Kreuzberg, Wedding, or Friedrichshain. Instead, they looked for and found apartments in the bourgeois Berlin around the Gedächtniskirche, in the western districts of Charlottenburg, Schöneberg, and Wilmersdorf—residential areas that reminded them of bourgeois neighborhoods in Saint Petersburg and Moscow. It's difficult to imagine that, in Berlin in the 1920s, 185 Russian publishing houses were founded, which published more than 2,000 Russian-language titles through 1924. A Russian periodical market also flourished, as did Russian cabarets and stage shows. There is virtually no important Russian author who didn't spend some time in Berlin in those years, including Andrei Bely, Vladislav Khodasevich, Ilya Ehrenburg, Maxim Gorky, Sergei

Yesenin, Vladimir Mayakovsky, Vladimir Nabokov, Aleksey Remizov, Viktor Shklovsky, Aleksey Tolstoy, and Marina Tsvetaeva.

One mystery remains: How and why did this enormous Russian diaspora, which took root in Berlin for a while, disappear almost without a trace from the city in the early 1930s—before Hitler had even seized power?

A few Russians did remain, including Tatjana Gsovsky, a dancer from Moscow who had immigrated to Berlin in 1924 with her husband, the dancer Victor Gsovsky, and lived on Fasanenstraße. She sheltered the Jewish musician Konrad Latte after his escape from the collection point on Große Hamburger Straße. Having survived the Nazi years in Berlin, she was engaged as a dancer and ballet teacher at the State Opera after 1945, and founded her own ballet school shortly thereafter, which gave guest performances throughout Europe and influenced European dance for decades.

Berlin has paid little attention to the Russian legacy that the October Revolution swept its way and that was one of the important influences on the city in the 1920s. By chance, sixty years later, I stumbled on one of the places Nabokov used to frequent: the previously mentioned tennis courts on Cicerostraße.

The courts were so well hidden by towering poplars and Erich Mendelsohn's residential complex that newcomers often failed to find them, even when they were standing directly in front of the entrance. From there, all you could see was a ground-level booth surrounded by bushes and a few wooden tables, which looked like an outdoor pub. The commercially run facilities, which were managed by Jutta Felser-Utrecht and her mother for decades, were a meeting place for a rare mix of patrons. Berlin journalists, academics, writers, artists, and dancers from the Theater des Westens (Theater of the West) crossed paths with nightclub and bar owners from the Kurfürstendamm. The latter, who spent the majority of their lives on these courts, liked to pull up in their sports cars, even though it would have taken them barely ten minutes to walk there from their places of work. The others arrived by taxi or bicycle. Psychoanalysts, especially, came in such great numbers—always reserving in advance—that it sometimes felt to spontaneous players like me that all the best courts had been booked by shrinks through the end of the year. Their profession was one of the few flourishing sectors in Berlin at the time. Of course, you would also come across the occasional patient on the courts; but these patients never played with those whose couches they had only just spent eighty deutsche marks to lie on.

Erich Mendelsohn had included the tennis courts as part of his residential complex in the 1920s. Of Berlin's tennis courts, they are among the most venerable, well located, and successfully integrated into their surroundings; today, they are a designated landmark. In the 1920s, Nabokov, still unknown as a writer at the time, earned some extra money as a tennis instructor here. A photograph shows him in long white pants and a black jacket, carrying a tennis racket as he makes his way to one of the courts with Svetlana Siewert and her sister Tatjana. The screenplay writer Jochen Brunow, a regular on Cicerostraße, remembers meeting a Jewish couple from the United States at the fence surrounding the premises. The old gentleman told him that he had once worked there as a ball boy for a few groschen. Back in those days, when frost was still guaranteed in the cold months, the courts would be flooded in winter to serve as an ice-skating rink. On weekdays, Berlin's skating mavens would glide along in loops to the sounds of a gramophone amplified by loudspeakers; on weekends, a live band would play.

In the postwar years, other patrons who would only become famous later also frequented the courts. Not all of them wanted to play tennis. Some were happy just to stand beneath the poplars and listen to the relaxing, rhythmic sound—improbable in this central location—of tennis balls being hit back and forth. One of these observers was Willy Brandt. The bestselling author Johannes Mario Simmel is also said to have penned one of his novels while sitting on the hard benches of the garden pub. In the mid-1980s, a few years after I had discovered the entrance to the tennis courts, the second wave of Russian immigrants arrived in Berlin. As is generally known, unlike in Nabokov's day, these immigrants were not members of the Russian aristocracy and bourgeois educated classes—they were the Russian nouveau riche of glasnost. They conversed in shouts even when they were sitting at the same table and sent their wives and daughters to the instructors on the courts—despite the fact that the facilities weren't exactly in the sort of condition that millionaires from the land of tennis had grown accustomed to expect. You could really only play on courts one, two, and three; the others were off-limits to the uninitiated. There, the prehensile roots of the old poplars caused serious court flaws; the facility's drainage system was so inadequate that after a downpour players would have to dry the courts using buckets, rags, and sponges. In fairness to the leaseholder, there was a watertight Nazi bunker buried beneath the sand of the rear courts, which was transformed into an underground garage in the 1960s. It actually would have made sense to install a few hard courts there.

Because no one was a member and anyone who paid was welcome, the courts became a biotope for individualists from every sector, and for unusual experiences and spectacles. The courts opened as soon as the March sun made its first incisions into the gray wall of clouds that hangs over Berlin in winter, and only closed when the first snow fell. I once played there on a sunny day in December, with gloves, on the already frozen sand strewn with poplar leaves. In the spring, a barrage of young talent from Berlin's fancy clubs, still closed for the winter, would invade the courts. In this brief "preseason," shots usually only seen in Wimbledon or at the U.S. Open were suddenly exchanged on the defective courts. This mirage would last for two weeks at most, then the scene would once again be under the control of the core troops—the artists, "new Russians," and bar and club owners from around the Kurfürstendamm. Since the latter worked nights, they only showed up around noon to play—not tennis, though, but backgammon or poker, often for thousands of deutsche marks. Sometimes they'd hit the courts to work out some crazy bet. Then you would see these elderly, no longer entirely sober warriors, often with impressive bandages around their knees, thighs, or elbows, step up for a showdown. Their game was clumsy, malicious, and completely lacking in style, but every insider knew that a great deal was at stake—sometimes life itself. The ballerinas from the Theater des Westens were unforgettable, floating like pixies over the courts and reaching the net seemingly on the tips of their toes to parry some really wicked drop shot. After a match, authors and screenplay writers would think about how to immortalize the courts fictitiously at least, if they failed to survive in actuality. There was a lot of talk about a television series titled *Matchpoint*, but it was never made.

The tennis courts on Cicerostraße still exist. But seeing them today just makes those who loved them want to cry. Even the better courts are now overgrown with man-high sumac shrubs. The red sand is covered with moss and grass everywhere. The branches of the sky-high poplars droop now, seemingly missing the sound of tennis balls that had energized them since Nabokov's day. Maybe even the residents who used to complain regularly about the noise from the courts miss this sound now in their quiet apartments.

A few years ago, the property was bought by a globally operating British real-estate company called Shore Capital. It is currently offering to rent the facilities for an absurd price. Those who know the courts and buyers willing to invest consider it a pure sham offer and suspect that the company has something entirely different in mind for the facilities. Once enough sumac shrubs have grown on the sand, the deeply indebted city of Berlin is likely to repeal their landmark status.

I fear they may be right. Berlin's landmarks preservation society claims that of course the courts' landmark status won't be revoked. Yet if no operator for the courts can be found, Erich Mendelsohn's original development plans will probably be resuscitated—after all, he only designed the courts because his client at the time ran out of money and couldn't finish all the buildings planned for the property.

LOVE IN DIVIDED BERLIN

The swinging life reestablished itself while the city still had quadripartite status—in West Berlin. During a trip to the Soviet Union, I met a former KGB officer by the name of Vladimir, who, after three glasses of vodka, boasted that he had had a German lover in every section of the city at the time. Needless to say, this cavalier made no mention of the fact that his army's ordinary soldiers had taken thousands of German women by force after capturing Berlin. As it happens, discussing these "incidents" was also taboo in West Berlin until the 1980s—Germans were never to be seen as victims. But it was clear that the KGB man still hadn't got over the fact that his erotic jaunts to the various quarters had become more difficult after the Wall went up.

Like the removal of the speed limit from Berlin's AVUS highway, it was seen as a sign of western freedom that, as night fell, ladies for hire would take over the destroyed Kurfürstendamm between Olivaer Platz and Uhlandstraße. Besides, how could the half-city, suddenly teeming with dozens of secret service agents, be expected to manage without prostitutes? At the time, the majority of these women were from Germany, and some worked on their own, without a pimp. The immigrants from Yugoslavia, Poland, the Czechoslovak Socialist Republic, and Thailand that poured in during the 1970s and 1980s were still a minority, not welcomed by their German colleagues. They had a reputation of working for pimps and their gangs, and of pushing down prices. West Berlin's first feminists were up in arms about this love for sale. But they had to contend with the equally militant defenders of the business, who fought for social recognition of the term "whore" and its corresponding profession. It never occurred to a single one of Berlin's senators of the interior to outlaw prostitution.

There were no red-light districts or official "houses" for women for hire in East Berlin. But prostitution flourished there as well. After the Wall was built, the Friedrichstraße train station and Interhotels became preferred places for establishing contact. Needless to say, every halfway experienced customer from the West knew that he—like every client of Salon Kitty before him—was being observed.

Meanwhile, a secondary branch of GDR prostitution sprouted in East Berlin thanks to the so-called guest workers: Turkish and Greek laborers from West Berlin who initially traveled to the Friedrichstraße station in the city's eastern half mainly to buy cheap cigarettes and vodka at the Intershop. Making the acquaintance of the East German ladies around the station, these visiting guest workers soon discovered that sex in the other half-city could often be had for as little as a carton of western cigarettes, a small bottle of perfume, or a pound of Jacobs brand coffee. A question West Berlin guest workers typically asked one another in the 1950s was, "Got granny?" This referred to those widows who generally lived alone in enormous apartments in West Berlin and were open to affairs with guest workers. After the Wall went up, the new question became, "Got Monika?" The reference now was to young women in East Berlin who were willing to return the favor, as it were, for a carton of Marlboros.

"You had to exchange twenty D marks into GDR marks, but with twenty marks you were king over there," recounts Andreas, who was a waiter in the 1960s and now owns a Greek restaurant in Charlottenburg. "You'd go to Café Moskau or Hotel Sofia, you'd light a cigarette with your Ronson lighter, and already you'd be surrounded by a swarm of gorgeous young women." At the time he and his friends had Cypriote passports. As a result, the VoPos, East Germany's People's Police, treated them with particular courtesy; as the first western nation to recognize the German Democratic Republic, Cyprus was considered a "friendly country." A VoPo who was familiar with Andreas from his constant visits even knew that he always buried his leftover currency in preparation for his next visit. He left Andreas alone.

"We regularly drove to the East, partied and drank over there, and before long each of us had a girlfriend," another witness to those years explains. "You know, in West Berlin the German women didn't want anything to do with us, but the Monikas in the East were different. Maybe also because we brought them Marlboros, Milka chocolate, and Jacobs coffee, like we were used to doing from our vacation trips to Turkey."

Inevitably, some of these "hour acquaintances" turned into solid relationships—even into second families with multiple children. For their wives on the other side of the Wall, the "oriental" fathers spun fables worthy of *One Thousand and One Nights* about their positions in the West, where they purportedly managed or owned car dealerships, film studios, or rug meccas on the Kurfürstendamm. When the Wall came down, so did most of these illusions, which had been nurtured for years for and by the second families in the East. When mothers from the East and their children visited their Turkish daddies in the West, they discovered that they didn't own carpet stores or manage gourmet restaurants in Grunewald but at best ran cheap kebab stands on Kantstraße and lived with their large first families in two-room apartments in Kreuzberg.

Of course similar relationships also existed between West German men and East German women, but they didn't last long because the Casanovas from West Berlin and West Germany were more aware of the consequences and feared them.

Experienced johns from the West who took up with East German women knew perfectly well that sooner or later these ladies would receive a visit from the Stasi and would have to report their "contact." Of course West-East love stories born of attraction taking its natural course were no less threatened by suspicion. It was as good as certain that at some point Erich Mielke's secret service would also get wind of these furtive "establishments of contact" and would do everything in its power to blackmail the partners into collaborating in one way or another—either by threatening to refuse right of entry to the western partner or by offering to facilitate meetings between the lovers.

Nevertheless, despite this airtight surveillance, German-German love stories took root in the Stasi observers' blind spot. The need for secrecy and fear of discovery fanned the flames of passion. Under the pressure of knowing that forced separations were possible at any moment, emotions and conflicts flourished the likes of which most people in western democracies knew only from Shakespeare's dramas and the novels of Balzac, Stendhal, Tolstoy, and Flaubert. Star-crossed love, which in classic romantic dramas was the result of insurmountable class differences, feuds between two families, and moral laws, for German-German lovers was caused by the hostility between the two political systems. The threat that travel into or out of the country might be banned inevitably exalted all feelings to the heights of greatness, not to say melodrama. Who could be trusted? Every false move could have dramatic consequences; every decision necessarily entailed familial, social, and political conflict. In applying for an exit visa, the eastern partner risked her professional life and consequences for her family. The Romeo from the West had to decide if he was prepared to bear this enormous responsibility. And, if his lover's exit visa was denied, would he be willing to organize her escape and take the risk that she might end up in an East German jail? What if she had children and insisted on taking them with her? Mothers caught trying to escape were separated from their children; the mothers were sent to prison, the young children given up for adoption, placed with the families of civil servants loyal to the system and fed bogus stories about their backgrounds.

The fate of these mothers and children was also hushed up in the western half-nation. To avoid jeopardizing détente conversations, West German politicians avoided terms such as "forced adoption" or "child stealing" at all costs. The mothers involved, for whose release from eastern prisons West Germany generally paid a ransom, found their adopted children only after reunification—if they ever found them at all. Yet, by that point, they could barely communicate with their now grown sons or daughters, who often didn't remember their original names. These mothers had spent years, decades even, filled with hatred against the communist regime and couldn't understand that their children, who had been raised in households loyal to the regime, were genuinely upset by the fall of the Wall and the disappearance of "their" German Democratic Republic.

It is only recently that newspaper reports and television accounts have begun to commemorate these dramas. Fortunately, they include a surprising number of stories about lovers who achieved the supposedly impossible: against all odds and defying every danger, they managed to be together in the West after a successful escape and were finally able to live out their love unchallenged by the Stasi and transit points. And still, not all of these couples survived this more ordinary love.

LOVE AFTER THE FALL OF THE WALL

The revolution of November 1989 swept away all the dictates and rules of the game that had applied to amorous relationships and services in the border zone. For commercial love this meant that western freedoms immediately also found their way to the East. In fact, it seemed as though the streets and buildings near Hackescher Markt had a historical memory, as though the cracked walls, which hadn't been replastered since the war, were whispering the news to the descendants of the women who had last presented themselves there half a century ago: *It's okay, you're allowed to again*. In any event, within weeks of the fall of the Wall, the pioneers of the profession had taken over Rosenheimer Straße, as though reclaiming their ancestral territory. Of course these girls from Thailand, Hungary, Poland, and the two German states didn't know that before them other young women, long since forgotten, had worked in the shadows of these same walls. But they willingly inherited the place. Nothing like the suits of armor they wore, however, had been seen in the 1920s or on the Kurfürstendamm during the West Berlin years. The new girls stood there like heroines from a comic-book movie: thigh-high stiletto leather boots, towering hairdos, boobs and behinds squeezed into latex uniforms. The prices they named through the open windows of the cars that rolled by at a walking pace weren't intended for Trabant drivers either.

The latter made up for it in West Berlin. In the late 1980s, near the Zoo station, establishments had sprung up that went by a name previously unheard of in Germany: peep shows. Invented in the U.S.A., these locales promised sexual satisfaction without risk, contact, or danger of infection. Men who weren't put off by the sight of a usually dark-skinned cleaner with a bucket and rag wiping away the previous patron's legacy would take their place in one of the circularly arranged booths. For five deutsche marks, a window would open onto a stark-naked lady offering herself up from every imaginable angle on a rotating platform.

For many family men from the East curious to find out what western freedom was all about, these peep shows near the Zoo station became the second must-see destination, after the *Schaufenster des Westens*, or "Showcase of the West," as the KaDeWe department store with its delicatessen department was known. When the East German writer Stefan Heym expressed his disgust at the ignoble behavior of his fellow countrymen, who pressed their noses against KaDeWe's display windows, he was rightly accused of hypocrisy. As a famous writer who had been enjoying the privilege of traveling freely between East and West Berlin for years, he didn't have to stop at gazing into KaDeWe's display windows—he could enter and shop there. His censure might have gone over better had he criticized his compatriots' curiosity for peep shows. But he wouldn't have got very far with that either. Because it wasn't just the scorned masses in their stonewashed denim uniforms that wanted to know what these peep shows were all about—East Germany's intellectuals did too. My writer friends Heiner Müller and Thomas Brasch—and probably Stefan Heym himself—simply couldn't resist the temptation to do some "research" of their own.

The explorations of the first East German tourists near the Zoo station in West Berlin deserve a commemorative epilogue. Regular West Berlin customers, who hid behind their collars and looked around surreptitiously before slipping into these establishments, soon saw, to their great surprise, scenes the likes of which they never could have imagined suddenly play out at the entrances to the peep shows. Entire East German families stood in front of the glowing red-and-purple signs discussing the upcoming event. One mother's announcement to her children has become legendary: "Daddy's just going to go have a look now. We'll stop by again in fifteen minutes to pick him up."

The degree of tolerance and solidarity that East German nuclear families demonstrated for their paterfamilias' exploratory urges was completely foreign to West Berlin customers.

Shortly after reunification, while taking the S-Bahn to the East, I saw a priceless headline in one of Berlin's biggest tabloids: WOMEN IN EAST GERMANY MORE ORGASMIC! Since I was reading my neighbor's paper, I couldn't just turn the page; I had to wait a long time before he finally got to the continuation of the article inside. "Experts fear the degeneration of GDR sex," the piece continued. "At 37 percent, the rate of orgasm for women in East Germany is clearly higher than in West Germany: 26 percent."

This announcement was the fruit of a new area of inquiry. Pouncing on the previously unplumbed subject known as "GDR sex," sex researchers tried to take its measure using the rules of their art. Thousands of questionnaires were sent out and analyzed, interviews carried out with hundreds of sexual partners who had never been interviewed before, new themes with peculiar names described. "The Sexual Unification of Germany" was one title; "Socio-culturally Determined Differences in Sexual Behavior" another. Researchers from the East and West turned their gazes to the bedrooms of the disappeared state's citizens, unsettling West German readers with their alarming figures. "The number of women who never reached orgasm was three times as high in the Federal Republic of Germany as in the Democratic Republic of Germany. Accordingly, significantly more women in East Germany than West Germany reported always reaching orgasm. Moreover, they more frequently described sexual activities as exciting and satisfying." A big guessing game began: What was at the root of these differences? Why had it worked so much better on former East Germany's regular, standardized mattresses than on West Germany's expensive, spine-friendly latex bedding? Were East German men, who had remained virtually unchallenged by the women's lib debates, ultimately the better lovers? Or were East German women more spontaneous and passionate, or simply less demanding, than their West German counterparts?

As always happens when it comes to the truly interesting questions concerning the relationship between the sexes, the researchers' answers were tenuous and failed to provide any real clarity. The researchers themselves seemed to be completely deaf to the laughter that their jargon-riddled academic papers inspired in impartial readers. Undaunted and supported by generous grants, they persevered in their investigations.

Yet their research overlooked the most exciting phenomenon in the reunified city's love life. Initially, this phenomenon didn't attract attention because it spoke German and looked German. In fact, it took a decade before the love market in the western half-city finally picked up on it. It was a long time before it showed up in the fantasies of western men. While the more obtuse among these men searched for playmates in the Far East or browsed through thick volumes of photographs of the Ukrainian and Russian selections offered by the relevant agencies, an unfamiliar creature emerged from right under their noses to take center stage: the East German woman. It was only in getting to know her better that this creature's exotic qualities became apparent.

The East German woman had a job, was economically independent, self-confident, and divorce-happy; at a time when only 50 percent of West German women made their own money, 90 percent of women in East Germany were employed. The East German woman tended to be quite young when she had children, who as a result were already grown up when she divorced for the first time and embarked on her second or third life. She was guaranteed rights—the right to an abortion and to a kindergarten spot, for example—that her West German counterpart had to fight for. National—albeit authoritarian, not to say military in their approach—daycare centers ensured her work-life balance.

For all these reasons, the East German woman didn't consider her male partner an enemy but rather a partner who, economically speaking, had little or nothing on her. Indeed, the average East German man, unless he had managed to gain a foothold in the regime's upper echelons—but what woman would want a man like that?—wasn't in a position to boast any typically macho privileges. He couldn't show off with money, fast cars, or a house on Ibiza. He had to rely on his potential talent as a lover and his qualities as a father and partner. As a result, he tended to cultivate a rather "soft" masculine image. He may have smoked excessively, had one too many all too often, and expected a warm meal on the table at the end of the day, but—provided he was firmly reminded often enough—he was willing to help change diapers, go grocery shopping, do dishes, and take down the trash every now and then. A divorce, he knew, wasn't hard to get in the divorce-happiest nation in Europe—and most divorces were instigated by women.

And, on top of all this: the suppression of all free movement in public in East Germany had led both sexes to develop a relatively uninhibited attitude toward sex. What other unregulatable pastime did East Germany have to offer its citizens? When she invited a stranger to her place for a glass of wine, the East German woman wasn't just looking for a future provider. First and foremost, she was looking for a good lover, and if she felt let down in that respect, she had no qualms about nipping the adventure in the bud then and there.

After relocating to West Berlin, the East German writer Thomas Brasch baffled me with his idea for a film set in 1980s

East Germany. The hero of the proposed project was a textile salesman who proved to be something of a "roving gigolo" during the many house visits he made free of charge. The dramaturgy of the story as Brasch told it remained hazy to me, but the film's title was set in stone: it would be called *Im Reich der Sinne*—In the Realm of the Senses. Sadly, he never found anyone willing to produce this unusual work.

The number of East-West couples has grown considerably in recent years. They account for only 4 percent of the total number of marriages, but most East-West couples don't get married, preferring to live together out of wedlock. Yet a perplexing imbalance jumps out in these relationships: East German woman–West German man matches are seven times more common than the reverse. It seems as though western men, their confidence shaken by feminists, have finally recognized the treasure that was right before their eyes all along, unnoticed. The East German woman stands on her own two feet professionally but isn't willing for a second to relinquish the natural prerogatives of the fair sex. During the East German era she hadn't been in a position to openly reject erotic accessories such as perfume, lipstick, and stilettos—a rejection her emancipated sisters in the West engaged in eagerly during the 1970s—since these items were virtually impossible to get ahold of at the time anyway. She displays her charms discreetly but rebels if it becomes expected of her. Plastic surgery, Botox, and the toys peddled by the sex industry are anathema to her. She is immune to the theory that differences between men and women are nothing but a social construct; the mention of "gender studies" makes her yawn. The idea of being financially supported by a man is foreign to her. Like the woman from the West, she demands equal rights, but she isn't interested in settling scores when it comes to who does the dishes how often, who cooks for whom, and who brings down the trash. If necessary, she would rather pitch in a bit more than to let these issues erupt into a battle of principles. She laughs off accusations that she is a traitor to her sex. She insists on her personal homemade blend of femininity: employed, self-confident, decisive, yet also womanly. Above all, she is still in the mood for men.

In the past few years, seven couples in my immediate circle of friends and relatives have committed themselves to the East German woman–West German man model. It seems to be a recipe for success. On the other hand, I hardly know of any couples of the opposite combination.

In the eyes of the West German woman, the East German man appears to be a dying breed, a kind of mountain spirit of the male species. He sports a beard, neglects his appearance, drinks too much, and doesn't bother to shower before getting intimate with his partner. At fifty or sixty, he doesn't earn a decent living, maybe even lives off Hartz IV social-security benefits—he is incapable of promoting his talents on the market. At the same time, however, at home he demands certain privileges he is used to from the East German days: a warm dinner and the right to dominate the conversation when it comes to rambling on about the superiority of the vanished East German state. The soft masculine image that had always been his point of reference hasn't equipped him to figure out the complicated desires of an emancipated woman from the West: yes, she definitely wants a soft, infinitely sensitive man, but at the same time he should be strong and decisive when it comes to certain things.

Nevertheless, there is an opportunity for the East German man: the single West German woman let down by the world of men who has finally divorced the father of her children after endless and ultimately irreconcilable disagreements. In this situation, the East German man appears as a good companion; he consoles her. He knows all about separation and divorce from his life in East Germany, he doesn't take either so tragically. He's been dealing with his own or a stranger's kids since he was twenty. He doesn't mind bringing the West German woman's kids to school in the morning or pushing them around the park in a stroller for hours.

Used to family solidarity, he extends his affection to these usually grossly spoiled kids, helps them with their homework, and proves himself to be a patient playmate. Carefully—and only when their mother isn't around—he tries to teach them some basic manners. And, once he has finally passed this long trial period, at long last his western lover opens the door of her bedroom to him.

CLUBS

Even during the years of the Wall, West Berlin's nightlife was already wilder than Hamburg's or Munich's. The explosion of places and types of entertainment after the Wall came down, however, was unprecedented. This development was spurred above all by a condition that didn't exist in any other capital in the world: a surfeit of abandoned, relatively central urban wastelands, which offered creative spirits the perfect opportunity for new beginnings. On the eastern side of the old border in particular there was a plethora of deserted warehouses and factory sites just waiting to be revived. According to some veterans of the scene, in the early years, soldiers of the British Army played a pioneering role in this revival. Roaming these wastelands at night, they would strip out of their uniforms and change into party outfits they had brought along to live it up with beer and drugs in the artificial caves of the vanished state.

These abandoned lots were owned by the unified city—that is, large municipal or semigovernmental operations such as Deutsche Bahn (the German railroad) or Berlin's waste management. Caught off guard by the fall of the Wall, these owners initially had no idea what to do with this legacy of East Germany. The alternative scene was faster; without wasting a lot of time asking questions, it staked a claim to the abandoned plots and ruins. As it happens, these new venues were all located in areas no pedestrian would just happen to wander into after dark. There were no bars, kiosks, grocery stores, or even any paved roads anywhere nearby. But you could reach them by foot or bicycle, and there was usually a U- or an S-Bahn station relatively close by.

What these clubs promised was the possibility of another life, one that celebrated the moment, the now. They were driven above all by the desire to escape from the real, everyday world of capitalism and to create a parallel world according to one's own rules. Instead of "bread and circuses," these places offered drugs, dancing, and games of love—and, if necessary, protest as well. The old ritual of *Feierabend*, or quitting time—workers going out dancing on Friday or Saturday nights, letting off steam, and falling into bed—no longer made sense to ravers. Wresting away just one or two nights from the daily routine wasn't enough for them— they also wanted the subsequent morning and long days; even half the week, if possible. Berlin invented a new opening time: midnight. The stamp on the inside of your wrist was good from Saturday night until Monday or Tuesday afternoon.

It's obvious that Berlin's social conditions have contributed to this probably unique extension of "quitting time." No other German city has so many young people living off welfare and a couple of undeclared side jobs, or working without any job security. The clubs have adapted to this reality: cover charges are relatively modest—under ten euros—and drinks cost about seven euros. Somehow, a lot of young people manage to scrape together the money they need to spend two or three nights and days in a club. And the world's youth identifies with this novel mixture of poverty and bohemianism. For the cost of one drink in a techno club in New York, London, or Paris, in Berlin they can party all weekend long. They flock here from every corner of the world, these clubbers—from Japan, Israel, and Australia; from Italy, Spain, and Portugal—all wearing the same uniform: T-shirt, jeans, and sneakers, and a tattoo on the upper arm and a piercing or two in the nose or lips for subtle variety. And the club operators are right, of course: no one under thirty who comes to Berlin is interested in the Philharmonic or Museum Island. They're interested in the clubs, and the clubs is where they go.

An article in *The New York Times* in 2009 touted Berghain as the best club in the world. There probably isn't another famous club out there located in such absurd surroundings. Berghain opens at midnight and can be reached only by S-Bahn—that said, the S-Bahn runs all night long. The building is in the middle of a wasteland; in the neon-lit sky behind it, only a few abandoned industrial buildings, a car fleet, an Aldi discount store, and the distant O_2 World temple of entertainment vie for attention. My companion and I didn't take the S-Bahn but came by car instead. After turning off Karl-Marx-Allee, we drove through dark, completely empty streets, past buildings without so much as a single light still on. Eventually, a dark colossus we assumed must be Berghain rose up to our right, floating in the sky like the enormous domino in Stanley Kubrick's *2001: A Space Odyssey*.

When you go clubbing in Paris or New York, you expect and encounter urban density, traffic jams, honking horns, boisterous groups of people, excited chattering. Berghain sits there like a dark castle on an island. To reach it, you have to swim across a black ocean. In June, we trudged past sumac shrubs, the vegetation of Berlin's ruins, doing our best to avoid the many puddles left behind by the soggy summer.

Berghain is an offshoot of the techno club Ostgut, which closed in 2003. Its operators, Norbert Thormann and Michael Teufele, had succeeded in acquiring a former heat and power plant on the grounds of the old eastern Ostbahnhof station and refurbished it for their purposes. The neoclassic-style industrial building from the early years of the German Democratic Republic appealed to them. The fact that not everyone can get into the club adds to Berghain's mythical status. Since I'm no longer of suitable clubbing age and was worried I would be turned away, I'd had myself put on the manager Norbert Thormann's guest list. Even so, my companion and I decided to get on the line outside the entrance, which was still short at midnight. We wanted to get an idea of Berghain's clientele and the bouncer's selection criteria. It seemed like almost everyone trying to get in had read the comments online and followed the advice to avoid flashy and eccentric outfits. There they stood all in a row, well behaved and inconspicuous, most of the men in sneakers, jeans, and T-shirts, the women a bit more colorful, but only a few in dresses or miniskirts, and not a single pair of stilettos anywhere in sight; some men, in anticipation of hours—or days—of dancing, had even showed up already in their undershirts. They spoke every imaginable language, but a certain uniformity about the crowd was apparent even so: everyone was between twenty and thirty years old, in good spirits, and easygoing—a friendly, pleasant crowd looking for a good time, not trouble.

The bouncers already attracted attention even from a distance. There were three of them, and each one apparently had a different function, though what exactly this was wasn't entirely clear to the patrons. The arbiter who granted or refused admission, on the other hand, commanded respect and was impossible to miss: Sven Marquardt—not a thug so much as a postpunk rocker with a belly, bushy beard, and gray hair in a ponytail. The steel lip piercings, heavy earrings, and hefty iron chain around his neck lent him a certain sense of unpredictability. He stood in front of the entrance like a statue, hardly moving at all. Every time two or three patrons were let in, a torturous pause followed. The entrance overlord would size up the next pair, absorb the data their clothing, expressions, and body language transmitted to him, and organize this input, comparing and evaluating it according to criteria he alone was privy to. With an imperceptible signal, he communicated his decision to his helpers—was it a sign of his hand or head, or a blink of his eyes that meant either yes or no?

There are countless stories and rumors about Sven Marquardt on the Berlin scene. A group of young regulars who didn't want to wait for hours and got on the short guest-list line told me that Marquardt had let them in even though their names weren't actually on the list. One of them had told Marquardt he was the cook at KaterHolzig—Berghain's biggest competition. Another member of the group, however, was asked to leave after being frisked and caught with a bag of cocaine. According to my source, Marquardt might have been willing to turn a blind eye, but one of his colleagues had decided to honor the established precept. Apparently this well-oiled team operated according to the policy that no one was ever to question anyone else's decision.

The couple right in front of us was turned away at the door and toddled off to the side without protest. Marquardt politely wished them a good night as they left. Obviously we wondered what it was about their outfits, glances, appearance that had tipped the scales so cruelly against them. After all, we told ourselves, the two of them must have done something wrong to fail the test. Unfortunately, we hadn't seen them from the front. From my perspective, I had only noticed a certain bagginess about their T-shirts and something matted about the man's hair. Slightly taken aback, I interrupted my train of thought. In trying to figure out the bouncer's criteria, I was already identifying with the selection process. Weren't the two of us—my companion in her little red leather jacket and I in my black linen suit—just as suspicious? Especially considering I was a good thirty years older than the average patron, even in the eyes of a generous judge? Nonsense, I told myself—the truth is, there aren't even any criteria! It's all just about the ritual of granting or refusing admission, and the more arbitrary it is, the better it works.

Sven Marquardt has often been asked about his selection criteria on talk shows and in interviews. Obviously he has been smart enough to refuse categorically to answer the question. The closest thing to the truth is probably that these criteria are a mystery even to him. It may be that his practiced eye can pick out potential thugs and troublemakers. But the main point of the procedure is probably just to create a barrier that separates the inner temple of Berghain from the outside world. Visitors must pass a test before being granted admission to the mysterious, dark cement mountain—a test for which they cannot prepare. That's all it takes for this place—a composite of the names of two Berlin neighborhoods, Kreuzberg and Friedrichshain—to assume a mythical quality. Anyone standing at the threshold of Berghain can't help but think of Kafka's castle, to which poor K. was denied access—also entirely without justification, as it happens.

"You don't really look like someone who goes to Berghain every other day," Sven Marquardt told my companion as he subjected her to his visual test. There was no way of knowing whether he was referring to some positive or negative quality about her. "That's true," she said, "but I'm on the guest list." Too bad, I thought to myself, now we'll never know if we would have made it in even without this prerogative. As Marquardt waved us through to his helpers, I couldn't resist tapping him on the shoulder. Would he have let an old guy like me in even if I hadn't been on any list? He looked at me for a while without really looking at me. Then he said, "Yeah, I think so."

Once inside, we were overcome by the same stupid satisfaction everyone feels after passing a test: we did it! Suddenly we were no longer part of the masses outside, whose line was growing longer by the minute. We were inside, accepted! Evidently our sense of triumph was shared by the young couple a few stairs above us who joined us at the window, laughing and waving to the crowd below, which had swelled considerably and stood in the encroaching fog still waiting to pass the test. "Look how many people are out there now! It'll be another two hours before they get in—if they even get in at all!"

The inside of the club stirs up exalted feelings, heightened by the thrill of having crossed the threshold. Interrupted only by a few staircases and mezzanines, the bare walls rise up some seventy to one hundred feet into another civilization, whose heartbeat is defined by the pounding electro music. The bass beats immediately seek out their echo inside the body. In the low light, which reveals only a hint of contours, the tremendous space is reminiscent of a gothic cathedral in whose galleries you can dance and drink cocktails. The soaring walls of windows reinforce this impression of a sacred space ruled by an unknown religion. Climbing the steel stairs takes you to another level, arrayed with bars, dance floors, and DJ consoles. Each of these levels, brimming with a massive body twitching in unison to the music, can be seen from the level above it, which in turn serves as a multiuse stage, resulting in the illusion of a large-capacity theater on each of whose floors various rituals are being performed simultaneously to different music. At any moment, a protagonist on the dance floor can turn into a spectator, and vice versa. The fact that there's no interference between the expensive disc jockeys' various strains of electro music is one of the masterful coups of the interior design of this temple of entertainment. Following the advice of our grown children, we had brought along earplugs. But the onslaught of decibels was entirely bearable and we didn't feel the need to use them. The price of a gin fizz or Campari-orange was also entirely reasonable: well under ten euros—affordable even to recipients of Germany's BAFöG state student loans and grants.

In the background, the two stages dissolve into a labyrinthine confusion of hallways that intentionally create physical proximity and lead to smaller rooms, niches, and nooks with sofas. Apparently, it is in this labyrinth and in the dark rooms on the ground floor that, in the early morning hours, the orgylike excesses take place that, together with its bouncers, have contributed to Berghain's mythical status around the world. And, as is often the case with such myths, fantasy considerably outstrips reality: a single instance of excess is all it takes to give birth to a lasting legend. As the case may be, in walking around the club, we didn't notice anything that might have corroborated this aspect of Berghain's reputation. On the other hand, the owner of another club told me that the liberality in some Berlin clubs actually far surpasses the rumors. Apparently there is nowhere else in the world where the police are similarly indulgent in this respect. Only dealing drugs in clubs is liable to prosecution; their consumption is tolerated.

We saw a rapidly swelling mass of young people on the dance floors abandoning themselves freely to the loudspeakers' command. What people do to the sound of electro and techno music can hardly be called dancing as I know it. It's more of an enraptured stepping in place, an oscillation of bodies to the prescribed rhythm. The lack of space alone precludes any individually willed dancing, audacious moves, or acrobatic improvisations. No one would even notice them anyway, since the strobe lights cut up all motion into freeze frames. Whether someone's movements are smooth or choppy or altogether outside the music doesn't matter— all that's ever left of any dance move, any body, is a series of split-second-long snapshots. The collective rapture that gradually takes over depends on patience and hours of swaying along to the prescribed rhythm.

Hardly anyone in this sea of jerking limbs stands out because of his or her distinctive clothing, particular dancing style, or unusual behavior. Many women dance with their purses slung across their hips—after all, where are they supposed to check them? Some men dance up to their partners with a cigarette in one hand, beer bottle in the other, the sleeves of their jackets—if they have one—tied around their waists. The concept behind Berghain doesn't reward the urge to stand out. Since my early days in Berlin, I've never cared for the tradition of generational culture, strictly divided by age group. Whenever I would end up in a hotspot in New York or Paris, I'd find myself surrounded by representatives of all three sexes and every age. As far as I can remember, in Berlin there have always been restaurants, bars, and clubs for people in their twenties, forties, or fifties. It's not that I felt in any way sharply cut off from or excluded by the under-thirty-fivers in Berghain. But I couldn't help but feel like someone who didn't belong there.

"Come on, let's dance," I prompted my girlfriend. "No point watching, whining, or resisting—if you don't stomp along with everyone else here you're lost!" It took patience and a lot of time for the cerebral apparatus to reduce itself to the reptilian brain and the individual body to merge with the mass body. But eventually we, too, managed to enter that blissful state free of doubt and could imagine continuing to dance on the spot like this for hours, or even days.

Then something unexpected happened. A thirty-year-old, who had been trying in vain to get her companion sitting by a corner window to dance, kissed me on the cheek and announced: "You're the best man here by far." I was too stunned and in a trancelike state to react, but the same thing happened to my girlfriend. Another woman danced up to her and shouted through the boom of the basses: "You're the most beautiful couple in the whole club—it's awesome you're here!"

So much for generational culture! Far from wanting to exclude the older and old generation, the young generation actually welcomed us in its temple! "E" was the cool verdict pronounced by my son, an experienced clubber, when I later told him about this scene, referring to the popular drug almost no one goes out without taking, since it promises sustained euphoria. Not hiding my disappointment at his sobering conclusion, I retorted that drugs only heighten feelings that are already there.

"We're just going to go grab some breakfast," I told the bouncer as we left the club that bright Sunday morning, leaving it open whether or not we'd be back in an hour. The stamp on the backs of our hands was good until Monday afternoon. Marquardt gave me the same look he'd given me when he'd let me in. It betrayed nothing—neither interest nor dismissal. How did he keep it up, standing by the entrance for eight to ten hours, evaluating people's suitability? Did he take ecstasy as well? "By the way," I continued, "I'm writing a book about Berlin and would like to interview you sometime!" "You'll have to get in touch with my agent," he replied, handing me his card.

Apparently there isn't a profession in Berlin for which you can't get famous.

The now legendary club Bar25 was a typical postmillennial Berlin creation. It all started with a silver '68 Nagetusch trailer. Its two owners had converted the trailer into a whiskey bar from which—techno music blaring in the background—they served a choice selection of whiskeys. They christened their mobile watering hole Bar25—the "25" referring to their trailer's maximum speed. The business thrived, so the operators looked for a fixed location for their bar. Underneath the Jannowitzbrücke S-Bahn station, they found an empty plot with a makeshift fence around it. It was on the sunny side of the Spree River and, as part of the former border area, had been equally accessible to West and East Berliners before the fall of the Wall; the actual, heavily guarded border had been in the middle of the Spree. The only building was an abandoned garage at the edge of the grounds, which had once belonged to East Germany's now defunct Wasserschutzpolizei, a special police force responsible for patrolling the city's waterways.

Jumping the fence, the two whiskey-peddlers began gathering wood from the area to cobble together a provisional club in the style of a Western saloon—made entirely out of wood. From the very first day, acquaintances and other sympathizers from Friedrichshain and Kreuzberg showed up wanting to help. At first there were a couple dozen helpers; soon there were a hundred and then some. The club's opening on July 24, 2004, turned into a party that lasted for eight weeks.

After the party, with the help of some of the guests, the carpentry and bricolage continued. While some perfected the club, others set up shanties. Initially there was no master plan for the quickly expanding assembly of wooden shacks that sprung up week after week. Everyone could build whatever they wanted and create their own spaces using materials they found or brought along. But because the plot was big—some 130,000 square feet—and because more and more people joined in, the improvised settlement soon turned into a village of sorts, with the club at its center. The club wasn't initially intended for outside guests but more as a sort of focal point for the life of the "village residents." Of the latter, hardly any had a steady job, few aspired to bourgeois careers, and all were more or less unemployed; it was this village and this club that they wanted to create. To accommodate the many collaborators' individual building projects, a small group had to draw up a general plan of sorts. In this way, over the course of the year, a playground for young adults took shape, with a restaurant, wellness area, and its own radio station; a theater, open-air movie theater, and circus tent were also added.

As the range of things on offer expanded, the audience and personnel changed as well. Professionals were needed to perform on the various stages—DJs, bands, cooks, projectionists, directors. The founders succeeded in attracting a very colorful bunch of aficionados to the club, most of whom came from Kreuzberg and Friedrichshain. As the club's reputation spread, people who went to work in dark suits and ties suddenly also wanted to join in. Anyone who showed up with a "capacity for experience" was admitted, explains Christoph Klenzendorf, one of the two founders from the trailer, drawn as they were to the community's life philosophy: "If you want to do something, do it! And do it with love and passion!"

The founders of Bar25 had started with empty wallets and an ingenious energy cocktail of euphoria and protest. The protest followed the usual neighborhood call to arms against plans to extensively develop the Spree waterfront—in short, against gentrification, a term that originated in English social history and refers to the expulsion of a neighborhood's "native population" by real estate developers and their clients. But unlike the permanent protesters from the anarchist camp, the operators of Bar25 skillfully coupled their protest to their own concrete interests. They wanted to hold on to the once wild waterfront along the Spree, which they had discovered and cultivated, as it were, and to continue to expand their village. However, conflicts with black bloc extremists were unavoidable. On several occasions, dressed in hoodies, the anarchists put up a threatening front outside the club, demanding to know the operators' intentions and worldview. Inviting them into the club and offering them drinks usually helped to appease them.

Negotiating with the owner of the plot, Berlin's waste management company, on the other hand, proved to be significantly more difficult. The city-owned business suddenly announced its intention to sell the property to the well-funded Mediaspree group, which planned to build luxury apartments, offices, and hotels on this sunny section of the Spree waterfront. The survival of Bar25 was under threat. Faced with this predicament, the operators discovered that their active cultivation of public relations from the start paid off; they networked not just with young Berlin politicians but also with influential friends of the club around the world. Thanks to their lobbying efforts, they managed to postpone the eviction several times after it had already been scheduled. They were able to point to a letter of protest signed by influential sympathizers on six continents.

Christoph Klenzendorf had spent the postreunification years in the new trendy bars and at basement and bunker parties. He had driven from one improvised open-air concert to another in his mobile whiskey bar. In the delirium of those nights, the desire "to create new, beautiful places" had taken root. With Bar25 on the banks of the Spree, he and his collaborators had made this dream come true, almost like in a fairy tale. When, in 2008, the first eviction notices started arriving, the founders asked themselves and then the city: Why are we being given notice? Why should we of all people leave? Aren't we part of this city's culture, an operation that is subsidized by no one yet brings money into the city and contributes to its reputation as a party town?

Berlin's waste management, however, was able to provide an irrefutable justification: the ground on which Bar25 had been building and partying for four years was polluted and urgently needed to be decontaminated—a sulfur factory had been operational there during the East German years. Nothing could be done: everything that had been wrought by four years of individual efforts had to be torn down completely and without compensation.

The clubless club people came up with a bold plan. Taking a look around on the facing riverbank, they found an obsolete soap factory. They reached an agreement with the owner to lease the building and surrounding property for eighteen months, a solution that really only made sense if they were going to move back to their old club grounds afterward. And even though there was next to no reason to entertain that possibility, they believed in it. But, first, they had to refurbish the soap factory for their purposes. Masters of the art of living, who had considered it a sin to look as far into the future as the next morning, turned into hardworking entrepreneurs and investors overnight. They succeeded in getting well over a hundred collaborators on board for their project. Gutting the building, they renovated the supporting structures, broke dozens of windows into the walls, installed a gourmet restaurant on the top floor and a room for bands and artists below it, and built an open-air amusement park on the jagged riverbank, replete with bars, food stands, areas for sitting and reclining, and secluded nooks for lovers. They poured a total of 1 million euros into facilities they would be allowed to use for only eighteen months, which also meant they had only eighteen months to recoup their expenses to avoid going broke. And they did: "We reached the break-even point," Klenzendorf reported, not without pride.

When I went to the club—now known as KaterHolzig—for the first time with my son and his friends, I felt like I had arrived in an unknown civilization: half pirate island, half ethnological museum, Department of Indigenous Peoples. The rambling grounds on which the club stands, surrounded by an impromptu 6.5-foot-high fence, is marked by a disused smokestack and two brand-new factory towers belonging to the power company Vattenfall. The soap factory, refurbished into a temple of entertainment, rises into the sky like a fortress, its windows cut asymmetrically into the walls. Only the chain of lights of a passing S-Bahn on the opposite riverbank reminded me that I was in the middle of Berlin— near the former Heinrich-Heine-Straße checkpoint, which I had passed through so often during the years of the Wall without once looking to the left or right.

We couldn't get on the dance floor. There was a wedding party going on inside, we found out, that had begun on Thursday and was supposed to last until Tuesday afternoon. But it was less the wedding itself that was restricting our access than the wedding present: a wide table, generously spread with every trendy drug in the world: speed, cocaine, ecstasy, et cetera. The wedding guests, we heard, were welcome to help themselves to any of it. That this privilege was reserved for the wedding guests made sense to us. After all, this "dowry" probably amounted to a six-figure total just for a hundred guests. At one point, the bride in tattered white tumbled out the door giggling, but her wedding guests immediately pulled her back into the party inside.

When I told a friend in New York about this, she surprised me by wondering, "What do the parents do at this sort of wedding?" In Berlin, no one asks questions like this anymore.

While we were keeping out of trouble by the pizza stand, a clubber joined us, reporting a personal record with obvious pride: after thirty-seven hours here, he had only just had his first vodka.

He was convinced that after another vodka and some other re-
freshments he'd last another thirty-seven hours.

Another young man, who worked as a cook at KaterHolzig,
where he was in charge of vegetable side dishes—a vacation, he
said, after having been responsible for prepping meat, his arms
covered in grease all the way up past his elbows—told us his
dream: a career as a disc jockey. He already spun in smaller clubs
and was confident that soon he would be able to work exclusively
as a DJ. The most successful DJs, I learned, charge between ten
thousand and twenty thousand euros per gig; some even earn up to
seventy thousand euros. One of these stars, Paul Kalkbrenner, for
instance, flies from one continent to another on his private jet. As
a kid in East Germany, he listened obsessively to RIAS 2 (a popular radio station broadcasting from the American sector in West
Berlin), helped edit the music broadcasts, and, at the age of fifteen,
showed up in a youth club in Berlin-Lichtenberg with a stack of
twenty vinyl records. He had spun there, but had had to stop every
night at eleven to catch the last tram home. Today, Kalkbrenner
performs in soccer stadiums and enormous music domes. He
travels the world with a team of twenty, and the only thing he still
carries himself is his small Rimowa suitcase. Naturally, the cook
and future DJ continued, these days star DJs release their own
albums. GEMA, Germany's music rights group, can't touch them
with their claims because the DJs create new virtuoso mixes out
of other people's music and their own.

Nowadays, he explained, if a world-famous DJ wants to matter on the international scene, he has to perform in Berlin at least
once a month. After all, techno was invented in Berlin, electro in
Frankfurt.

I never managed to see the inside of KaterHolzig that night;
I would have to come back again—and soon.

After all, the club's closing date was moving closer. The owners
stepped up their schmoozing with Berlin's assemblymen and the
managers of its tourism industry, involving them in discussions

about the city's future. What do you want Berlin to look like in twenty years? they asked. Do you want it to become a city like Manhattan or London, where only bankers, fat cats, and a few stinking-rich artists can still afford the rent? Should all the real estate be hawked to the highest bidder, so that only hotels, luxury apartments, and office towers end up being built? When putting a property up for sale, shouldn't a city also consider its social and cultural value?

The debate reached the media and finally also Parliament. "The funny thing was," reports Klenzendorf, who grew up in a leftist environment, "the CDU suddenly showed up at our doorstep." Young representatives of the Christian Democratic Party, which governs Berlin together with the Social Democratic Party, saw a chance to make a name for themselves as advocates for the ravers. Together with the Greens, they drove the discussion forward in Parliament. A public campaign against the extensive development of the Spree waterfront strengthened the club's position. An unexpected alliance between left and right developed. "The two most discussed projects in the city," Klenzendorf opined with a touch of megalomania, "were the planned new international airport and KaterHolzig club." The city government finally gave in to the demand for a "sales moratorium." Without the guarantee that they could do whatever they wanted with the site, Mediaspree and other interested investors backed out. The only bidders who stuck around were the hippie investors, who only knew the term "planning reliability" from newspapers. In the fall of 2012, a decision was reached across party lines: the club was given the right of first refusal. But more important, a new clause was introduced for the sale of municipal properties. Until then, the law in Berlin had been that real estate belonging to the city could only be unloaded for the highest price. In the future, social and cultural factors would also be taken into consideration.

But how was the club going to come up with the roughly 10 million euros it needed to buy the property? The operators suggested a lease-in-perpetuity to the Senate. According to this model, the city would remain the owner of the property and, in exchange for a leasing fee, would guarantee the club its use for ninety-nine years. The city rejected the proposal. The operators then looked for a buyer who would purchase the site and lease it to them in place of the city. They found a Swiss foundation—a pension fund called Abendrot, which was an outgrowth of the antinuclear movement and was looking for a safe way to invest its policyholders' money. The Swiss came, took a look at the club and its project plans, and sealed the deal that same evening.

"So now we're paying rent to a Swiss foundation instead of to the poor city of Berlin," Klenzendorfer notes.

KaterHolzig closed at the end of 2013; the new club on the other side of the Spree has opened under the name Holzmarkt. Having anticipated the move, KaterHolzig's team used mostly mobile components in refurbishing the soap factory—anything that isn't a ceiling, floor, or wall can be unscrewed, taken apart, and transported to the other side of the river. An operational cooperative composed of thirteen people decides what will be built and where. But their task is limited to establishing a platform for various spaces that it will then be up to independent special-purpose entities to build. Klenzendorf himself, together with seven colleagues, will handle the event side of things. Others are developing a hotel with 120 rooms—"a special hotel," of course, "where the concierge will welcome adventure-hungry guests with a monkey on his shoulder." A student hostel and start-up center are also planned, as are art and music studios (which will produce their own labels), physical therapy studios, hair salons, and retail stores. The rooftops of all the facilities will be dedicated to "skyfarming"—agriculture and fish farming, that is. The idea, in short, is to create a self-sufficient village in the middle of the city—a *Gesamtkunstwerk*, or universal work of art, of sorts.

Klenzendorf responds tentatively to a question concerning the bookkeeping: of course there are a few professionals involved by this point. But he is convinced that they will also spend their free time at the club and that at those moments, at the very latest, they will remember its life philosophy, which, based loosely on Pippi Longstocking's motto, is: Do things the way you like. That's the only way to make sure they turn out right!

The approximately 750-square-foot bar with the off-putting name Kumpelnest—roughly, "buddy nest"—belongs to a completely different category of nightlife. Its location alone—on Potsdamer Straße in the West, historically a site of prostitution—predestines it for a much more colorful crowd. Since the fall of the Wall, the street has lost a lot of its grubby charm. Its few fun spots—the Wintergarten vaudeville, new casinos, and old corner bars—are so far apart from one another that most stretches of the street are dead by midnight. Even so, Kumpelnest is one of the liveliest places in Berlin. One rumor has it that it opens only at three in the morning, but when we got there just before this supposed opening time, the place was already packed. Anyone who dreads skin-to-skin or body-to-body contact shouldn't even bother going in. The space, decked out with dark wallpaper with a pale gold ornamental pattern, creates a forced proximity between patrons that would be sure to cause mass panic anywhere else. Forget sitting down; the bar stools and sofalike protrusions along the walls are always already taken. Active standing in place is a necessary part of the strategy for survival at Kumpelnest. Techno music also dictates people's movements here, but, unlike Berghain, Kumpelnest doesn't live off the charisma of its architecture or reputation as Berlin's hottest nightspot—it lives off the charisma and extroversion of its patrons. Everyone crammed together here shimmying and shaking has worked on their image and is showing it off. Whether they're wearing a leather jacket, wife-beater, red suit jacket, knickerbockers, or a daring top paired with a shimmering miniskirt, they will also always be sporting some additional accessory to mark their individuality: a crazy hat, absurd scarf, unprecedented socks. *I am me, and the rest of you are different—* that is the message. Sven Marquardt, the bouncer at Berghain, would fit in perfectly here, come to think of it. Instead though, he keeps watch at the entrance to his club to make sure that no one who might try to compete with him and his outfit crosses the threshold.

I had heard a number of languages other than German at Berghain and KaterHolzig—mostly English, Italian, French, and Japanese. The patrons we were crushed up against at Kumpelnest on this particular morning looked like they came from every part of the world. Afghans, Italians, Turks, Palestinians—but, except for the Americans, they were all speaking German with one another, mostly with a Berlin accent. This was a new experience for me. It had been at least twenty years since I'd last stayed out until morning at a trendy Berlin dance bar on Lehniner Platz. There, too, there had been countless "foreigners," as they were called at the time. But they had kept to themselves and would answer in broken German or English if you spoke to them. Something fundamental had changed in the time between my last white night and this one. The twenty-, thirty-, and fiftysomething "foreigners" I met at Kumpelnest all spoke German perfectly; they didn't have to make the slightest effort—whether or not they had a German passport, they were real locals, native speakers, who happened to have different complexions. German was their first language, they were at home in Berlin and in this bar in particular.

In their midst, other "minorities" also felt at home. Two older ladies perched on wall seats, on the lookout for one last customer. A representative of the third sex, who, struggling to catch people's attention in the cramped space, finally did a solo turn on a small platform, which garnered lukewarm applause. And there was another thing I liked about this bar. It didn't follow the Berlin rule of being a "generational bar," it was home to night owls of every age. You were among your own kind here—your own kind being anyone else, young or old, who wanted to party the night away. And then—it must have been around dawn—two otherworldly-looking women dressed in white entered the scene: one creature at least six foot six with an enormous chest, and her somewhat shorter companion, who was still a good half head taller than me. The colorful troop of smokers in front of the entrance froze in awe and stepped aside; inside the bar, the crowd divided as the two transvestites strode through like royalty. They took a seat at the bar, ordered shots, knocked them back, and left again. Someone hailed a cab. The two empresses got in, the tall one letting her overlong, bent leg trail outside for a beat before she pulled it into the cab and slammed the door. No sooner were they gone than the spaces that had opened up in the crowd fused shut, and everyone stood and moved tightly packed together again.

Just as my girlfriend and I left Kumpelnest, the sun unexpectedly broke through the cement skies of that gray summer. Both of us were surprised by how cheerfully and utterly shamelessly we had managed to lose ourselves in the bog of Berlin's nightlife once again.

The Bunker on Albrechtstraße, where the Berlin club scene's first parties were held after the fall of the Wall, has made an unusual career for itself. Like a relic from another age, the square, sixty-foot-high monstrosity with its six-and-a-half-foot-thick outer walls and embrasurelike windows sits between expensive apartment buildings and the Deutsches Theater, a five-minute walk from the Friedrichstraße S-Bahn station. Slave laborers built the Bunker for the Nazis in 1943. Even as the Allies had already begun to bombard Berlin, the architect apparently still found the time to add his own stylistic touches. The roof is reminiscent of the battlements of a fifteenth-century Italian fortress. In May 1945, the Russians captured it, and the bunker became a war prison.

Beginning in 1957, East Germany used it to store dried and tropical fruits.

No sooner had the Wall fallen than the first DJs were already occupying the building, filling its spaces with their music. The Bunker, which had once served as a bomb shelter for tens of thousands of civilians, now became a playground for the Berlin underground. The organizers who later went on to found successful clubs like Ostgut and Berghain practiced throwing their first parties here. One of the last to do so hit on the strange idea of presenting the Bunker as the Red Cross Club, though he was forced to drop the name after the Red Cross sent him a warning letter; he found a way around it with the name Ex-Kreuz-Club—"Ex–Cross Club." Following several crackdowns, the Bunker became the focus of so-called fuck parades, which protested against the "suppression of the Berlin subculture" and ended their rallies in front of the Bunker's locked iron doors. This scene, however, which was driven more by a thirst for adventure than real protest, soon shifted to former factory sites, cooling towers, abandoned tunnels, and other ruins, of which there is no shortage in Berlin.

In 2003, the story of the Bunker took a typical Berlin turn: a rich advertising executive from the western city of Wuppertal by the name of Christian Boros bought the building and turned it into a museum for his collection of contemporary art. During the remodeling, he made sure to include a penthouse apartment for himself and his small family on the 10,000-square-foot roof.

Entering Boros's art bunker was a strange experience. As a child, I had only known bunkers as places you ran to when the rising and falling wail of alarm sirens announced an attack from low-flying aircraft.

Boros had the five-story building restored with a certain reverence—if such an emotion can be said to exist for bunkers. Instead of having the walls plastered over, he had them painted white so the original layering of the concrete beams can still be seen. The ventilation flaps, iron doors, and even the test filters for the early detection of potential poison-gas attacks have all been preserved. Even the faded traces of black paint from the club-party era have been reverently conserved in the "darkrooms." The decisive modification, which has freed the Bunker of its oppressive atmosphere to a great extent, are the large, staggered openings cut into the ceilings of the rooms. As you go upstairs, from each floor you can always see down into the exhibition spaces of the floors below. These openings create breathing room and a certain sense of freedom for both the works of art and visitors in the otherwise confining space.

It was the sounds in the art Bunker that surprised me most of all. If Boros set out intentionally to produce this effect, it was a smart choice. Because anyone sitting in a bunker in the middle of a war barely sees anything—and doesn't want to see anything; what he pays attention to are sounds, or, as the case may be, the absence of sounds: the anxious silence among hundreds of women and children, loud screams when bombs strike nearby, the wait for a sign that the danger has passed.

Of course the sounds I heard some seventy years later in Boros's art bunker were of a completely different nature. Right after entering, I was unsettled by a sound installation by Alicja Kwade. A young art student explained where the sound was coming from: the artist had attached microphones to several coldly glowing fluorescent tubes on the ceiling, which transfer the frequency noise of the lights to loudspeakers and to steel plates bent into wavelike shapes. On another floor, you could hear the ticking of time. The sound came from a big clock, whose face Kwade had hidden behind a curved mirror.

Klara Lidén's installation *Teenage Room* also announced itself through sound first. If you walked in through a door instead of through the rectangular hole in the wall, an ax came crashing down as soon as you let go of the doorknob. In the far corner of the room stood an iron bunk bed painted black, in which the nightmare objects of an unhappy student life were presented and immortalized—also in black and made of iron: a pile of books, backpack, computer. And, already on the ground floor, you could hear a constant "plopping" from the upper floors. This came from a popcorn machine on the fourth floor, which uses a dryer to pop each kernel and apparently will keep doing so until the entire room is filled with popcorn. The corn is organically grown, the art student assured me, which inspired me to help myself to a handful, even though I have never really eaten popcorn. But when I went to get a second helping, I was distracted by an irritating filing sound next to the explosion of corn kernels, caused by a rotating car tire endlessly grinding itself down against the Bunker wall. According to the art student, it would continue to do so until it had ground itself up for good.

Probably for reasons related to my personal history, the pieces I have mentioned here are ones that primarily engaged my ears. But there were also numerous works of art that challenged the sense of sight: the spectacular *Tree 2011*, for example, amassed and assembled from numerous trees and tree remains by the Chinese artist Ai Weiwei. Apparently several of the Bunker's balustrades had to be dismantled so the twenty-foot-tall tree could be hauled up to its position on the fourth floor. Ai Weiwei's bare tree, composed and screwed together out of dead swamp wood, really does look like the primordial form of a tree, even as its Chinese parentage is undeniable.

In Berlin, it seems, in the end everything becomes either art and/or memorial, irrespective of whether you're dealing with the Holocaust, World War II bombardments, or the division of Germany. And maybe that's a good thing. Boros has done a clever and impressive job in staging his unusual exhibition rooms. That said, even if I could afford it, I'd never have an apartment with a spectacular view built for myself on the roof of a bunker. I would be reminded too often of the sights and sounds of the hundreds of thousands of people who once sought shelter on the floors below the penthouse. But these are the afflictions of a seventy-year-old. Christian Boros and his family belong to another generation. And, as such, they enjoy what the former German chancellor Helmut Kohl once referred to as "the blessing of a late birth."

WHAT HAPPENED TO THE WALL ANYWAY?

While it stood, the Berlin Wall was the city's most famous and infamous structure. Yet just a year after November 9, 1989, it had already largely disappeared—pulverized or sold off around the world. At best, tourists near Checkpoint Charlie today might encounter a few street vendors selling coins, medals, gas masks, and uniform jackets from the vanished system.

A national Berlin Wall Memorial opened on Bernauer Straße twenty years after the fall of the Wall. The location was a point of contention for years. This was where more than three hundred (mostly failed) attempts to flee had been made; this was where—because of the especially solid ground—several escape tunnels had been built. City councilmembers wanted to preserve a relatively long section of the border area to keep its memory alive at least in this one part of the reunified city. But residents of the western side of Bernauer Straße had a strong case against them: they'd had a view of the Wall for twenty-nine years; they didn't want to spend the rest of their lives looking at it.

There were valid objections on the eastern side as well. During the East German era, the administration of Sophienkirche (Saint Sophia's Church) had had to accept border guards controlling visitors to its cemetery and patrolling among the graves. When the Wall was built, more than a thousand of the deceased were moved to new graves; moreover, part of the border area had probably been established over a preexisting mass grave for soldiers killed in action during World War II. In the first ten years after the Wall went up, residents in the East had only been allowed to visit the graves of their relatives with a "grave certificate," while West Berliners had been completely barred from visiting their dead: when the Wall finally came down, initially neither East nor West Berliners wanted to be reminded of it anymore.

The Wall Memorial on Bernauer Straße is a compromise. A piece of the original Wall has been preserved. Several gaps are marked by Wall-high vertical iron posts, between which visitors can slip to reach the "death strip" on the other side. The so-called death strip, however, has changed to the point that it no longer conveys the brutality of the original arrangement. A memorial with embedded photographs of the victims of the Wall shows the several dozen people who lost their lives along this section of the internal German border. In the name of political correctness, the eight border guards and members of the People's Army who died "in service to the Wall"—and who were honored as heroes for this in the East German propaganda—are also commemorated. In reality, they lost their lives while trying to stop escape attempts; in most cases, they were shot by their own fleeing colleagues. With an archaeological thoroughness bordering on the absurd, the remains—or foundations, rather—of the border security facilities have also been unearthed. An excavated area reveals: the paltry vestiges of the foundations of the lighting system, but not the lighting system itself, which ensured an illumination as bright as day even at night; the underpinnings of the border fence in the ground, but not the border fence itself, which set off an alarm when touched; the foundations of the guard post, but not the guard post itself, from where the border guards kept watch. For those who knew the border area, these remains on display seem strangely harmless. Why haven't the facilities they invoke been restored or re-created to give a more realistic impression of the insanity of a state that willingly walled itself in? The most striking evocation of the border area is a transverse rust-red wall installed specifically for the memorial. Significantly higher than the Wall itself, it symbolizes the latter's insurmountability far better than the vestiges of the border area do.

Perhaps the most vibrant memorial is the so-called Mauer-park—literally, Wall Park—that separates the West German district of Wedding from the East German Prenzlauer Berg. All that remains of the Wall here is a roughly two-hundred-yard-long section of the *Hinterlandmauer*—the wall that fugitives from East Germany had to scale in order to reach the cordon sanitaire of the actual Wall. This stretch of wall has since been plastered entirely with graffiti in flashy colors.

If nothing else, it's a sign of life that the area around the former death strip has turned into an enormous green playground for a mostly young public. These days, a flea market, amphitheater, climbing wall, puppet theater, music groups, and playgrounds attract thousands of visitors every weekend. The pop remnant of the wall has become a recreational ghost, as it were, protectively watching over the colorful goings-on. It used to be that at the end of every Sunday night the muddy lawns would be strewn with beer bottles. A cleaning-up culture of sorts has taken root in the meantime. Ever since Joe Hatchiban started hosting karaoke parties in the amphitheater and handing out trash bags to the audience afterward, Mauerpark has become clean and green. You could even say that Mauerpark has become the Tiergarten—Berlin's version of Central Park—for a young public. But, as always happens when a large inner-city area opens up in Berlin, its future use is in dispute. There are public campaigns to reserve the area for recreational activities and as a "lung" for the city. So far, it has only been by agreeing to enlarge the park that city planners, faced with a growing shortage of housing, have managed to get permission to build a residential building with six hundred apartments at the northern end of Mauerpark.

At more than fourteen hundred yards, the so-called East Side Gallery is by far the longest remaining section of the Wall. In reality, however, it is also part of the former *Hinterlandmauer*; in other words, it only became possible to paint on it after the actual Wall had fallen. After reunification, the Council of Ministers of East Germany commissioned a series of internationally known artists to paint and spray-paint a number of impressive images onto the long wall. But because the *Hinterlandmauer*, unlike the actual, reinforced concrete Wall, was made of the cheapest material, it didn't hold up to weathering. The East Side Gallery crumbled and fell apart. And so began one of those landmark preservation actions that it seems can only be concocted and implemented in Berlin. The steel reinforcement of the disintegrating *Hinterlandmauer* was laid bare so it could be treated for corrosion. The resulting gaps were filled with special concrete, spackled and primed. The artists of the damaged pieces were invited to Berlin and asked to repaint their old images on the renovated wall. Not all of them were still alive, others couldn't be tracked down, and still others didn't want to come. All the same, 87 of the surviving 115 artists showed up to re-create their pieces, receiving a 3,000-euro "compensation" to reimburse them for their time and expenses.

One can argue about whether paintings in open-air galleries inevitably weather and disintegrate sooner or later. After all, unlike the wall paintings in Pompeii or Leonardo da Vinci's *Last Supper* in the Dominican convent of Santa Maria delle Grazie in Milan, the creators of these artworks consciously exposed them to the influence of wind and weather—not to mention to unavoidably being painted and doodled over by fellow practitioners of the graffiti arts. In fact, a number of the East Side Gallery artists simply couldn't warm up to the idea of reproducing their work— especially not for the remuneration offered. Disagreements regarding the copyright of the images also arose. The print media and publishers had made money on coffee table books about the

East Side Gallery, without first having cleared copyright issues. But did these rights even exist? Whom did the Wall belong to anyway—with or without these paintings?

In the meantime, other artists jumped in to fill the gap. The photo artist Kai Wiedenhöfer wanted to paste thirty-five panoramas onto a 380-yard-long stretch of the East Side Gallery. Originally, he planned to cover the section of the Wall put at his disposal with large photographs of the Israeli–Palestinian border. Yet due to differences about the project between the many groups involved in the East Side Gallery, his plans fell through. An agreement was apparently reached over a subsequent project—mounting photographs of eight different border areas from around the world, including the border stronghold between North and South Korea, the border between the Turkish and Greek parts of Cyprus, and the "wall" between the United States and Mexico—but this project too is still being disputed.

In the fall of 2012, I came across a Wall memorial worthy of the name. It takes the form of—this being Berlin, what else?—a simulation: a panorama painting by the Berlin artist Yadegar Asisi. Displayed on the inside of a round tower built especially for the piece near Checkpoint Charlie, it presents the drama of the former border system so well that all other memorials created after the fall of the Wall pale in comparison. The Berlin principle—illusion, trompe l'œil—proved to be more powerful and realistic than all the "real" places that have been transformed into museums.

In the 1980s, Asisi lived near the Wall, and he has condensed his emotions and memories of the time into a fictional snapshot. Irreverently, he has compressed buildings and scenes that are actually far apart in time and space into a single view set in the 1980s. When you enter the tower to take in the panorama, the first thing to jump out at you is the ridiculous curving progression of the Wall. It is the late, the fourth, version of the Wall, that the painter has consolidated into a meandering monster that dominates the city under dark November skies. Naturally, Asisi hasn't failed to include the hackneyed warning sign YOU ARE LEAVING THE AMERICAN SECTOR, or the graffiti on the main western Wall, or the carefully concealed door in the Wall, which the border guards would sometimes open to recapture spray-painting East German refugees who mistakenly believed themselves to be safe: only experts knew that the western side of the Wall, including a 6.5-foot-wide strip beside it, was actually located on East German ground. The border police sometimes used these doors to white-wash graffiti before state visits by high-ranking foreign representatives. They would enter the West with brushes and buckets of white paint and, undisturbed by the Allied military police, paint over the graffiti along a sixty-five- to one-hundred-foot stretch of the Wall—precisely where, according to information from the state security service, the anticipated visiting luminary from the West would appear at the podium to hold his or her obligatory Wall speech.

Needless to say, graffiti artists lost no time repainting the whitewashed stretches of the Wall. It probably never occurred to those who later bought large and spectacular pieces of the Wall to subject their expensive and extremely heavy specimens to closer inspection. With any luck, they might have discovered earlier, possibly brilliant, works of art underneath the visible paintings.

But back to Asisi's panorama painting. Behind the Wall that faced West Berlin, lit up by the icy light of the lampposts, the artist shows the death strip and one of the watchtowers with its primed border guards. You can make out the antitank obstacles behind the Wall, the strip of asphalt for the border guards' jeeps, the dog patrol areas, and the *Hinterlandmauer*. What Asisi can't show using his means are the traps beneath the sand: jumping from the *Hinterlandmauer*, clueless fugitives would land on beds of nails hidden in the sand, which would pierce their feet and ankles; with every second or third step, they would become entangled in electrically charged wires, which alerted the border guards in the watchtower. Nevertheless, Asisi has succeeded better than anyone else in conveying the menace and inhumanity of the border system. At the same time, he also communicates something very different: the astounding ability of those who lived near the border to accept and adapt to the situation.

Behind the border area, Asisi has conjured up the perfect likeness of a crumbling nineteenth-century building near the border, its bottom floors walled up. There is light in the windows only on the upper floors, indicating the presence of a few occupants. In one of the lit-up windows, you can make out the silhouette of a woman, though it isn't clear if she's looking "over to the other side." Insiders know that only people loyal to the party were allowed to live directly by the Wall and that they could only access their apartments near the border using a special permit. In some cases they were childless couples devoted to the East German regime, who were given the children of attempted escapees to adopt. With magnificent accuracy, the painter has captured the disintegration of this East Berlin apartment building's façade, exposed down to its bricks, with only the turn-of-the-century decorations still intact. To its left, he shows the new East German buildings near the border and, still farther to the left, several *Plattenbauten* from the 1980s, which detractors referred to as the late-gothic phase of the Honecker era. At the center of the panorama, the massive, somehow surreal TV Tower rises up into the dark November sky.

But the painter has also depicted the false idyll on the West Berlin side. There is a dilapidated building near the border area that has been occupied by squatters. Those familiar with the story know that these squatters had just one enemy: the West Berlin police and Senate, which regularly issued eviction notices. I can't remember a single one of the squatters' slogans having anything to do with the fate of the Germans imprisoned on the other side of the Wall. In front of the squat, you can make out homeless people warming their hands by a fire next to a trailer. In the shadow of the Wall, they have cultivated vegetable patches as well as a small zoo with unidentifiable animals. The rickety cars, abandoned Shell gas station, Berlin corner pub, and Turkish grocer next door—everything exudes the cozy desolation of the 1980s. To the left, on the West Berlin side, a narrow street is visible; its apartments overshadowed by the Wall. Old mattresses no one wants to sleep on anymore are being carried into or out of an apartment. Kids kick a ball against a wall, which happens to be the Wall.

With his panorama painting, Asisi has achieved something that Berlin's city planners and memorial functionaries will never manage: he has captured a snapshot of a neighborhood in a divided city, in whose nooks residents on both sides have made themselves at home. There is nothing to suggest the imminent events that would soon change the course of world history.

And what became of *the* Wall anyway—the real Wall? Those who had put it up hadn't cut any corners, using the best reinforced concrete for what was by far the most expensive example of East German architecture. Apparently West German and Swedish suppliers of reinforced concrete and barbed wire also made a tidy profit from the Wall. Needless to say, the real Wall wasn't torn down by thousands of "Wall woodpeckers." Armed with good equipment, a technically adept Berlin friend of mine set to work on the Wall for two days; after many joint-punishing hours, he still hadn't managed to break off much more than a few pieces. Twenty years later, he had to decide whether to throw out or keep these chunks, which he had been storing in his basement. He decided to incorporate the heavy pieces into a sculpture, for which he required the help of a tombstone expert because of its weight. The sculpture now sits in his garden.

Professional demolition machines were required to definitively tear down the real Wall. In this respect, it is misleading to speak of the "fall of the Wall." The Wall did not fall on November 9 or in the ensuing days; instead, initially several openings were broken into it with the help of building cranes, and then specialized companies gradually carted it off piece by piece. Today, sections of the Wall can be found around the world; 360 of the Wall's 45,000 pieces were selected as artworks and divested for up to 40,000 deutsche marks. Among them were 81 pieces auctioned off in Monte Carlo in 1990. One of the buyers was the cognac heiress Ljiljana Hennessy, who secured a piece of the Wall for the park on her country estate. Other owners include not just the CIA and many museums, but also the former president of the Federation of German Industries (BDI) Hans-Olaf Henkel, and King Taufa'ahau Tupou IV of Tonga. One section is on the Honolulu Community College campus in Hawaii. Pieces of the Wall are now located in at least 125 sites around the world, all of which are duly listed in *Die Berliner Mauer in der Welt* (The Berlin Wall in the World), edited by Anna Kaminsky and published by Berlin Story Verlag. Yet the majority of the Wall was reprocessed—the steel melted down, the concrete ground to sand—and used to build new highways in the former East Germany. Drivers racing over some of the smooth-as-glass highways in the new federal states today are oblivious to the fact that the ashes of the erstwhile monstrosity lie beneath the asphalt. Anyone driving to Berlin Schönefeld Airport or to the Baltic Sea is traveling over the remains of the Wall. And so, in the end, in its shift from vertical to horizontal, the Wall turned out to be good for something after all.

EPILOGUE

In early March 2013, a demonstration at the East Side Gallery brought about an unexpected turn of events. Unlikely slogans could be heard near the section by Mühlenstraße in the Friedrichshain district: "The wall must stay," groups of demonstrators shouted, while others chanted, in English, "Mr. Wowereit, don't tear down this wall!"—a play on Ronald Reagan's famous call from 1987, "Mr. Gorbachev, tear down this wall!" The reason for the demonstration was an investor's attempt to cut out a sixty-two-foot-long section of the East Side Gallery to clear the way for the entrance to a new apartment tower. The plans called for the removed sections of the *Hinterlandmauer* to be set up again at another location. The investor had a valid contract in hand, signed by the district's mayor, a member of the Green Party. But the demonstrators, many of whom hadn't even been born while the Wall still stood, were attached to the East Side Gallery and didn't want to relinquish a single chunk of it. They pointed to the millions of euros in taxpayer money that the city had only just invested to renovate the East Side Gallery—and now the landmark was supposed to make way for an investor? The protest quickly swelled into a mass rally with some six thousand demonstrators, capturing the media's attention. Young protestors were joined by older Berliners, who, now—twenty years after the fact—wanted at all costs to hold on to what was left of the cursed wall. One twenty-year-old announced through a microphone that even a tiny gap in the East Side Gallery would destroy the sense of constriction and imprisonment that had reigned here during the years of the Wall—a feeling he was keen to preserve. A man from the landmarks preservation society went so far as to say that Berlin was "the modern Rome of archaeology" and had an obligation to protect the monuments of the past.

Berlin's mayor Klaus Wowereit made the matter a top priority. He saw no reason, he asserted, why the East Side Gallery shouldn't be preserved—he would talk to the investor and district mayor. But, in the end, at the break of dawn, the construction vehicles advanced again after all, biting a chunk out of the wall. The demonstrators hadn't woken up in time for the investor's surprise coup; Berlin's mayor acted shocked. This tug-of-war is sure to continue for a while.

Yet, with or without a gap, it seems the East Side Gallery will be preserved—an astounding reversal in the history of Berlin's attempt to define itself. For there is virtually nothing authentic about this wall that is now being protected: the meager *Hinterlandmauer* itself was but a shadow of the real Wall, and all the paintings on it date to after the fall of the Wall. But isn't it decidedly better to maintain at least a fake—an ersatz—Wall in Berlin than nothing at all?

THE AMERICAN SECTOR IS LEAVING YOU

The entire world marveled at how quickly after the fall of the Wall the city reconsolidated its two halves and filled its vacant lots with new buildings, not to say entire neighborhoods. But just as quickly as the city redeveloped itself, it also cut itself off from the structures and systems that had shaped its recent history, including the structural legacy of the American occupying power, to which the western half of the city owed its democratic survival after the war. It was a rejection that occurred almost soundlessly. Yet had the presence of the western Allies really only saved democracy in West Berlin? Let's assume that the Allies had accepted Berlin's capture by the Soviets, that the Americans hadn't exchanged the departments they already controlled, Saxony and Thuringia, for Berlin's western sectors. In that case, "the German question" probably would have been settled then and there; East Germany could have declared the undivided city of Berlin its capital. It was only thanks to the western Allies' insistence on maintaining a political-military presence in Berlin that the postwar fate of Germany and Berlin remained an open-ended question.

No other site in the city is a more compelling reminder of the three West sectors' successful resistance to the Soviet blockade than Tempelhof Airport. Beginning on June 26, 1948, for an entire year, every ninety seconds, aircraft of the U.S. Air Force and Royal Air Force supplied the half-city with deliveries of fuel, food, building materials, and all other essentials. The *Rosinenbomber*—literally "raisin bombers," more commonly known as "candy bombers" in English—took their name from a gift given to Berlin's children by American airlift pilots. In April 1945, as a five-year-old, I had witnessed the arrival of the U.S. Army in Grainau in Upper Bavaria. Already then, the occupying forces had spoiled us with chewing gum, candy, and chocolate. This tradition was revived—apparently unprompted by any orders from above—on the initiative of a U.S. Air Force pilot by the name of Gail Halvorsen. Initially, when his was still the only plane delivering candy, he would announce himself to the children on the ground by wiggling his wings, which earned him the nickname Onkel Wackelflügel, or Uncle Wiggly Wings, among his young fans. Other pilots soon followed suit. Before landing at Tempelhof, they would throw handkerchiefs filled with all sorts of candy suspended from tiny homemade parachutes to the children, who by this point stood expectantly on a mountain of rubble in Neukölln waiting for them.

The Berlin Airlift was the first time the West stood up to the demands of their former ally, the Soviet Union. Thanks to their perfect organization, the flying skills of the British and American pilots (who dropped off supplies at Berlin-Tempelhof at intervals timed down to the second and virtually without any accidents), and the western Allies' successful counterblockade, Stalin ended the Soviet blockade in May 1949. Countless movies, from Billy Wilder's *One, Two, Three* to Wim Wenders's *Wings of Desire*, which shows the airport's underground tunnels, have contributed to the mythical status of Tempelhof, which was once the largest commercial airport in the world.

The airport continued to be used well into the new millennium, until, on July 31, 2007, the Berlin Senate decided to shut it down in favor of the planned new Berlin Brandenburg (BER) international airport. A public campaign passed a referendum against the closing of Tempelhof. But even though 530,000 Berliners spoke out in favor of keeping it open, they failed to hold their ground against the majority of residents opposed to it. Surprisingly, most of the votes to keep the airport open came from the residents of the Tempelhof-Schöneberg district, who were most afflicted by the aircraft noise pollution, along with a slight majority of West Berliners. They were defeated by a clear majority from the districts of former East Berlin.

This was one of the first major decisions that gave the reunified city a taste of the power of its eastern half. What probably tipped the scales against Tempelhof for East Berliners was the fact that they didn't associate any positive memories with it—after all, the Soviet blockade had cut off the West Berliners, not them, from all supplies. And it wasn't their freedom, but that of the West Berliners, that the candy bombers had defended. The majority of East Berliners probably still saw Tempelhof Airport as it had been presented to them in the communist propaganda: as a former Nazi airport that had been turned into a base for "U.S. imperialism" after the war. *Their* "home" airport was Schönefeld Airport; in 1945, Soviet troops had occupied the grounds and facilities of the Henschel aircraft company located there and began, two years later, to transform them into the "capital" airport of East Germany. Today, Schönefeld Airport is being partly integrated into the new international BER Airport located to its south.

In the summer of 2012, I visited the Tempelhof field, which stretches out on either side of the two runways. Already from a distance, the old airport's new users catch your eye. Instead of airplanes, the sky over Tempelhof is filled with landboarding and hobby kites. The wide, still intact tarmac is teeming with skateboarders, cyclists, and stroller-pushing mothers and fathers; occasionally, adventurers in low-lying self-made vehicles with thick wheels zigzag across the grass, pulled along by flapping sails. In the distance, a few old airplanes are still parked in front of the former terminal, and you can't help but wonder how they'll ever be removed from here—presumably not by air.

Separated from the public traffic on the airfield, so-called hay meadows have been set aside for "highly endangered" species "protected throughout Europe," including tall oat grass, bellflowers, cleavers, and red fescue, as well as butterflies, spiders, beetles, small mammals, and birds. The skylark in particular, according to one information sign, requires a peaceful habitat in order to breed. To protect and glorify the skylark, a series of wooden steles topped by fretwork depictions of birds taking off or landing have been set up—a pioneering project by seventy schoolgirls, completed with the help of five woman sculptors. "Flight instruments, rook flight games, and flight signs" are also on display here—all made out of wood and exhibited on sixteen-foot-tall wood columns. There are special areas set aside for everything dear to the hearts of environmentalists and community gardeners: dog runs, minigolf grounds, sports fields. Yet I searched in vain for a sign explaining the proper handling of dog waste.

Amateur gardeners have made themselves at home in some of the fenced-off areas, displaying and lovingly watering their plants in dirt-filled shopping baskets and plastic containers of the kind used in supermarkets to transport food and building parts. Apparently the city has forbidden the gardeners from planting anything directly on the Tempelhof field, resulting in the emergence of a troop of ambulant gardeners, who can pick up and move on anytime with their zucchini and tomato plants and apiaries. The terms "art" and "creative industries"—so generously applied throughout Berlin—are very much in evidence here too. There are "art and exhibition projects" at every step—the "nonprofit pioneer-project city field," for example, which creates a "connection between city and nature," as one poster boasts. An art project titled *Parallelen* (Parallels) by the avant-garde artist Harun Farocki, on the other hand, sits abandoned on the Tempelhof field—except for the presence of one lone guard. The former Sixty-Eighter and film artist Farocki has made a mistake for which the locals refuse to forgive him: he expects people to pay to see his installation! If you want to associate with the environmentalists, you have to meet one basic requirement: free admission!

There are posters everywhere mentioning nonprofit gardeners, "commons," and "urban agriculture." Yet not a single sign along the runway, let alone an original memorial, commemorates the candy bombers who landed here every few minutes from 1948 to 1949.

On a trip to Bucharest, I had been surprised to see mainly potato fields, cow pastures, and orchards on my way into the city from the airport. When I mentioned this to a friend of mine in Bucharest, a cosmopolitan architect, he was amused. "Haven't you heard? 'Urban agriculture' is the latest craze in modern city architecture. Thanks to our backwardness in Romania, we're suddenly at the forefront of the avant-garde!"

Apparently Berlin is well on its way to outstripping Bucharest.

The American Embassy made a mistake when it decided to phase out another, rather unprepossessing, icon of the American presence in Berlin: the Amerika Haus on Hardenbergstraße, which was West Berlin's most important showcase for American culture during the years of the Cold War. The former ambassador John Kornblum, who more than any other American diplomat is associated with the history of the United States in the city, ascribes the decision to security concerns. Ostensibly it isn't possible to sufficiently secure the building, located diagonally across from the Zoo station, which has been demoted from an actual train station to a mere S-Bahn stop.

With all due respect, I would object that the obsession with security that took hold of the United States after 9/11 is unwarranted in this case. I can't imagine that it would be necessary to close off Hardenbergstraße and the Zoo station for an appearance by Richard Ford, Jonathan Franzen, Siri Hustvedt, or Paul Auster. Another argument I've often heard makes even less sense to me:

the United States doesn't need a cultural association like the Goethe-Institut; Hollywood and Apple are already spreading American culture around the world—without any government funding. Fortunately, however, there is more to American culture than highly salable products. As a student, I read *The New York Times* at the Amerika Haus in Berlin; it was here that we saw our first Jackson Pollock paintings, listened to jazz, and experienced the avant-garde of modern dance. And it is precisely defiant, unpopular works like these that invite people to look beyond the preconceptions and clichés about the United States. It's true that the Amerika Haus, with its flat roof and its entrance hall with glass windows and mosaic walls, was never a beauty. But—together with the eggs that were thrown and splattered against its windows in 1966 during a demonstration against the Vietnam War—this small building is part of the American history of Berlin.

I also can't make peace with the closing down, or relocation, of the American Memorial Library, a gift from the Americans to the Berliners. When the foundation stone was laid in 1952, the mayor at the time, Ernst Reuter, described the library as an enduring symbol commemorating the people of Berlin's resistance against the Soviet blockade. On a decorative wall in the foyer, you can still read a wonderful—generously rededicated—sentence by the third president of the United States, Thomas Jefferson: "This institution will be based on the illimitable freedom of the human mind. For here we are not afraid to follow the truth wherever it may lead, nor to tolerate any error as long as reason is left free to combat it."

As students, it was here that we read the original English versions of books by the Beat generation, as well as those of the Black Panther movement and Latin American revolutionaries. The library was always a bit less organized, but also less bureaucratic, than the Free University library: it was easier to gain access to books, but volumes listed in the catalog were often impossible to locate. Sloppiness alone probably wasn't to blame for this; it was also due to the library's proximity to the border. Before the Wall was built, the library had also been used by information-hungry East Berliners. According to a famous and true story, one user from East Berlin borrowed a book from the library in early August 1961. Because the Wall subsequently went up, he was unable to return it for twenty-eight years. Apparently, during that entire time, he was troubled by the fact that this book was so long overdue. Just a day or two after the Wall came down, the good man made his way to the American Memorial Library to return it.

The Berlin Senate now wants to move the library's inventory to a so-called central library, to be built on the Tempelhof field. No one has any idea where the debt-ridden city will find the money for this pet project of the current mayor, Klaus Wowereit. One CDU opponent suggested housing the planned central library, including the holdings of the American Memorial Library, in the asbestos-riddled International Congress Center (ICC) near the Radio Tower, a building desperately in need of renovating. This would allow the city to save a great deal of money, since the ICC renovations will cost 320 million euros—exactly the projected cost of the new central library planned for the former airport grounds.

This proposal may make sense in the context of the reigning renovation mania, which has the city lurching from one closing and opening to the next. But why in heaven's name does a city with more than 60 billion euros in debt want to close down a functioning library in favor of a new building it can't afford? And have Berlin's city council members completely lost their sense of the value of iconic buildings and spaces? Of course you can move the American Memorial Library to the ICC or to Tempelhof Airport; position a candy bomber on the lawn in front of Schönefeld Airport, where no such plane ever landed; or re-create Checkpoint Charlie in the Berlin-Spandau district. But once a memorial site is gone, it remains gone forever.

THE GHOST OF BER INTERNATIONAL AIRPORT

The new international Berlin Brandenburg (BER) Airport is re-unified Berlin's biggest, most ambitious, and most expensive project. At the same time, it is also the city's biggest scandal. The idea for the new super airport arose shortly after the fall of the Wall. It was the result of the delusions of grandeur that seized the city's politicians at the time; having learned above all how to wheedle subsidies out of the federal government, they now egged one another on to think big, plan big, bring big projects into being.

With a wry smile, a friend of mine, the Polish writer and theater scholar Andrzej Wirth, told me about the Polish airline LOT, which offered a daily direct flight between Warsaw and New York. Its business class was always full. Major carriers, including Delta, Lufthansa, and Air Berlin, had repeatedly tried to set up a similar service from Berlin, but always ended up canceling the connection because they only ever found economy-class customers. Berlin has a wealth of ideas, start-ups, clubs, and all manner of masters of the art of living—but no business class.

Whose idea was the international airport anyway? asked a story about BER in the newspaper *Die Welt*, on July 31, 2012, reaching the conclusion: "No one really knows anymore!" After all, Berlin already had three functioning airports: Tegel, Tempelhof, and Schönefeld. From the very start, the venture turned into a provincial farce with billions at stake, a full cast of combative actors, and surprising plot twists. Berlin's mayor Klaus Wowereit was the chairman of the supervisory board, whose members also included the prime minister of Brandenburg, Matthias Platzeck, and the CEO of the airport, Rainer Schwarz. The two senior politicians didn't make much time for their new entrepreneurial duties—the supervisory board met only four times a year.

It all began with the precautionary acquisition of 300 acres of arable land by Flughafen Berlin Brandenburg (FBB), which also ran Berlin's three existing airports. Speculators who learned of the plan beat FBB to the punch, buying the properties in question from their owners and thereby driving up the price. Farmers who had been living off European Union agricultural subsidies became multimillionaires overnight. No sooner was the acquisition made than it became apparent that the layout of the airport needed to be completely reoriented—from one day to the next, the expensive property became worthless and once again available for cultivation. The airport corporation was half a billion euros in debt before ground had even been broken.

In the meantime, other locations were considered. Environmentalists who feared that the airport would endanger the survival of a rare species of crane piped up. Consulting the files, residents discovered that airplanes don't fly straight after takeoff, but veer fifteen degrees off their path—meaning that they would fly over entirely different parts of the city than indicated in the plans. Citizens also felt betrayed by the airport corporation's misinformation regarding noise control. Public campaigns were started, which turned into demonstrations. A raft carrying opponents of the airport floated up to the private lakeside home of the airport CEO Rainer Schwarz and blasted it with eighty-five decibels—the approved level for flight traffic. A policewoman using a noise-measuring device made sure the sound didn't exceed this level.

Nevertheless, preparations for the construction of the airport continued. The first target date was set: October 30, 2011.

However, by this point—at the height of the financial crisis—banks were no longer willing to issue loans for construction of the airport, and private investors backed out. The banks demanded that the public shareholders—the states of Berlin and Brandenburg, and the federal government, which now had to guarantee a 2.4-billion-euro loan—provide collateral. There was no way the originally planned opening date would be met; the target date was pushed back to June 3, 2012.

It turned out that one structural element—which Berliners, and probably the politicians on the supervisory board as well, were hearing about for the first time—was causing unexpected difficulties: the fume extraction system. The flaps that were supposed to remove poisonous smoke from the buildings in the event of a fire didn't work. To meet the target opening date, the technical director suggested a "man-machine-interface": hiring seven hundred unskilled workers to stand by the fume extraction system during the opening celebration to open the flaps manually in case of an emergency. The supervisory board deemed this Chaplinesque proposal a good solution and stuck to the new target date. But on May 8, four weeks before the planned opening, Chairman of the Board Klaus Wowereit declared, on behalf of the board, that the airport would in fact not be able to open because the Technical Control Board and building authorities wouldn't sign off on the fire protection system. And so Berlin was spared the spectacle of an opening celebration with seven hundred hired helpers ensuring the functioning of a supposedly automated system.

The cost overrun for the fume extraction system added half a billion euros to the budget; on top of that, residents had legally obtained provisions for improved noise protection that ran to an additional 600 million euros. Not included in these calculations, because they haven't been negotiated yet, are the claims for damages made by the airlines and other companies that had been counting on the June 2012 opening. The airlines found themselves obliged to move all their baggage-handling logistics back to Tegel. Hundreds of shops that for a year had been preparing to open in the new airport had to let their employees go and make new plans; some went bankrupt. Trains operated by Deutsche Bahn had to run constantly back and forth through the tunnels of the underground BER ghost station, without any passengers on board, just to prevent mold from forming. In the meantime, residents near the old Tegel Airport, which had been slated to close long ago, had begun to revolt. Tegel was designed for 7 million passengers a year, but now handles 17 million. The noise level had increased along with the number of flights, and residents were seeking monetary compensation. These combined lawsuits will probably cost the airport corporation several hundreds of millions of euros more. Needless to say, the third target date—May 17, 2013—could not be met either. The opening date was once again rescheduled, this time for October 27, 2013.

No sooner was this new date announced than yet new defects came to light in the fire protection system, which was already in the process of being revamped, and, in December 2012, Chairman of the Board Klaus Wowereit admitted that the new opening date couldn't be guaranteed either. Yet another cycle was set in motion: every time a deadline is postponed, costs go up, which in turn threatens the new deadline. Sure enough, experts are already discovering new problems: the new airport doesn't have enough check-in counters; the distances between gates are too short, leading to passenger congestion; the eight planned baggage conveyors don't provide enough capacity; there aren't enough runways (two!). In the meantime, the fourth deadline has also been scrapped and, as a precaution, a new one has yet to be announced. The authority of Berlin's popular mayor, Klaus Wowereit, whose name has long been bandied about as a candidate for more important positions, has suffered badly as a result of his role in the construction of the airport. Instead of withdrawing from his position as chairman of the supervisory board and admitting that he was out of his depth, he made a complete fool of himself with a speech he gave in the Berlin Parliament: he had nothing to blame himself for; everything had had to happen just as it did, the disaster was actually a success, Berlin was proud of its new airport. There are jokes going around Berlin now along the lines of "No one intends to open an airport"—a reference to the June 1961 claim by the East German head of state at the time, Walter Ulbricht, that "No one intends to build a wall." Apparently seventy thousand Berliners have registered to attend the "opening" on the practical-joke date of April 1, 2026. One jokester proposed the mayor's hundredth birthday as the definitive opening date. Considering that Wowereit is nearing sixty, this seems fair enough.

It's debatable how wise it was to shut down Tempelhof and, eventually, Tegel Airport. I don't know a single major city in Europe that doesn't have at least two operational airports. "The real question," declared the newly appointed CEO of BER airport Hartmut Mehdorn in March 2013, "is whether Berlin doesn't perhaps need two airports!" Mehdorn might as well have stuck his hands in a hornets' nest. Criticism rained down on him from all sides: the minister of the interior, Berlin's mayor, and the airport corporation all tried to bring the new manager back into line. Binding contracts and endless legal proceedings were cited; as agreed, Tegel would have to be shut six months after BER became operational.

In one survey, an overwhelming majority of Berliners expressed sympathy for Mehdorn's offensive. There's no end in sight to the dispute—let alone an opening date for the new airport. According to another popular joke making the rounds in Berlin, the city has three airports—none of which actually works, unfortunately. This biting quip isn't fair to Tegel Airport, which was slated to close a long time ago but meanwhile handles more than twice as many passengers as it was originally designed for. Still, as a criticism of the chaotic planning efforts, the joke has merit.

What is wrong with the Germans? the international press asked. Is this nation, famous the world over for its "good engineering" and efficiency, incapable of building an airport for its capital with a functioning fire protection system? In the meantime, Berliners are being entertained by special local television programs investigating why virtually all the major projects managed by politicians (see: Elbe Philharmonic Hall in Hamburg and Stuttgart 21 train station) go pear-shaped or end up costing twice as much as planned. One answer comes to mind: if the actual cost of these major projects had been announced from the start, they probably never would have got off the ground.

It's one of the paradoxes of Berlin that atmospheric and creative projects succeed seemingly all by themselves, while major plans for the world capital get tangled up in provincialism and dilettantism. Under the aegis of the finance senator Thilo Sarrazin, Berlin's water supply company was hawked off to private operators—with the result that Berliners now pay more for their water than residents of any other German city. Deutsche Bahn, the operator of Berlin's S-Bahn, possibly the city's most important emblem after the Brandenburg Gate, went so far in streamlining the subway system that it's been breaking down regularly for years. All in all, it seems that the famous/infamous Prussian virtues are more at home today in the anti-Prussian south—in Bavaria, Baden-Württemberg, and Saxony—than in the reunified Berlin. For the time being, Berlin is glad it still has the

small but brilliant Tegel Airport, designed by the architect Mein-
hard von Gerkan when he was just twenty-five years old. As for
the new international airport, designed by this same von Gerkan, it remains in the state of incompletion that the city likes
best.

THE STASI LEGACY

The Socialist Unity Party (SED) of East Germany built up the largest—in relation to the number of citizens—and most absurd secret service in history. The Staatssicherheitsdienst, or Ministry of State Security, known as "the Stasi" in the vernacular, was the country's largest employer, with 100,000 permanent and 185,000 so-called informal employees. Over the course of the decades-long history of the German Democratic Republic, hundreds of thousands of citizens made themselves available to the Stasi as informal collaborators—in other words, as snitches. When, in the fall of 1989, participants in the civil rights movement stormed the local headquarters of the ministry around the country, they came across tens of thousands of files in every reasonably large East German city. If all of these files were placed back to back, they would span sixty-nine miles.

In his short story "El rigor en la ciencia" ("On Exactitude in Science"), the Argentinian author Jorge Luis Borges speculates that a precise and complete charting of the earth would require a one-to-one scale representation. But this map would be useless since, like the earth itself, it wouldn't provide any oversight and would be impossible to unfold.

Erich Mielke, the head of the Stasi, seems to have had a similar project in mind for surveying the country. He instilled the motto "In principle, everyone is suspect" in his subordinates. Based on this ground rule, anything that suspects—in other words, citizens—did, said, thought, or planned was of interest to the Ministry of State Security. Mielke's delusion led to the creation of a comprehensive catalog of the external and internal movements of East Germany's citizens. Yet because this enormous amount of data wasn't digitalized, but recorded by hand or mechanically with typewriters, it was impossible to organize it clearly. The material collected vastly exceeded the capacity of those who evaluated it—in other words, most of it was never read. The result was that even some declared "enemies of the state" remained undiscovered—not because the snitches had failed to notice them, but because the evaluators couldn't keep up with their reading. Important evidence sometimes drowned in the sea of unimportant information.

The greatest failure of Mielke's Stasi was that it fell short of the most lofty task of any secret service: preventing, or at least predicting, the collapse of the country it was in charge of monitoring. Its only enduring "success" was the internal poisoning of East German society. Mielke's people managed to create a climate of distrust and suspicion throughout the country through an elaborate system of blackmail and bribery, malicious gossip, career destruction, arbitrary jail sentences, and *Sippenhaft* (or kin liability, by which entire families were held responsible for the actions of any of their members). Neighbors weren't safe from one another, nor brothers from their sisters, wives from their husbands, parents from their children, teachers from their students, and vice versa.

The rule of thumb regarding the omnipresence of the Stasi among my acquaintances in East Germany was a derisive variation on the words of Christ: where five or six are gathered together, one of them is a Stasi informer. This virus of distrust afflicted practically every dissident I met in West Berlin before the fall of East Germany.

The dispute in Germany over whether Mielke's monstrous legacy—the Stasi files—should be preserved and opened to the public or destroyed was long and heated. For the second time after the war, the personal responsibility of the individual citizen was at issue. To mitigate the debate, the federal chancellor at the time, Helmut Kohl, spoke up, saying that he couldn't be sure that he himself wouldn't have become a Stasi informer had he grown up in East Germany. At the time, I also wasn't sure I could answer this question unequivocally. But I believed that if I had in fact become an informer for the Stasi and betrayed my best friend, then I could and should be judged a failure.

In the early 1990s, a friend of mine, the East Berlin writer Jurek Becker, who had already lived in West Berlin before the fall of the Wall, received a call from a close acquaintance from his East German days. The caller, a doctor from the Charité, East Germany's largest hospital, was hoping to be rehired there. A new rule had recently been introduced for the reappointment of civil servants and public officials from East Germany: they had to submit a form attesting to the fact that they had never worked for the Ministry of State Security. Surely Becker must remember him, the caller said, and could confirm that he had never been a follower, let alone a snitch. It would be a great help to him, the doctor continued, if Becker could back him up and call the hospital administration to affirm that he had never suspected the doctor of being a Stasi informant.

Just a few months earlier, Jurek Becker had begun to inspect his Stasi files. The author of *Jakob der Lügner* (*Jacob the Liar*), Becker was an internationally recognized writer even during the East German years. As a result—and because he had signed a letter of protest against the expatriation of the singer Wolf Biermann, East Germany's most well-known dissident—the Stasi had had its eye on him for a long time. His file consisted of roughly twenty binders comprising some three hundred pages each. When the doctor called, Becker had got as far as the seventeenth binder without having come across the man's name. So he agreed to do the favor and put in a good word for him with the hospital administration. A few days later, Becker pulled out the eighteenth binder and started browsing through it. Several dozen pages immediately jumped out at him: detailed reports from this very same doctor to the Stasi about the health of patient Jurek Becker, about his— unfortunately both very funny and cutting—jokes about the East German leaders, and otherwise questionable opinions. "And then?" I asked. "Did you call back the hospital administration to let them know?" Jurek shrugged and laughed. He'd always had something against informers, he said, so he couldn't even get himself to inform on this informer. The doctor got the job.

Other victims of informers didn't find it so easy to come to terms with their betrayal. In reading his Stasi files, another friend, the writer Hans Joachim Schädlich, discovered that his older brother, the historian Karlheinz Schädlich, whom he saw two to three times a week for decades, had been an informal Stasi collaborator since 1975. This brother had filed a report with the Ministry of State Security about almost every one of his visits. Hans Joachim Schädlich was far less interested in whether and to what extent this duplicity had harmed him than in the unbelievable damage it had caused to his relationship with his brother. Because the older brother refused to admit to the betrayal, feigning surprise instead, the two never reconciled. Joachim Schädlich tried to come to terms with his shock by writing a cool narrative that deliberately relies on emotional distance. In his inimitably laconic way, he summed up his attempt to overcome the incident: "What I had to say about it, I said in my text 'Die Sache mit B.' [The Thing with B.]. What my brother has to say about it, he said by not saying anything. Done. For me."

But the situation wasn't done for his older brother. In December 2007, almost twenty years after the dissolution of East Germany and the Stasi, he shot himself to death on a park bench in Berlin.

The story of the once-married actors Ulrich Mühe and Jenny Gröllmann is another spectacular example of the poisonous effect the Stasi had on the inner lives of East Germany's citizens. Jenny Gröllmann was a successful theater and film actress in East Germany before going on to play leading parts in numerous West German productions. In obituaries written by her colleagues, they lauded Gröllmann as the "Romy Schneider of the East." She was also compared to Catherine Deneuve and Claudia Cardinale—in short, in the eyes of many of her peers, Jenny Gröllmann had the stuff of a world star.

Ulrich Mühe, whose career took off with his legendary East Berlin production of *Macbeth,* became famous thanks to his starring role in Florian Henckel von Donnersmarck's Academy Award–winning *The Lives of Others.* In this film, he plays a Stasi officer whose intense spying on the suspicious lovers Georg Dreyman, a playwright, and Christa-Maria Sieland, an actress, brings him into conflict with his position. Identifying increasingly with his victims, he falls in love with the actress and ends up working against his Stasi employers. Originally von Donnersmarck hoped to film several scenes in the infamous Stasi prison Hohenschönhausen, which is now a memorial. So he wrote to its director, Hubertus Knabe, to request permission. When I visited the memorial, Knabe told me about von Donnersmarck's letter. He had read the screenplay carefully, Knabe said, and ultimately turned down the director's request. For he didn't know of a single case in the files of the Stasi Information and Documentation Center in which a Stasi officer had taken his victim's side.

Knabe wanted to know my opinion about this. I disagreed with his decision. After all, I argued, the movie was fiction, not a documentary, and a filmmaker has the right to overstep reality. To date, only part of the Stasi files have been examined. And even if it turned out that not a single "good" Stasi officer could be found in any of them, such a figure nevertheless remained possible, and inventing him was a legitimate provocation. Not unlike the protagonist of Spielberg's *Schindler's List*, an exception like this put the masses of obedient subordinates to shame much more enduringly than the depiction of an average case.

Hubertus Knabe stuck to his opinion. As far as I know, von Donnersmarck had to film the corresponding scenes in the studio. His movie proved that he didn't need to rely on either a "typical" Stasi officer or the actual Hohenschönhausen prison to portray the perfidiousness of the Stasi system.

When Knabe and I had this conversation, there was no way we could have known that the story the movie told would eventually seem relatively harmless compared with the drama that developed between Ulrich Mühe and Jenny Gröllmann. For a companion book to the film, its director, Florian Henckel von Donnersmarck, interviewed Mühe. In the interview, Mühe accused Gröllmann, his former wife and the mother of his daughter, of having been a Stasi informer. Due to the movie's international success and its leading man's celebrity, the accusation spread around the world. The actress, who from the start vehemently denied the accusations, began a descent into a hell of public suspicion and self-justification.

The existence of a Stasi file that listed her supposed contacts and reports spoke against Gröllmann's claims of innocence. She swore under oath that she had never had contact with the Stasi, at least not "knowingly"—referring to the fact that Stasi officers often didn't reveal themselves as such to the people they were sounding out. In their reports to their superiors, in which they generally highlighted their "successes," the spies then often made it sound as though their interlocutors had collaborated willingly. Since her ex-husband refused to recant his statement, Gröllmann had no choice but to sue. She was able to prove in court that her supposed case officer, Helmut Menge, had indicated meetings with her in his reports that never could have taken place: Gröllmann had been onstage at the Gorki Theater at the time six of the purported meetings occurred. On top of that, this very same

Helmut Menge spoke out in her favor to the press. He revealed that he had always introduced himself to Jenny as a detective and had never told her that he worked for the Stasi; he had even made up parts of his reports to impress his superiors. Moreover, Gröllmann had never signed a declaration of commitment. Apparently Menge was a fan of the actress, bringing flowers to several of her premieres without including their cost in his Stasi expense reports.

Still, the expert opinion of the historian Jochen Staadt of the SED-State Research Association of the Free University of Berlin pronounced Jenny Gröllmann guilty: "The available records of the Ministry of State Security of different provenance unequivocally show Ms. Jenny Gröllmann to be an unofficial collaborator of the Ministry of State Security."

The dispute surrounding the famous divorced couple, covered extensively by the media, dragged on for two years and through several courts, turning into a veritable bloodbath. Of course Jenny Gröllmann's relationship with Helmut Menge also invited speculation. Why did she meet with the supposed "detective" at all; what had taken place between the two? Was it possible that Helmut Menge might be the "good" Stasi officer who had failed to turn up in the files, that he had fallen in love with the woman he had enlisted and was now providing her with an alibi after the fact? Or was he doing it for ideological reasons—as a die-hard defender of the system, dedicated to protecting his colleagues to the very end? Or was it the other way around: was Helmut Menge, as one newspaper put it, a "seduction officer"—one of those legendary, Stasi-trained "Romeos"—who had tempted Jenny Gröllmann into collaborating?

A sort of serial novel emerged from the newspaper articles, television reports, and finally books, which gave credence either to Jenny Gröllmann's or Ulrich Mühes's assertions. Seemingly of their own accord, the opposing camps took sides in line with the old patterns: most of the liberal media, including *Der Tagesspie-*

gel, Der Spiegel, Stern, and the *Süddeutsche Zeitung,* sided—
somewhat skeptically—with Gröllmann, while the conservative
media—led by the newspapers of the Springer Group and the
magazine *Focus*—beat its drums for Ulrich Mühe's version of
the events. The *Frankfurter Allgemeine Zeitung* broke rank with
the cohort of conservative Mühe supporters and took Gröllmann's side. The case offered an ideal screen onto which to project
speculations and long-cherished "core beliefs."

In the end—much too late—the debate turned into a long-
overdue reckoning with the question of whether and to what extent the files in the Stasi Information and Documentation Center
could be trusted.

In April 2008, the Kammergericht, Berlin's supreme court,
deciding in the case brought by Gröllmann's then husband against
newspapers that had printed the rumors, concluded that the Stasi
accusation against Jenny Gröllmann was unreliable. In the media, only a "report of suspicion" was permissible, provided that it
also listed the evidence in support of Gröllmann's innocence.
Henceforth no one could print the claim that Gröllmann had
been a Stasi informer.

Ulrich Mühe and Jenny Gröllmann, the protagonists of the
dispute, didn't live to hear the supreme court's verdict. Jenny
Gröllmann died of cancer in August 2006. Less than a year later,
in July 2007, Ulrich Mühe also passed away—of cancer as well. In
December 2006, forced by the verdict of an earlier court, he had
signed a statement indicating that he wouldn't repeat the accusations against his ex-wife. But after signing it, he had uttered a
quote by Heiner Müller: "Words fall into the gears of the world,
irrecoverably."

A year later, Helmut Menge died—also of cancer.

The only thing still missing from this cycle of public taking-
of-sides are conjectures about whether the Stasi was capable of
causing cancer. The answer to this riddle has to be that the Stasi
itself was the cancer.

Yet, the tragedy didn't end with the deaths of Mühe and Gröllmann. On July 11, 2012, a day before the fifth anniversary of Ulrich Mühe's death, his third wife, the actress Susanne Lothar, died. She was the daughter of a famous West German actor-couple and had entered Mühe's life as his "new great love." The two children from this marriage were adolescents when their mother passed away. Several papers indulged in speculations about Susanne Lothar's alcoholism, her increasing instability after Mühe's death, her possible suicide.

I knew Ulrich Mühe, albeit only from a few encounters—at a premiere gala, birthday party, and the Rot-Weiß Tennis Club. Sometimes he would call me to set a date for a match, speaking with his exceptionally lovely voice and particular modesty. Of the two of us, he was the slightly weaker player, and he usually apologized for calling. Among tennis addicts, it's easy for the less practiced player to develop the vague apprehension that his partner is being charitable when he agrees to play. That was out of the question in our case. We played only "friendly games," and neither of us was particularly strict about keeping score. Even so, Muhe and I often had absurd exchanges on the phone: "I'm perfectly aware that my backhand can't stand up to yours." "But you double fault less often than I do!" "I think your serve has improved a lot! And your terrible forehand . . ." "Uli, if Federer had asked me, I would've told him that I had an important appointment. But for you, of course, I have the time—it's an honor . . . !"

After we played, we would talk about all the current rumors and gossip, about our mutual friend Heiner Müller, about our respective projects. During these chats, I always noticed Ulrich's modesty, his discretion when it came to things that concerned him and others—he was the opposite of a show-off. In tennis as in his work, he tended to hide his light under a bushel. In fact, it was the discreetness with which he played his many leading roles, his quiet, unassuming intensity, that made him one of the most impressive actors of his generation.

The idea that the Uli I knew had accused his ex-wife of a betrayal of this magnitude without good reason and had used this suspicion to promote his own worldwide success doesn't fit with the image I have of him. I can only imagine that he himself genuinely believed in his former wife's guilt. But that doesn't mean that his suspicions were warranted. Savage, previously unvoiced suspicions and emotions can gain the upper hand in a divorce. And this was precisely the only—the diabolical—power that the Stasi wielded: sowing rumors, sparking suspicions, infiltrating and undermining people's private lives. It's impossible to rule out that, in the battle over custody of his daughter and the decision regarding her future home, Ulrich Mühe embraced the suspicion of Gröllmann's Stasi involvement: if you can denounce your ex-wife and the mother of your child as a Stasi informer, all other arguments and pain seem to become superfluous. But I find it hard to believe this version.

Admittedly, I also know Claus Jürgen Pfeiffer, Ulrich Mühe's successor in Jenny Gröllmann's life, fairly well. Pfeiffer spent the last seventeen years of Gröllmann's life with her—and with Gröllmann and Mühe's daughter, Anna. His first reaction to the file, he told me, was incredible surprise. But he couldn't deny that it unsettled him, Stasi virgin and paperwork-trusting West German that he was. "But it says it there—black on white," he told his wife. And she had answered, "I don't know why it says it there either." On the other hand, he couldn't imagine Jenny as a Stasi snitch. He had always seen her as a free spirit—a free spirit full of contradictions, yes, but the idea that she should have worked for the Stasi simply didn't fit with his image of her. Uli Mühe's behavior puzzled him as well. As far as he knew, Mühe had never tried discussing the matter with Gröllmann—which really would have been the most natural way to react to the emergence of this kind of suspicion. Especially since the accusations against Jenny didn't concern the period when they had been married, but the 1970s, when she didn't even know her later husband Uli Mühe and was living with another man. In fact, Mühe had admitted on several occasions that, to his knowledge, his wife had never reported anything about him to the Stasi. But, ever since his interview with von Donnersmarck shortly before the world premiere of *The Lives of Others* in 2006, the rumors had taken on a life of their own. The former husband and wife had never had a private conversation about it. Instead, lawyers and the press had taken over.

One day when the media circus was in full swing, Claus Jürgen Pfeiffer recalls, while riding the tram, Mühe's lawyer had called Jenny's cell phone to inform her that Mühe wanted to "hash things out." Pfeiffer had decided to take his gravely ill wife's case into his own hands, filing a suit against Mühe's claim—made in the 2006 interview with von Donnersmarck—that Gröllmann had been a Stasi informer. He had witnessed how their shared circle of friends had gradually thinned out. While some actively took sides with Gröllmann and against her premature condemnation by certain members of the press, others found some pretext or other to take to their heels when the conversation turned to the case and never came back. It had taken weeks of conversations and research to expose the file as a hodgepodge of untenable allegations and distortions, insinuations, and falsifications, including intercepted phone calls of Jenny's that were passed off as conversations with her case officer. Apparently, Pfeiffer explains, her case officer had suffered from a compulsive need to write. Keeping full-time Stasi spies occupied also happens to have been a "socialist job-creation measure"—they wanted to or had to deliver material constantly to their superiors to convince them that they were indispensable. Pfeiffer had gone on to win all the proceedings, all the way up to the highest court.

After this initial case against Mühe, Pfeiffer had sued the papers that had repeated his claim that Gröllmann had been a Stasi snitch. As a result, the most arduous proceedings, which continued even after his wife's death, no longer had anything to do with Ulrich Mühe and von Donnersmarck's accusations, but with issues related to freedom of the press. Not wanting to admit under any circumstances that they had erred, major papers and magazines committed to Jenny's guilt contested the court decisions. They forced Claus Jürgen Pfeiffer to take the cases to the highest courts— this time to combat these papers' presumed claims of infallibility. Jenny's husband took on and won this battle as well. He did it above all to defend his wife and her daughter, Anna, against defamation—but also because he absolutely refused to give in to the calculation of a widely circulated magazine that the fear of the cost of yet another trial would be enough to make Gröllman's poor husband settle. On April 18, 2008, with the verdict of the Berlin Kammergericht, which was validated by the Bundesgerichtshof, the German Federal Court of Justice, and cannot be appealed, Pfeiffer achieved his goal. Yet it wasn't an absolute exoneration. In a media world specialized in unmasking and self-affirmation, a ruling from the highest court that forbids the allegation of a fact, but still allows "reporting" on a related "suspicion," offers only partial protection. It is a verdict that unwittingly pays belated homage to the most diabolical aspect of the Stasi's poison: once a suspicion is on record and publicly established, it is impossible ever to eradicate it again.

Claus Jürgen Pfeiffer says that he is 100 percent convinced of his wife's innocence. But, he adds, the final 5 percent of certainty in a matter like this depend entirely on faith in one's own instincts and in the person one loves. Without this 5 percent of faith, he notes ironically, you can't cope in a love story like this.

Pfeiffer makes no secret of the fact that he believes that Florian Henckel von Donnersmarck used the scandal to market his movie and forced Ulrich Mühe to give the interview. This much is certain: it was the interview that unleashed the media frenzy of suspicion against Jenny Gröllmann; when the same suspicions had been voiced in the newspaper *SUPERillu* two years earlier, they hadn't provoked any response whatsoever by the media. Von Donnersmarck had repeatedly hinted that there was "a true story" behind *The Lives of Others*. And he seems to have persuaded his leading actor to divulge this "true story" just in time for the movie's premiere. The interview can't have been easy for Ulrich Mühe— he knew at the time that his ex-wife was dying of cancer. As did von Donnersmarck.

After the deaths of Jenny Gröllmann and Ulrich Mühe, Claus Jürgen Pfeiffer wrote a letter—which remains unanswered—to Florian Henckel von Donnersmarck:

> I find your attempt to romanticize the final months of his [Ulrich Mühe's] life, against the backdrop of tears that were shed in our home due to his and your behavior, unbearable. I can't accept your objection that Uli didn't agree lightly to giving the interview. Your claim that he only spoke to you hesitantly and with long silent pauses, and your conclusion that it was difficult for him to talk about these things, only makes the entire matter even more egregious. Suspecting, or at least considering the possibility, that it might lead to something terrible, he nevertheless spoke. Why didn't he, supposedly a lifelong seeker of the truth, begin his investigation in the most obvious of places—with Jenny, who lived a hundred and fifty meters [500 feet] away from him? . . . I find the argument you used to convince your friend Uli to do the interview for the book—that the press would drag the rumors back to light in any case, so Uli would be better off explaining himself at length now without any imposed word limits—unbelievable. Beating someone to death because otherwise someone else will do it later is one of the most disgusting lines of reasoning I have ever encountered. To redeem yourself and Uli, no attempt to legitimize your behavior after the fact is too tasteless for you. Just one conversation, just taking a serious interest in the circumstances, and Uli might have been able to find peace.

After the movie won an Academy Award, reproaches like these apparently couldn't dampen the euphoria of its director. Upon his return from Hollywood, von Donnersmarck greeted waiting journalists at Tegel Airport by holding up his Oscar and exclaiming, "We're Oscar!"

It was a crude play on a brilliant headline that had appeared in *Bild* after Cardinal Ratzinger was elected Pope, proclaiming: WE'RE POPE.

Erich Mielke, the head of the *Firma*—or "company"—as the Stasi was popularly known, seems to have been as oblivious to the devastating effects of the poison he spread as he was to his impotence during the year of the revolution. Unlike his world-famous and literarily gifted subordinate Marcus Wolf, who met with his boss at least twice a week and was unquestioningly devoted to him for decades, Erich Mielke didn't give rise to a legend or leave behind any traces in the media landscape. In the few portraits that exist of him, he looks like a small, stocky peasant with shrewd little eyes. Nothing is known of any hidden, dark passions in his private life. He stood out neither for being particularly intelligent nor for any other talents. He wasn't a good speaker and rarely wrote in full sentences, at most jotting down a few key words on the documents he was handed—key words that resulted in terrible consequences. He had neither charm nor charisma. Almost all of his hundreds of thousands of permanent employees and freelancers feared him, few respected him, no one loved him. He led an unremarkable married life with his wife, Gertrud, with whom he had a son called Frank; they also adopted a daughter called Inge. His only known passions were hunting and a downright insatiable craving for order. His greatest love seems to have been for his dog—a Yorkshire terrier called Airen.

Four days before the fall of the Wall, on November 5, 1989, Erich Mielke made his last public appearance. During the session of the Volkskammer, the East German Parliament, the man whose presence had made East Germany's citizens quake for decades, stuttered: "I love—but I do love all—all people—but I do love!"

After a moment of incredulous amazement, the Volkskammer acknowledged the declaration with liberating laughter. After being sentenced to six years in jail for an ancient act of violence—in 1931, Mielke had demonstrably murdered two German policemen on Bülowplatz (now Rosa-Luxemburg-Platz) in Berlin, a crime for which he was convicted only in 1993—the old man was soon deemed "unfit for detention" and released. Mielke died nine years after reunification—on May 21, 2000. Shortly before his death, the caretakers in his nursing home had found him yelling at invisible inferiors and ordering them to find his dog Airen. Apparently he no longer remembered—or refused to believe— that his wife, Gertrud, had left him and the apartment they had shared, and had given his beloved dog to an animal shelter. Mielke was as alone in death as he had been in life.

AN "ENEMY OF THE STATE" BECOMES BOSS

Among those on whom the Stasi set its sights early on was a student in Jena by the name of Roland Jahn. In 1976, during a seminar at Jena University, he protested against the expatriation of the singer Wolf Biermann. The leader of the seminar, a Stasi collaborator, squealed on him, and the university initiated disciplinary action against Jahn. Yet they wanted his expulsion from the university to be carried out in a "democratic" manner: the student group itself was to file the application for his expulsion. During a private meeting with Jahn, his fellow students all assured him that they would vote against his expulsion. But when the time came to vote, all of them—except for one—did precisely the opposite. Afterward, they whispered him their apologies: "Please understand, my father's a big gun in the party . . . ," "My wife is expecting our second child . . . ," "I'm on your side, but my spot at the university . . . !" To everyone's great surprise, nothing happened to Ulli Waller, the only one who had stood by Jahn and who had expected to be punished for it. He was able to continue his studies undisturbed. "Sometimes there was no price to be paid for being decent," Jahn explains, "but you'd only find that out after the fact."

Jahn was disappointed in his fellow students, but didn't condemn them outright. After all, he knew that his protest would put not only himself in danger but his parents as well. Until he was expelled from the university, he had always shown consideration for his father, who held a prominent position with Zeiss in Jena. Accordingly, his father had put pressure on him: "Lie low— speaking out will only cost you!" Or: "Is it really worth risking your father getting fired and our family's happiness with your protests?"

At the next official May Day rally, on May 1, 1977, Jahn stood out for the unusual accessory he was carrying. Instead of a red flag or a banner with a patriotic slogan, he held up a sign that had nothing written on it. Children pointed their little index fingers at the blank sign and cried out, "Look, Daddy, there's nothing on there!" Several adults approached Jahn and asked him what he was trying to say with his sign. Jahn told them that he had been expelled from the university because he had opposed Biermann's expatriation and explained that he was demonstrating against his expulsion. By protesting, he wanted to show the university and his fellow students that they had left him in the lurch. Some of his interlocutors elbowed him and whispered, "Man, I think it's great that you're doing this!"

It was Jahn's first public act of protest. Even though his sign was much smaller than the placards and banners others were carrying, it attracted significantly more attention. For the first time, Jahn says, he was amazed by the major impact an individual using minimal means can have in a dictatorship.

In September 1982, Jahn was arrested for riding his bicycle with a small Polish flag that said "Narodni Polski" on it, which he had bought at a stationery store for eighty cents. With a marker, he had added the word "Solidarność" above the printed text and the German translation underneath: "Solidarity with the Polish people"—a stock phrase he had often come across in the party newspaper *Neues Deutschland*. But combined with the Polish word "Solidarność," which was also the name of the Polish protest movement, the stock phrase became a political demonstration.

Jahn was sentenced to twenty-two months in prison for "contempt of national symbols."

The little flag, Jahn explains, was the incitement, but not the reason for his imprisonment. "They round you up when they've had enough." Previously, he had demanded information regarding the death of his friend Matthias Domaschk, who had died under unclear circumstances while in custody. From that point on, the Stasi no longer listed him as an "opponent," but as a "Central Operational Case"—*Zentraler Operativer Vorgang*, or ZOV, in German—under the name "Weinberg." ZOV indicated the highest level of persecution, and several departments were deployed to handle such cases.

Jahn was imprisoned and counted on being ransomed by West Germany. He spent most of his time in solitary confinement. It seemed unrealistic for him to hope that he might be released in East Germany, or that the protest movement might spread. During his trial, he had seen how state-controlled judges had thrown him in jail for a trifle—a little flag on his bicycle! What weighed on him most heavily were the threats that had been made during the interrogations: "We consider it very unlikely that you will see your daughter on her first day of school!"— the little girl was only three at the time. His East German lawyer, Wolfgang Schnur, urged him to apply for an exit visa to West Germany. By this point the Stasi had started to allow dissidents who had proven intractable and were fairly well known to leave for the West. If Jahn didn't apply for an exit visa now and waited to be released from prison years later, his lawyer warned him, there wouldn't be anyone left at the gate waiting to pick him up. His significant other would also be in jail; his friends would long since have emigrated. But if he filed an application now, his sentence might be over in just a few weeks. At the time, there was no way Jahn could have known that his lawyer worked for the Stasi. After the Stasi files were opened, Schnur was convicted of being a snitch.

Jahn had already had several brief breakdowns in jail; he was no longer capable of making decisions. Going against his instinct, he filed the application. After six months in prison, Roland Jahn was released "for good behavior"—not into West Germany, however, as he had been expecting, but into East Germany. At first he wondered about the reason for this turn of events. Did the Stasi consider him to be particularly dangerous—or, on the contrary, particularly obedient? Was he suddenly considered "assimilable"? It was only after his release that he realized that the reason he had been set free had nothing to do with him or with his behavior during the interrogation. "In dictatorships," Jahn explains, "decisions concerning the fate of an individual are almost never made based on consideration of the individual case." Instead, his release was due to a shift in the international political climate. During Jahn's detention, the peace movement in West Germany had grown increasingly influential. In Bonn, its supporters demonstrated against the stationing of American Pershing and cruise missiles in West Germany—an objection entirely in keeping with East German foreign policy. A small group of demonstrators had made signs demanding the release of Roland Jahn and other political prisoners in East Germany. West German newscasts had broadcast these images. Releasing Roland Jahn from prison in February 1983 was a political gesture with which the East German leadership, which of course saw a natural ally in the West German peace movement, hoped to impress its desired partner.

Roland Jahn, the stunned beneficiary of this situation, was quick to appreciate his new freedom. Just a month after his release, together with friends, he founded the Friedensgemeinschaft Jena—"Jena Peace Community"—and began organizing demonstrations in Jena. His reasons for replacing his old watchword "freedom" with "peace" were purely strategic; among his fellow campaigners, he left no doubt that what he meant by it was a life of freedom and justice.

The group from Jena participated in the officially organized peace demonstrations in East Germany with its own signs. The advantage of this form of protest was that the members of the group were now "only" beat up, and no longer arrested, by plainclothes Stasi people. The Jena example caught on, and soon there were peace communities in other East German cities that also participated in the official demonstrations with their own slogans. The result, however, was that Stasi officials now paid Roland Jahn a visit every few days to remind him of his application for an exit visa. Jahn declared the extorted application null and void. On the record, he said that he preferred to stay in his "homeland." Eventually he was ordered to go to the police station under some pretext. There, he was told that he was being relieved of his East German citizenship that very day; he was to return to his apartment immediately to get his luggage. His was the second case of compulsory expatriation—after Wolf Biermann, who had been refused reentry into East Germany after a concert in Cologne. As a rule, wishing to avoid comparisons with the Nazis, who had used similar tactics, the East German authorities shied away from this practice.

Instead of following the functionaries' instructions, Jahn fled to a friend's house. But a horde of Stasi people followed him. Shackling his wrists in handcuffs, they forcibly led Jahn from the apartment just as he was, dressed in a shirt and pants. As they shoved him into a paddy wagon, he called out to the gawking neighbors, "Please don't think I killed anyone. They're arresting me because I *don't* want to go to the West!"

It was a grotesque situation: in handcuffs, Jahn was forced to accept a privilege that countless East German citizens longed for—departure to the West.

A motorcade brought him to the border, where he was dragged onto the train platform, his wrists still shackled. When he asked the official he was fettered to what he would do if a similar fate were to befall his son, the man tightened the chains around Jahn's wrists until he cried out. The official only removed the handcuffs once Jahn was on board the train.

Jahn's arrival in West Berlin on June 8, 1983, became a media sensation. Never before had an East German citizen been brought to the West under duress. *Bild* ran the title FIRST TIME YOUNG GERMAN IS TAKEN FROM HOMELAND BY FORCE! The outcry over the deportation cut across all political lines. Jahn wrote letters of protest to leading politicians in the West and East; he appealed to the president of the United Nations and demanded his immediate repatriation. The East German government remained unimpressed—Jahn was barred once and for all from entering the country he hadn't wanted to leave. But—though neither the East German government nor Jahn had any way of knowing it at the time—this "once and for all" would last only for another five years.

As he dealt with the flood of invitations he received after his deportation, Jahn was plagued with worry about his father's fate. He knew the ways of the "company" well enough to predict that it would make his father atone for his son's escapades. Since by this point his father had retired and received a disability pension, the Stasi could no longer punish him by firing him from Zeiss in Jena. But Jahn found out that Mielke's avenging angel had nevertheless found a way to hit the old man where it hurt most. From an early age, Jahn's father had been an enthusiastic and talented soccer player. As a young man he had wanted to pursue a career as a professional athlete, but the loss of a leg in World War II prevented him from realizing his childhood dream. Nonetheless, he didn't abandon his passion; no sooner was he home from the war than he established the Carl Zeiss Jena Soccer Club and began to coach young players. Over the course of a lifetime spent mentoring, he fostered twenty-three national players. Some members of the senior Jahn's club played for the East German national team in a historic game against the West Germans, which the East Germans won. For many years, the senior Jahn was the Carl Zeiss Jena Soccer Club's number one honorary member.

Mielke's people made sure that the old man lost his honorary membership and was barred from the club. They trampled his life's work. Yet, for Jahn's father, the fact that "his club" gave in to the Stasi virtually without resistance may have been even worse than his debarment.

When Roland Jahn found out what had happened, his father's old question came back to him with full force: Had his protest, which had brought misfortune on his father, really been "worth it"? Hadn't he gone too far, hadn't he shown too little consideration for his parents? In prison, he had witnessed former friends and comrades-in-arms, blackmailed by the Stasi, founder and agree to compromises. He had sworn that he would never let himself be blackmailed. His father's fate changed his view of these "failures." It heightened his awareness of the fact that in many cases these individuals hadn't given up their resistance out of fear for their own well-being, but because they were thinking about the consequences for their families.

At the same time, taking into consideration one's relatives' fates was a complicated matter; the Stasi didn't follow any fixed pattern. In punishing dissidents and their families, the Stasi by no means adhered to a preset program. The problem, Jahn explains, was precisely that no one who defied the East German dictatorship could predict ahead of time what the costs would be for him and for his family. For Roland Jahn's father, his son's resistance had devastating consequences; in other cases, there were no consequences whatsoever. The Stasi acted according to the rule of thumb: punish one so that a hundred others live in fear. If you allowed this incalculable fear to determine your actions, you basically couldn't do anything at all—you gave in to a sort of preemptive obedience to the Stasi since, in principle, you had to expect the worst at any time. "*Sippenhaft*, or even just the threat of it," Roland Jahn concludes, "was the most effective means of oppression."

Roland Jahn returned once, illegally, to the country that had cast him out. On his way back from a trip to Prague, he was able to take advantage of inattentive passport controllers to get into East Berlin. Defiantly, he got on a train headed to Jena. For a long time—it felt like an eternity to him—he stood in front of the entrance to his parents' building, unable to get himself to ring the bell. He wasn't sure how his parents would react: would they welcome him home with open arms or heap reproaches on him? He didn't even know the state of his parents' health. He thought about his father's heart defect and feared that the shock of an unexpected reunion might be too much for him—let alone the commotion that would ensue if the Stasi were to confront him here and drag him from the apartment. He slunk away like a rejected dog—his involuntary defection to the West stood between him and his parents' front door.

In his Trabant, a friend drove Jahn to his comrades-in-arms in East Berlin, who included Bärbel Bohley, Ulrike and Gerd Poppe, and the pastor Rainer Eppelmann. The four of them made it clear to Jahn that he could do a lot more for the East German civil rights movement in the West—through his talks and his work as a journalist in the western media—than as a martyr in the Stasi's custody. "You're more valuable to us in the West than in the underground here." After two days and nights of draining discussions, they drove Jahn to the border. The Permanent Mission of the Federal Republic of Germany in East Berlin had ensured in advance that he would be able to leave East Germany undisturbed. Otherwise, if his latest, this time "illegal return" had been discovered, it could have resulted in a new jail sentence.

It was only at the moment he stepped onto West Berlin soil for the second time—and this time of his own volition—that he felt free and at peace with himself, Roland Jahn reports. It was only then that he really felt like he had left East Germany. The umbilical cord had been severed and, with it, the guilty conscience that consciously or unconsciously triggered defensive reflexes in almost all dissidents whenever West German newspapers or parties tried to tout them as a testament to the superiority of the western system. Roland was neither an "Ossi" nor a "Wessi"—he was German.

During the years of Roland Jahn's resistance, the thought of a reunified Germany had been just as far from his mind as it was from those of most dissidents in East Germany. What Jahn wanted was nothing more or less than the end of the dictatorship; he wanted democratic conditions established in the country that he called home. At the time, the reunification of the two German states had seemed like an infinitely distant possibility that had no real place in his mind.

On January 15, 1990, Roland Jahn participated in the storming of the Stasi headquarters on Normannenstraße. The aim of the campaign was to prevent the destruction and removal—already under way—of files by Stasi officials. An activist from the "citizens' committee" pulled a file from the shelves: one of the many collected volumes the Stasi had compiled on Roland Jahn. Jahn was the first East German citizen given the opportunity to take a look at his file—in front of the television cameras of the world.

Eleven years later, on January 28, 2011, Roland Jahn was named head of the agency responsible for processing the Stasi's enormous paper legacy. The appointment put him in charge of sixty-nine miles of shelves. In addition, there were also the destroyed files, which Stasi officials had fed into their shredders in the days after the fall of the Wall. Countless trash bags had been rescued and stored in the extensive inner courtyards of the Stasi headquarters. Resourceful software programmers developed a process by which the scraps of paper could be put back together again like the pieces of a puzzle, making them legible. What Mielke left behind is the legacy of a monstrous and paranoid spy apparatus. It is a testament to the corruptibility of people, to subjugation and betrayal; yet, at the same time, it also provides evidence of the moral courage of those citizens who resisted all efforts to bait and extort them.

By now, the ideological dispute over the agency has subsided.

Officials from the interior ministries of Poland, Hungary, and the Czech Republic have already visited the agency to study how Germans are handling the legacy of the communist dictatorship. Initially, the administrations of these countries had chosen not to preserve or make available the files of their respective secret services. The main argument of those who opposed archiving the files was that forgetting is more blissful than knowledge—processing the documents would lead to a rift in society. But it soon became clear that it was precisely the prescribed forgetting and forgiving that was causing the rift. Seeing informers and the henchmen of oppression assume leading positions after democratic elections was unbearable to the victims of the communist oppression.

It seems to be a law of nature that, if they aren't forced to face up to their past, erstwhile perpetrators will try to fashion themselves as victims and rise to leading positions in the wake of a radical shift in the system they once served. In Germany, this law is exemplified by the state of Brandenburg, which, as Berlin's neighbor, was a stronghold of spying. When rehiring officials, the ruling coalition there, composed of members of the SPD and the Left Party (which succeeded East Germany's Communist Party), waived the usually required disclosures regarding individuals' pasts in East Germany. This "generosity" immediately resulted in the appointment of former Stasi collaborators, as well as of compliant East German judges and attorneys, to high positions in the state's police and judicial apparatus after reunification. A wave of distrust and indignation swept through the country. The only way to distinguish legitimate suspicions from false ones was through recourse to the records in Jahn's agency.

Roland Jahn, now the head of an agency with more than two thousand employees, considers his "company" a school for democracy. He wants to reveal the mechanisms that generate fear and subordination, but also to bring to light examples of moral courage and resistance—of which there are actually quite a few. And naturally it is important to him to prove that East Germany really was a dictatorship—a concept that many former East German citizens still angrily deny because it supposedly leads to equating East Germany with the Nazi regime. But comparing, Jahn retorts, isn't the same as equating. In reality, it's only by comparing that it is possible to differentiate. In fact, comparing the Stasi to the Gestapo leads to an astonishing conclusion. The Gestapo had at most 45,000 employees, out of a population of 80 million. The Stasi, which kept watch over just 18 million citizens, employed well over 100,000 officials, along with another 100,000 unofficial collaborators. Apparently the Nazis could count on the compliance of the country's citizens significantly more than the ruling communists in East Germany could. Unlike the Gestapo, the Stasi resorted to murder and torture only in exceptional cases. Instead, Mielke's secret service relied on the power of widespread suspicion: each citizen had reason to mistrust every other. Mielke had come as close to achieving this goal as possible. Jahn's agency has shed light on the prerequisites for this success, the most important of which was East Germany's own ruling party: the Socialist Unity Party of Germany, or SED.

THE NEW RACISM

One of the many unforeseen consequences of the opening of the Wall was an eruption of overt and violent racism. A rise in xenophobic incidents, the likes of which hadn't been seen since the war, occurred throughout reunified Germany. In the East German cities of Rostock and Hoyerswerda, but also in West Germany, in Solingen, Lübeck, and Mölln, people of different skin colors were persecuted, and hostels for asylum-seekers set on fire. In the days after the opening of the Wall, the phrase "Foreigners, don't leave us alone with the Germans" could be seen scrawled across its perforated concrete. The brute response to this nostalgic slogan wasn't long in coming, demanding: "Germany for the Germans!"

In early 1990, while doing research for my book *The German Comedy*, I came across a strange story, which I called "the last wall jumper." On March 14, 1990, four months after the fall of the Wall, a man balanced precariously on the rounded crest of the Wall, walking at a reckless pace, turned around abruptly, and headed back in the opposite direction. It was only when he turned for a second time that passersby realized that he wasn't putting on a show. On the western side of the Wall, like a shadow, a zealous East German border guard was running alongside him. Several eyewitnesses approached and asked the official whom he was trying to arrest and under what law. He murmured some-thing about "international agreements"—apparently referring to German-German agreements—that obliged him to detain fugi-tive Vietnamese and bring them back to East Germany. For the first time, the curious bystanders from West Berlin realized that the new right to cross the border marked by the Wall applied only to Germans. The Vietnamese fugitive took advantage of the argu-ment between the border guard and passing pedestrians to jump from the Wall and flee to West Berlin. He was one of the first of thousands of Vietnamese who sought asylum in West Berlin in the subsequent months and years.

It was only after further research that I discovered that the first "Workers' and Farmers' State" on German territory, which had prided itself so much on its "internationalism," had been home to at most 1 percent of foreigners. Until the end of its existence, East Germany had been Europe's "most foreigner-free" nation. Half of East Germany's roughly 160,000 immigrants came from Viet-nam, the others from Mozambique, Angola, Poland, and Cuba. When the "Fijis"—many East German citizens associated the Vietnamese with the Fiji Islands and stuck to this misnomer even after being geographically enlightened—entered the country, the East German authorities immediately stripped them of their pass-ports, committed them to residential barracks, and pocketed 12 percent of their wages—as compensation for East Germany's "brotherly military assistance" to the Vietcong. Outside of work, the "Fijis" had virtually no contact with the locals; any meeting or conversation that took place after the end of the workday had to be reported. Most of the Vietnamese workers were women em-ployed in East Germany's textile industry. If they became preg-nant, they were given the choice between an abortion and deportation. Some women escaped this fate through suicide. The "Fijis" weren't allowed to leave the city without authorization and weren't permitted to enter regular restaurants. One worker, who had managed to become a representative in a regional parliament, recounts that, at her welcome party, she sat alone at her table in the packed room for the duration of the event. The "Mozis"—workers from Mozambique—were no better off. Only the Latin Americans and Cubans enjoyed certain privileges. With their guitars and revolutionary songs, some of them found lovers among open-minded East German women and succeeded in learning German this way.

East Germany's Vietnamese and Africans were the first to be immediately persecuted by the local neo-Nazis after reunification. Since the early 1960s, West Germans had been living together with millions of foreign workers—even though they doggedly denied the fact that their country had become a nation of immigrants. One of the first major misguided decisions by the drowsy West German "victors" was to plant hostels for asylum-seekers in the virtually homogenously German desert of former East Germany, in order to "fairly" distribute the asylum-seekers who were flowing into Germany from all over the world. Many East Germans, whose businesses were shut down after reunification, reacted with unbridled anger.

One of the worst incidents occurred in the East German city of Rostock. Between August 22 and 26, 1992, several hundred hooligans attacked a hostel for former Vietnamese contract workers, egged on by thousands of onlookers. The building was set on fire, and the attackers and onlookers blocked the local police and firefighters from reaching the hostel. The police retreated, leaving the Vietnamese stuck in the burning building to their own devices. They only managed to escape thanks to an emergency exit on the eighth floor that led to the neighboring roof and to a renewed intervention by the police, which came far too late. Sixty-five police were injured in the face-off with the unbridled hooligans, whose number had swelled to roughly a thousand. It was a miracle that not one person perished in the flames.

The international press presented the riots in Rostock as images of terror reminiscent of the Nazi era. *Bild* felt that foreigners were once again coming down unfairly on the Germans. Federal Chancellor Helmut Kohl resorted to an absurd attempt at an explanation straight out of the Cold War era, claiming that the Stasi had incited and directed the riots in Rostock-Lichtenhagen. Moreover, he categorically refused to visit the crime scenes and their victims. Through his spokesperson he let it be known that he didn't think much of "other politicians' condolatory tourism."

But then, in both of Germany's halves, a democratic mobilization against the new (old) barbarism began to develop, initiated not by any political party, but by civil society—or, more precisely, by individual citizens who joined together in protest. Together with some other like-minded people, Giovanni di Lorenzo, the editor in chief of *Die Zeit*, set the wheels in motion, organizing a candlelight vigil against xenophobia in Munich. Hundreds of volunteers helped, and tens of thousands of people participated. Similar events followed in Hamburg and other cities. A veritable candle-fever seized the Germans. The candlelight vigils became so popular so quickly that the Association of German Candle Manufacturers took the opportunity to organize an exhibition of the most beautiful photographs of the demonstration in Munich; a car manufacturer countered the feared collapse in sales of German cars abroad by creating advertisements with photos of the candlelight vigils for the foreign market. It wasn't long before the farthest edges of the political spectrum began to raise their voices in angry counterprotest. One left-wing activist, clearly envious of the success of the candlelight vigils, accused the organizers of "sloppy sentimentality," suggesting that only the egg-throwing, radical leftist *Autonome* were "real" protesters; an ultraconservative Berlin politician suspected the nerve center of a secret popular front of being behind the mobilization of these millions of candle-bearers; Brigitte Seebacher-Brandt, the second wife of the late Willy Brandt, claimed to see a direct connection to the spirit of the Nazis in the symbolism of the "fire magic."

Despite, but also because of, such suspicions, the candlelight vigils became a highly visible sign of civil society's determination to face down the outbreak of barbarism. They emboldened Jews and foreigners living in Germany to stay in the country of their choice.

Initially, Berlin, the German city with the largest proportion of inhabitants holding foreign passports (some 900,000 of its roughly 3.5 million inhabitants are of foreign origin), was spared any dramatic arson attacks or other large-scale murderous incidents. Nevertheless, even this cosmopolitan city became the site of a growing number of attacks against and murders of nonwhite citizens, usually in U-Bahn and S-Bahn trains and stations.

In October 1991, together with several colleagues and friends—journalists, writers, artists, actors, theater makers—I founded an initiative called Courage Against Xenophobia. After several flyer campaigns, we concentrated on going to schools, where, with the support of teachers and students, we implemented activities against racism and xenophobia. The basic idea behind these activities was to individualize abstract images of "foreigners" by giving them concrete faces and stories—in fact, the majority of our group's members were Berliners of foreign origin; at times, we spoke sixteen languages among us. Everyone was free to choose what form his or her "lesson" would take, and we compiled and evaluated our experiences to serve as models for future actions.

In the course of our appearances, we discovered that we were mainly being invited by schools in West Berlin whose students and teachers had already created similar initiatives. The "problem schools"—in the East Berlin districts of Lichtenberg and Hohen-schönhausen, for example—hardly ever took us up on our offer because the principals feared that accepting an invitation from our group alone would be enough to ruin their schools' "good reputation." Among enlightened Berliners, the commandment of political correctness, which dictated that the problem of the new racism was distributed equally across the West and East, quickly prevailed. A sort of competition of contrition had taken hold, making it difficult to state the obvious: that the new, eastern states were particularly susceptible to the messages of the new old racism.

An absurd rivalry for the crown of guilt developed among academically educated experts. No sooner did someone point to the extreme right-wing mind-set among East German youth than someone else produced evidence that it was at least as prevalent among West German youth—and vice versa. A glance at the geography of right-wing terror, however, unequivocally showed that, for two decades, this mind-set—and the electoral victories of Germany's right-wing National Democratic Party (NPD)—had been centered in the new states of Saxony, Saxony-Anhalt, and Thuringia. And if you ask Asians or blacks in Berlin which S-Bahn stations they tend to avoid after dark, the answer is just as telling. In November 2012, a representative investigation by the Friedrich Ebert Foundation, which has ties to the SPD, concluded that the percentage of East Germans "with a closed, extreme right-wing worldview" had doubled since 2002—from 8.1 percent to 15.8 percent. In the West, during this same period, a slight decline was seen—from 7.6 percent to 7.1 percent. According to the study, approximately 39 percent of East Germans have manifestly xenophobic views, despite the still extremely low fraction of immigrants (approximately 2 percent) in the former eastern states. It also revealed that new centers of extreme right-wing violence have developed in Germany's west: in the Ruhr district and in Schleswig-Holstein.

Fortunately, engaged citizens in the East and the West couldn't care less about this academic debate. For some time now, antiracist campaigns have focused on the so-called new states. Virtually no appearance by neo-Nazis isn't offset—or even prevented—by a counterdemonstration. Through citizens' groups, silent vigils, and antiracist networks, a steadily growing number of courageous citizens are publicly refusing to tolerate the so-called national liberated zones of right-wing extremism.

On the twentieth anniversary of the ignominious events in

Rostock-Lichtenhagen, thousands of Rostock's citizens assembled in the name of solidarity and humanity. The federal president of Germany, Joachim Gauck, gave a moving talk—and if anyone is capable of speaking rousingly about freedom and responsibility, it's the Rostock native Joachim Gauck. Germany was finally showing itself from its best side again: a prosperous nation facing up to the sins of its past with its head bowed. Indeed, there was no sign that day of the xenophobic mob that had tried to burn the residents of the hostel for asylum-seekers twenty years earlier. You had to wonder where all those people had gone. At the time of the attack, the Rostock racists had been of prime hooligan age; in 2012, they couldn't have been older than forty or fifty. According to the media, today, two-thirds of the population of Rostock-Lichtenhagen are new citizens—in other words, people who moved there only after the pogrom. Some of Rostock's older citizens preferred a different explanation: the mob at the time had come from Berlin and West Germany and had long since crawled back.

Oddly, no one was interested in finding out what had become of East Germany's Vietnamese after all those years.

VIETNAMESE IN BERLIN

Shortly before Christmas 2012, I visited five enormous show-rooms in Berlin-Lichtenberg, one of the city's easternmost districts. Located in the middle of a landscape of abandoned warehouses, they are part of the Dong Xuan Center, a mall. Inside, all sorts of services are offered—everything from personal care, tailors, hair and nail salons, psychics, and restaurants, as well as everyday and exceptional items: fresh produce and frozen fish; evening and wedding dresses. The walls are covered with posters in German and Vietnamese, advertising massages, car services, accountants, and lawyers. The cost of a haircut is eight euros for men, and fourteen euros for a wash, cut, and set for women. The stylists in the well-staffed salons are dainty young Vietnamese women with shimmering hair of all shades—the daughters, apparently, of the generation that included "my" last wall jumper. Most of them speak fluent German and immediately invite curious passersby who glance into their shops inside for a haircut. Many of them graduated from high school in Germany and help out their parents during the Christmas season. I had read in the papers that over 50 percent of Vietnamese students in Germany attend academic high schools—far more than native German students—and that they bring home better report cards too.

The most popular tattoo by far is an elaborately ornate dragon advertised on posters, which tattoo artists can probably ink onto their customers' backs blindfolded. Man-high bales of brightly colored scarves are for sale, piled on the bare floors of the roughly 320-square-foot salesrooms. There's no shortage of shops selling garments of all sorts—though naturally, for the most part, the available sizes aren't exactly suited to Central European customers. The busiest spots are the gift shops and general stores, where you can find everything from safety pins to corkscrews to sporty steering wheels. Near the exit of Hall 3, I discovered the most beautiful shop: in a space just over two hundred square feet large, all of the world's flowers were on display in such abundance that not so much as the tiniest sliver of wall was still visible. Standing by the entrance in a daze, I was convinced I could smell the perfume of all the flowers that grow on God's green earth—until I realized that they were perfect imitations.

The activity in the mall was so peaceful that it was impossible for me to conjure up the hate-filled screaming in Rostock twenty years earlier. German families with children, who in these surroundings looked like members of a slightly overgrown and overfed species, squeezed their way through the narrow corridors ponderously yet considerately before stopping to enjoy a bite to eat in one of the Vietnamese restaurants. The Dong Xuan Market is, after all, located in Berlin-Lichtenberg, a no-go zone for foreigners. Yet it is here of all places that, with tenacity and intrepidity, the Vietnamese seem to have succeeded in staking out a spot for themselves, which has become too big and attractive to be a target for neo-Nazi attacks. Twenty thousand to forty thousand Vietnamese—no one knows the exact number—live in Berlin today. They are considered one of Germany's most assimilated immigrant groups. The VietinBank has bought a five-story building in Berlin-Lichtenberg and opened a branch there. However, not a single Berlin politician showed up at the opening, which was celebrated in the presence of the vice president of Vietnam, Nguyen

Thi Doan. Why? Because the opening took place on a German holiday: Whit Monday. No doubt Berlin's politicians were all in church that day, praying for peaceful cohabitation throughout Germany.

In Berlin, some stories with awful beginnings end well.

ANETTA KAHANE AND THE AMADEU ANTONIO FOUNDATION

In 1998, the East Berliner Anetta Kahane and some like-minded acquaintances founded an association in East Berlin against xenophobia and racism, named after Amadeu Antonio. This Angolan had been employed as a contract worker in Eberswalde in the state of Brandenburg. On the night of November 24 to 25, 1990, a group of some fifty extreme right-wing youths made their way across the city with baseball bats to hunt for blacks. When they came across three Africans in a restaurant, they laid into them. While two Mozambicans were seriously injured but managed to flee, twenty-eight-year-old Amadeu Antonio Kiowa went into a coma from which he never awoke. He died two weeks later.

Today, the Amadeu Antonio Foundation is part of a network of hundreds of similar initiatives. It organizes demonstrations and rock concerts against right-wing and racist violence, and has the support of many public figures. Some 600,000 German citizens now work for antiracist initiatives. The Amadeu Antonio Foundation garnered worldwide attention when, following a series of murders by a neo-Nazi trio based in the former East German city of Zwickau, which took the lives of nine Turks living in Germany over the course of a decade, it published a list of all the fatalities of racist violence in the country. The figure it released diverged from the official crime statistics to a shocking degree: while the official figure for the period from 1990 to 2011 comprises a total of 63 so-called state security crimes, the Amadeu Antonio Foundation's list indicates 183 cases. It includes one Jewish victim, though it isn't clear that he didn't die of a heart attack.

The discrepancy between these figures is due mainly to the different definitions applied to the acts of violence. The official crime statistics excluded all cases not clearly motivated by racism as defined by its restrictive criteria. Under pressure from the documentation gathered by the Amadeu Antonio Foundation, the Conference of Ministers of the Interior has since changed its criteria for determining "politically defined crimes"; nevertheless, it continues to dispute the foundation's figures. Based on independent research, a report by the weekly *Die Zeit* arrived at the much closer total of 152 cases for the same period.

Nothing about Anetta Kahane seemed to predestine her for a career as a crusader against racism and champion of human rights. Any missionary tendencies, let alone any hint of the moral arrogance sometimes seen in human rights lawyers, are foreign to the petite redhead. She gives the impression of being quiet rather than confident; her disposition seems to tend more to doubt than incontrovertible truths. Her reserved manner probably has something to do with the East German chapter of her life, a time when she herself lost her moral moorings. If you look up "Kahane" on the Internet, after just a few clicks, a two-syllable word appears next to her name: Stasi.

Anetta Kahane is the daughter of German-Jewish communists who emigrated to Brazil at the dawn of the Third Reich, but returned to Germany immediately after East Germany was founded. One of her uncles was a rabbi; her parents were staunch Marxists who had turned away from religion and wanted to participate as loyal citizens in building "the first antifascist nation on German soil." Anetta grew up in the bourgeois district of Pankow in East Berlin, but searched in vain for a place of her own there— and in the new nation her parents so enthusiastically defended.

According to her parents, Kahane says, she was a failure. As a child, she had always looked for hiding places in her parents' apartment without ever finding a spot that felt right. She wondered where she would have lived and found shelter if she had been alive at the time of the persecution of the Jews. And what would have happened to her if she hadn't been lucky enough to be hidden away.

Jews in East Germany constituted a tiny and unique diaspora. For the most part, this group had immigrated to London, Mexico, or the United States during the Third Reich and returned with great hopes after the founding of the German Democratic Republic. The majority of them were secular and didn't particularly care about identifying as Jews or as victims of the Holocaust once they were in East Germany. They shared this reluctance with the Jews who immigrated to the United States in the 1950s and 1960s and, for their part, outright rejected any talk of a "unique Jewish fate," preferring to speak of the "fate of humanity." The Jews in East Germany looked to the future as communists and wanted to help build the new state. The Polish-born writer Jurek Becker, who had spent the first years of his life in the ghetto in Lodz and in the Ravensbrück and Sachsenhausen concentration camps, once told me about an argument he had with his father. Why had he brought him to Germany—the land of the murderers, of all places—instead of to Poland, Jurek Becker had asked. His father had responded with one terse sentence: "Please tell me in what country the anti-Semites lost the war!"

Kahane's father had fought in the International Brigades and, according to Kahane, had been a hardliner as a journalist, though he was liberal in his personal life. He never forbade his daughter from watching western television programs or from reading an issue of *Newsweek* that happened to be lying around. In the 1960s, Kahane's mother, an artist, had known the protest-singer Wolf Biermann. When, in 1976, three weeks after her death, Biermann was expelled, Kahane's father was shaken but didn't say a word publicly. A friend of Anetta Kahane signed a letter of protest and urged her to follow suit. Her self-esteem was so low in those days, Kahane says, that she asked herself, "Who in the world would care about my signature?"

Hundreds of other anonymous young people had probably asked themselves the same question at the time, yet signed the letter of protest all the same—with the result that they either weren't allowed to continue their studies or were arrested. Kahane was not among them.

In fact, she was hardly in a position to sign the letter of protest since, two years earlier, at the age of nineteen, she had allowed herself to be recruited by the Stasi, in whose service she remained for eight years. Kahane makes no secret of this major misstep in her life. Yet because she was often abroad and was studying in Rostock, she had only limited contact with her case officer, Hartung. As a result, she reported only limited and mostly trivial information to him, which she felt guilty about—she believed she had "failed" even in his eyes. The Stasi never gave her any awards or gifts. After separating from the agency in 1982, Kahane applied for an exit visa, but it was refused.

Kahane's feelings when she remembers this period, she says, depend "on her state of mind that day." If she happens once again to be depressed and distraught about herself and this phase of her life, she thinks, "My God, how could you, what in the world have you done?!" On other days—say, after a concert by the rock star Udo Lindenberg, who regularly performs for her foundation—she feels defiant and mockingly says to herself: "Man, Kahane, what a loser you are! Even the Stasi gave up on you! They had such high hopes for you. And you let them down so badly!"

It was two experiences that had made it impossible for her to continue her collaboration with the Stasi. The first was the East German government's smear campaign against the Polish protest movement Solidarność, with which Kahane sympathized. The second was her long work-related stays in Mozambique and São

Tomé in the Gulf of Guinea, where she went on various missions as an interpreter. From the very beginning of her assignment, a representative of the East German Embassy had made it clear that she was not to have any contact with foreigners. Who did he mean by "foreigners"? she had asked. "Well, all of them!" "The Mozambicans, you mean?" "Them too!" "But they're locals here, not foreigners!" She was told to kindly stop splitting hairs. "And what about the Soviet brothers who work here?" "Same thing!"

The attitude of the East German officials working in Africa and of some of her colleagues deeply unsettled her. Even before going abroad, back home in East Germany, Kahane had never managed to completely rid herself of the suspicion that more than just a handful of her compatriots who professed to be antifascist were actually closet anti-Semites. Now she was forced to recognize that, of all people, the East German instructors in Africa acted like flagrant racists. Some of them were so arrogant and contemptuous in their dealings with the Africans that it almost seemed as though they were trying to expose the phoniness of their prescribed "international solidarity." Kahane dreaded these countrymen of hers, who made their nasty racist jokes within earshot of the Africans.

When she returned from Mozambique, it was clear to her that it was time to "clean up." The failure of East Germany's antifascism became Kahane's leitmotif. It was precisely the antifascism she had been born into that had made her susceptible to recruitment by the Stasi; now, it was her own brand of antifascism—no longer the ideological one she had learned, but one that she herself had defined and according to which she lived—that stripped her of her faith in East Germany. In 1982, she broke off her collaboration with the Stasi.

Already before Kahane's travels abroad, friends in East Germany had told her that they and their Vietnamese or African acquaintances were being targeted by neo-Nazis, who would chase them down and beat them up. Whenever Kahane had talked about this with her parents and their friends, they had always only told her that these sorts of things didn't happen in East Germany, that she had a "false sense of perception." There was no room for her observations in her family circle; she remained alone with these stories and with her doubts about her intelligence and perceptive abilities. In truth, she adds with an ironic smile, she was never sure if she really deserved any place, any role, on this planet.

It was this doubt and despair that later led her to establish the Amadeu Antonio Foundation. Time and again she had asked herself how she could make people see something they were constantly telling her didn't even exist. The protest movement in East Germany gave her a chance to call public attention to her knowledge and to her commitment to foreigners and minorities in East Germany. In the summer of 1989, she made and posted signs advising people to turn to her for advice on these matters, indicating her address in Pankow as the location for a preliminary meeting. She couldn't believe her eyes when eighty advice-seekers showed up at the appointed time: students from Mozambique and Cuba, women from Vietnam who worked as seamstresses in East German factories, shattered veterans from the official East German solidarity committees, and a few curious local artists. She had borrowed an extendable table from a neighbor, and it was around this table, she says, that they now all ate the sandwiches Kahane had prepared or stood staring at one another expectantly. She herself didn't know what to say; she only knew that she had to break the silence at all costs. When she rose to address the group, for the first time in her life she felt like she could speak plainly and directly.

In the following weeks, like many other formerly voiceless individuals, she felt out her new role. She suddenly found herself included in roundtable discussions in which the future of East Germany was negotiated. She became a commissioner for the integration of immigrants and helped work on new laws and regulations during the final days of the East German Parliament. After the end of the East German regime, she became the first—and simultaneously last—commissioner for the integration of immigrants for the municipality of East Berlin. In 1991, she founded the Regional Centers for Issues Regarding Foreigners, Youth Employment, and Schools (RAA e.V.), whose main activities are supporting and sponsoring various intellectual projects in schools and other educational institutions. That same year, she was awarded the Theodor Heuss Medal in honor of "the peaceful demonstrators of the fall of 1989 in the former German Democratic Republic," on behalf of and together with others. In 2002, she received the Moses Mendelssohn Prize for her commitment to fighting xenophobia and right-wing extremism.

That same year, her past as an unofficial collaborator caught up with her. While she was under discussion for the job of commissioner for the integration of immigrants in the Berlin Senate, records from the Stasi authorities surfaced in the press that provided evidence of her eight years working as a snitch for the state security service under the alias "Victoria." But, according to Kahane, the facts contained in these records had been public knowledge since the early 1990s. In fact, Kahane didn't even have to withdraw her alleged candidacy, since she herself had never applied for the post. The senator responsible for the position had nominated Kahane as a candidate by popular demand before she had even had a chance to say anything—and her candidacy had been announced in the press without delay.

At the time, in 2002, she reports, she had told her closest colleagues about her work as an unofficial collaborator and had discussed the question of making a voluntary declaration. She had severed ties with the Stasi in 1982 and had admitted to her collaboration ten years later. Didn't that settle the matter?

In the end, she had decided against a voluntary declaration because she felt that there was no chance that her case would be given nuanced consideration in the context of the hysterical debate about Stasi informers at the time.

Indeed, there had been a grotesque reversal in the public evaluation of guilt and responsibility: provided they were prominent enough, the "traitors"—the unofficial collaborators—were named and shamed and morally bankrupted in hundreds of articles in the media, irrespective of what they had actually done. The real instigators of the betrayal—the case officers and their superiors in the Communist Party and in the Ministry of State Security—on the other hand, participated in talk shows, serenely meting out scant information. They didn't even have to defend themselves because no one was blaming them for anything—after all, they had just been "doing their job."

As a young woman, for three years, the writer Christa Wolf had drafted reports for the Stasi. This same secret service had kept tabs on her for decades after she refused to provide additional services. Shortly after the fall of the Wall, Wolf wrote an autobiographical story about her years in East Germany, titled "What Remains." Inexplicably, she doesn't so much as mention her three years collaborating with the Stasi in the book—even though making peace with this phase of her life in no way would have harmed her settlement of accounts; to the contrary, it would have increased its credibility and literary value. A flawed biography, the story of a perpetrator who becomes a victim, is certainly more morally challenging than a hagiography. In any event, Christa Wolf neglected to mention her own involvement with the Stasi for decades. Needless to say, the omission was exposed, and the culture sections of the *Frankfurter Allgemeine Zeitung* and *Die Zeit* lambasted the author. Suddenly not only her silence on this matter but her entire oeuvre were seen as deceitful—more despicable than the organization that had spied on her for decades. After the uproar over "What Remains," Wolf continued to try to come to terms with her "lapse" in failing to acknowledge her years collaborating with the Stasi (1959 to 1962), asking herself "why I completely forgot about it." Unsurprisingly, this question also became one of the leitmotifs of her final work, *City of Angels or, The Overcoat of Dr. Freud,* which met with unanimous critical success and tacitly helped re-establish Wolf's good reputation.

Anetta Kahane's decision not to take the offensive by making a voluntary declaration admitting to her activities as a snitch was wrong of course, and so what had to happen happened. The press held her Stasi activities against her, and a deluge of bitter criticism flooded the blogs and comments sections associated with the newspaper articles. The neo-Nazi scene especially, which considered Kahane its mortal enemy, went to town with its schadenfreude. "Once an informer, always an informer," said one reader's letter, while another wrote: "Today, the pinko Kahane is a leader in falsifying statistics about 'right-wing offenses.'" Another commentator drew a parallel between Kahane's red hair and her views: "For eight years, the red heroine, inside and out," had sent "people to their doom as a Stasi snitch."

This much is certain: if she really had sent people "to their doom," as the right-wing bloggers claimed, it would have come out. Kahane is in the public eye. Every journalist has the right to examine the Stasi files of a public figure like her.

Her answer when I asked her was terse: there were two people she feared she had harmed. She had spoken with both of them—and her fears had proved unfounded. Since then, she herself had carefully studied her files, and had even commissioned a report on them. The fact was that the information she had supplied hadn't resulted in any so-called Stasi actions against these individuals.

It seems obvious to me that someone who worked for the Stasi and is under consideration for public office should be vetted. The fact that this person provided intelligence reports at some point in the past, however, shouldn't be enough to condemn her. Each individual case should be examined to determine whether the person snitched on and harmed acquaintances or friends. If someone like Anetta Kahane makes up for her earlier lapse in judgment by creating the largest and most effective initiative against neo-Nazis and right-wing extremism, then society ought to give her credit for this achievement in the name of democracy. In my eyes, Anetta Kahane has redeemed herself through her work.

The Amadeu Antonio Foundation, which she cofounded, now has, in addition to interns, twelve to thirteen permanent employees whose positions are financed in part by the foundation, in part by various project funds. Projects need to be resubmitted and approved every year, so inevitably there is staunch competition among the hundreds of initiatives fighting for sponsors and public support. Today, Kahane's foundation has so much authority that other initiatives and the federal government turn to it for advice; it has contributed significantly to the broadening of civil society's mobilization against right-wing crimes. Yet Kahane is rather skeptical about the evident success of this mobilization. In her opinion, it's still the neo-Nazis and not the antixenophobia initiatives that are "swimming like fish in water." Ten years ago she was even convinced that the neo-Nazi mind-set was so deeply rooted in "the people" that opposing forces in civil society stood no chance against it. Since then, civil society has clearly made progress, but mostly in urban centers like Jena, Leipzig, and Eberswalde. Now as ever, the situation is worst in rural areas—in the eastern states of Thuringia and Saxony-Anhalt. Sometimes Kahane has to suppress the suspicion that certain regions are haunted by ancient evil spirits. The neo-Nazi strongholds are located precisely where the old National Socialist German Workers' Party (NSDAP) once held sway. "But the old Nazis aren't alive anymore," Kahane muses. "Besides, there's some degree—albeit minimal—of cultural diversity now. Still, when I compare the election successes of the old NSDAP with those of the new NPD, regional continuities jump out at me. It's as if the mountainsides, village streets, house walls had a historical memory! Already as a little girl I felt like the windows and walls were watching me and telling me stories—stories of death and destruction."

This analogy, Kahane continues, doesn't hold true as much for those neighborhoods and regions where the left was once strong. Apparently the scourge of Nazism penetrated much deeper than Marxism did.

As I see it, Anetta Kahane's moral continuity has its roots in this: her fine-tuned ear for and sensitivity to Germany's history of violence and persecution.

Toward the end of our interview, I ask her for her opinion about the growing number of acts of violence that can't be attributed either to racism or anti-Semitism. How does she classify crimes in which youths gratuitously start kicking completely innocent people in S-Bahn stations half or even completely to death? Does her foundation document these cases as well?

My question surprises Kahane. This isn't something she has concerned herself with, she answers, and she doesn't really want to. She holds these cases at arm's length. Why is that? After a pause, Kahane admits that she doesn't have an answer. But she considers it a sign of a good interview when she's asked questions she can't readily answer. In the end, she and her organization aren't responsible for dealing with every form of violence.

THE NEW BARBARISM

It's true that the city is facing a tide of violence that defies the usual categories. I don't know if comparable numbers of similar acts of extreme violence are happening in other big cities like Paris, London, or New York; if they are, I haven't heard about them. The fact that Berlin's crime statistics classify these incidents as "crimes of barbarism" or "youth-group violence" makes it impossible to draw clear conclusions about either their nature or number, or the perpetrators' motives. Perhaps the most accurate description of the phenomenon was a Berlin prosecutor's attempt to describe the motive behind an act of extreme violence by four youths in the U-Bahn station Lichtenberg. He characterized it as having "fun carrying out gratuitous violence against a weaker party."

This definition could be seen as an admission of being utterly at a loss about the violence, or even as minimizing it. After all, the "fun" evoked here generally includes the death of the victim of this supposed revelry. Nevertheless, the prosecutor's unusual definition seems to me the most apt description of a crime for which there is currently no category in the crime statistics. The following is a list of a few such cases.

On February 11, 2011, in the Lichtenberg U-Bahn station in former East Berlin, four young men attack the painter's assistant
Marcel R. and his friend, almost kicking the former to death with
blows to the head. One of the perpetrators then leans over the
unconscious victim, stealing his cell phone and wallet, which has
three euros in it. After weeks in a coma, Marcel R. pulls through;
his friend gets away with less serious injuries thanks to a burly
passerby who came to his aid. Initially, half of Marcel R.'s body is
paralyzed; the doctors speak of at least two years of physical rehab.
Apparently, during their attack, the perpetrators spewed invectives
such as "shit Nazi" and "We hate Germans!" The possibility of a
racially motivated act of revenge suggests itself. But the trial leaves
in doubt whether these expressions were actually uttered and
whether they can be considered as motives. The only thing that is
certain is that the perpetrators were drunk and had already ac-
costed other travelers earlier that night. The attack, the judges
decide, was "gratuitous" and happened "out of pure delight in
violence." Three of the perpetrators are minors. They are originally from Kenya, Kosovo, Bosnia, and Iraq; their two victims are
German.

On April 23, 2011, at three-thirty in the morning, the high
school graduate Torben P., out and about with a friend, forcefully
hurls a Coca-Cola bottle at the head of a total stranger. When the
attacked man, who was sitting on a bench, stands up, Torben P.
knocks him down with a punch to the face and kicks him repeatedly in the head. Though Torben P.'s friend seems baffled, he
doesn't intervene. The perpetrator turns away from his victim for
a few seconds, but suddenly turns back around and, taking a running start, jumps on his head again, kicking him repeatedly. A final deathblow is averted only thanks to a brave eyewitness, who
steps in Torben P.'s way. The perpetrator and victim didn't know
each other; both are German.

Early on the morning of September 17, 2011, Giuseppe Marcone, a cook, and Raoul S., a student, are on their way home. At

the Kaiserdamm U-Bahn station in Charlottenburg in the city's west, two men from Neukölln approach them, both without a profession and unemployed. They'd been drinking vodka "because we couldn't think of anything better to do," Ali T. later tells the judge. Acting like "inebriated idiots," they goad the two men and demand cigarettes. Raoul S., Marcone's companion, tells them that he has only two cigarettes left and makes his way toward the exit with his friend. During the questioning, Ali T. says he then threatened Marcone with "a one-on-one fight." When Marcone doesn't react, Ali T.'s buddy punches him. The two attacked men briefly defend themselves before running up the stairs. In court, the attackers admit that they provoked the confrontation and chased the two men. With the pursuer at his back, Marcone tries to cross the Kaiserdamm's five lanes. He runs into an oncoming car. His friend hears the thud when the car crashes into Marcone, runs to the site of the accident, and tries to resuscitate him. He watches Marcone die. The pursuers are German-born Turks from Neukölln, the victim an Italian.

In the early morning hours of Sunday, October 14, 2012, on Rathausstraße, right near Alexanderplatz in Berlin's east, seven men kick to death a twenty-year-old by the name of Jonny K. The young man was trying to help a friend, who went outside after a long night of partying at the Cancún club and asked one of the seven men for a cigarette. The group tackles Jonny K.'s friend, knocking him to the ground. Jonny K., who has no experience whatsoever with brawls, tries to defend his friend. The seven men abandon their original victim and start hitting and kicking the prone Jonny K. until he stops moving. A paramedic manages to resuscitate him briefly; the doctors at the hospital declare the young man dead and switch off the machines. Jonny K. is the son of German-Thai parents; the seven assaulters are Germans of Turkish origin.

No nationwide candlelight vigils like those seen after the racist attacks in the 1990s followed these and other similar incidents. The attacks didn't fit into the pattern of public campaigns against racism and xenophobia; they were difficult to classify. Nevertheless, the Berlin public reacted immediately in each of these cases—with dismay, grief, and anger. Irrespective of the victim's background, flowers and candles were left at the site of the crime, hundreds of mourners walked behind the caskets, sponsors commissioned memorial stones, and citizens' groups against violence were founded. Berliners extended their empathy to every one of the victims.

The fact that there is no official definition for these crimes makes it impossible to accurately determine their number. Most attacks like these, if they end in "minor physical injuries," don't even get reported. Yet, every year, there are more and more "gratuitous" violent crimes that end in life-threatening or fatal injuries. "The reason for these acts is often completely incommensurate with the brutal methods employed," writes Kirsten Heisig, the juvenile court judge for Berlin's Neukölln district in *Das Ende der Geduld: Konsequent gegen jugendliche Gewalttäter* (The End of Patience: Dealing Firmly with Juvenile Delinquents). "In order to do justice to the educational concept behind the Youth Court Act . . . it would be useful to know why an act is carried out without any regard whatsoever for the victim." Heisig feels that the police reports lack any indications or investigations to that end, and she vehemently disputes the police's palliative claim that there has been a drop in violent offenses by youths in recent years. A long-term comparison study would reveal completely different numbers, Heisig argues—as would taking into consideration the steady decline in the birthrate.

A layperson like me sees certain similarities in the acts of violence described here. They almost always occur at night or early in the morning, in public places, or in S-Bahn or U-Bahn stations. The victims are men of both German and foreign origin, and the same is true of the perpetrators, though roughly 70 percent of the latter are of immigrant background. The perpetrators are youths or young men; usually they have already insulted, jostled, or provoked other passersby or travelers before the attack. In almost all cases, alcohol and/or other drugs are involved on the perpetrators' side. The most important feature these acts of violence all share, however, is that the perpetrators don't know their victims and disregard all traditional rules of fair play. There is no precedent of conflict between the opponents. Only rarely can any sort of motive or trigger be discerned—a refused cigarette or an insult like "We hate Germans!," for example. The randomly instigated altercation isn't fought one-on-one, but takes the form of many against one or two. The attacking group doesn't lay off its victim even when he is lying defenseless on the ground. During the initial questioning or in court, the perpetrators will confess at most that they had been in an "aggressive mood." More often, however, they claim they were attacked and were just defending themselves. They almost never exhibit the sort of remorse typical of someone waking up with a hangover: *I'm sorry . . . I didn't mean to . . . I can't remember anything.*

It seems to be a question of a murderous pastime—a mental flash that, for a few seconds, gives the violent perpetrators the desire for complete power over a random victim. The fact that these acts of violence are usually carried out with reckless disregard for the presence of witnesses or surveillance cameras attests to the heady thrill they seem to involve. A fair number of these violent crimes have been caught on camera, which has also made it possible to solve some of them. Yet, because of the data protection act in force in Germany, sometimes footage is automatically erased before it can be evaluated.

For years the Berlin public has noted with outrage that the judges set the perpetrators free again immediately after their arrest, even when they have beaten their victim almost or completely to death. Defendants can be held in custody only if they are deemed a flight risk, or if there is the danger that they might suppress evidence concerning the circumstances of the crime. Individual committed judges, policemen, and even reformed perpetrators with firsthand experience of the judiciary's handling of violent young offenders regularly point out that, with their routine proceedings, the German courts are unprepared to deal with this type of crime. As one social worker put it, no violent repeat-offender juvenile delinquent could possibly take the German court system seriously. Young offenders who are sent home right after attempted or actual manslaughter never have a chance to grasp the gravity of their crimes. If they were locked up immediately instead—or at least stripped of their cell phones, stereo systems, and motorcycles—this would force them to confront the fact that they have done something terrible, something unforgivable.

Yet, in contrast to the Anglo-Saxon criminal justice system, the German penal code doesn't allow for such novel, incisive punishment. By the time the young offenders—who are usually adults by this point—are tried and sentenced to a few years of juvenile detention for homicide or manslaughter, two years after the fact, their friends protesting in solidarity, they already feel and act like victims of the justice system.

But it isn't just the courts that are struggling to deal with this wave of "senseless violence"—Berlin's liberal and leftist public is too. It is considered politically incorrect to point out that youths of immigrant background are significantly more likely than German youths to be reported as having caused dangerous and serious physical injuries—and that, in turn, young men of Muslim origin are disproportionately represented among these youths of immigrant background.

Beginning in 2008, Judge Heisig fought for recognition of these facts, taking on the criminal justice bureaucracy and pushing for an acceleration of the proceedings so that the connection between a crime and its punishment would be clear to perpetrators and thus have a disciplinary effect. She was immediately denounced as "Judge Merciless." In reality, she wasn't doing anything so radical as recommending that the age of criminal responsibility for youth offenses be lowered, or the penalty increased. Instead, she made the case that parents should exercise their educational responsibility, supervise their children's daily school activities, and help her to socially rehabilitate convicted youths. She went to the parents of the offenders and said, "I'm the one sending your son to jail and I'm not happy about it." Heisig reports that, after some initial resistance, many of the parents and Islamic associations she approached reacted positively. The criminal justice bureaucracy, on the other hand, did what it could to obstruct her—after all, speeding up proceedings would mean speeding up their work. It was only in July 2010, when Heisig committed suicide, that her voice was finally heard throughout the country.

After Heisig's death, several groups of experts took on the theme of youth violence in Berlin. Probably the most thorough and comprehensive study is the research report "114," published in 2011 by the Criminological Research Institute of Lower Saxony. It concluded that experiences of discrimination and violence at home significantly increase the propensity toward violence among youths of immigrant background. But the study also revealed another finding: a clear relationship between Islamic piety and the propensity toward violence. Of the nonreligious Muslim students surveyed, 6.9 percent indicated that they had committed at least one act of violence in the previous twelve months, while 13.5 percent of the more religious Muslims admitted to acts of violence; a converse relationship between religiosity and the propensity toward violence was revealed among Christian youths. The study explained that "norms of masculinity" were largely responsible for the comparatively high propensity toward violence among devout Muslims: religious Muslims agreed with violence-affirming notions of masculinity twice as often as nonreligious Muslims did.

A storm of indignation descended on Christian Pfeiffer, one of the two researchers in charge of the study. During a meeting in

Osnabrück, his German colleagues accused him of "populism," "intellectual arson," and "political motives."

Political correctness wasn't invented in Germany. Yet it seems that this mechanism for controlling what is considered acceptable thinking has found a home here. When politically sensitive topics are at issue, reporting research findings alone is seen as an indication of a suspect worldview—observations are treated like opinions. And yet, when naming the causes of an evil ceases to be acceptable, a society robs itself of the ability to fight it.

TURKS IN BERLIN

Immediately after the fall of the Wall, memorable scenes played out on the streets of West Berlin near the border: East Berliners holding maps of West Berlin in their hands for the first time—a large white expanse had been the only indication of West Berlin on East German maps—turned to helpful Turks for directions on how best to get to the KaDeWe and Kurfürstendamm. The Turkish Berliners greeted these visitors from the East in broken or perfect German and welcomed them to "their" city. Later, too—during the period of occupational retraining—there were other encounters of the third kind: young, academically educated Turks taught courses in which they introduced citizens from East Germany to the basics of West German democracy. Sometimes Turkish teachers also taught German to the so-called Russian Germans, who poured into Germany in great numbers after the fall of the Wall. It was a new reality: foreigners who were at home in Germany taught German to Germans from abroad.

The author and journalist Necla Kelek reports how, in 1991, having just received her university degree, she traveled to the new federal states to prepare former employees of the communist regime's municipal and district administrations for the West German social system. She taught labor, social, and constitutional law. The participants of one of the courses had refused to be instructed by West German lecturers, whom they perceived as arrogant know-it-alls. According to the school administration, the Turkish-born Necla Kelek was "politically unencumbered" and better suited to spurring the intractable group to cooperate. It was a noteworthy, an intelligent, step. Until then, almost no German administration had tapped into the potential of its new Turkish citizens to support reunification.

"I still remember November 11, 1992, perfectly," Kelek reports.

When I entered the assigned lecture hall, the first rows were empty. The roughly thirty-five participants, mainly middle-aged men in cardigans and suits, had sat down in the last rows, turned the chairs around, and had their backs to me. What could I do? I began my lesson without acknowledging the insult. The topic: What is a state? I drew diagrams on the board and talked and talked. I could understand how foreign the new citizens of the re-united Germany sitting in front of me must have felt having to listen to "Wessis" telling them what freedom, democracy, and personal rights are. But I was proud to be teaching precisely this subject.

It was only when Kelek asked her students, "But who is 'the people'?," drawing a big question mark after the word "people," that some of the adult students turned to her and laughed. "They were the people who were free now, but who also had to learn to emerge 'from [their] self-imposed immaturity' [Immanuel Kant]."

Yet enthusiastic prodemocratic immigrants were included in the process of German reunification only in a few isolated cases. Candidates of Turkish origin are also noticeably underrepresented in other areas of public life—in administration, schools and kindergartens, the police, and the German armed forces—a shortcoming that politicians have only recently begun to address.

Civil society has made significantly more progress in this regard. The previously discussed public campaigns and demonstrations against xenophobia and racism that followed the neo-Nazi attacks in Solingen, Mölln, Rostock, and Hoyerswerda are a strong indicator of successful coexistence in Germany. But perhaps nothing has promoted German-Turkish harmony more than the rise of Turkish soccer stars in Germany's many soccer leagues. When Turkish soccer virtuosos like Mesut Özil or İlkay Gündoğan score goals for the home team, suddenly thousands of fans can spell and even chant their names—which, however, doesn't prevent them from cursing and booing these same players when they play for an opposing team. At the same time, many Turks consider Mesut Özil a traitor for having chosen to play for the German rather than the Turkish national team.

The Turkish national team failed to qualify for the soccer World Cup in 2006, which was held in Germany. German-born Turks devised a German-Turkish flag for the matches—a black-red-gold tricolor with a half-moon and star in the middle—to express their affiliation with their second-favorite team. Two years later, when the Turks and Germans played against each other in the Euro Cup, some fans watching the game in Berlin also waved the German-Turkish flag. Despite all fears, the match ran its course peacefully. Watching Federal Chancellor Angela Merkel flirt with Turkish prime minister Recep Tayyip Erdoğan in the VIP box, TV viewers almost forgot which team actually won.

But there were also other, more alarming incidents between native Berliners and the city's largest minority. On the night of September 11, 2001, right after the terrorist attack on the World Trade Center in New York, residents of the western districts of Neukölln and Kreuzberg were startled by an unexpected spectacle. Rocket flares usually only seen in Berlin on New Year's Eve were launched into the sky from courtyards. Hardly an organized and compact fireworks display, it was more of a fitful celebration of joy, a fireworks display of the poor: two rockets here, three there. But the sum total was nevertheless hundreds of rockets launched into the sky to celebrate the attack of September 11, while the vast majority of Berliners were still at a loss for words to express their horror and compassion for the victims.

In the days after the attack, rumors and scattered reports in the Berlin press caused further consternation. Behind closed windows, cheering and spontaneous celebrations had broken out in some apartments and restaurants in Neukölln and Kreuzberg. Teachers in schools in these districts reported that Muslim students remained seated when invited to stand for a moment of silence. They justified their refusal by arguing that no teacher had ever called for a moment of silence after an Israeli massacre of Palestinians.

At the time, many Berliners asked themselves for the first time with whom they were actually living side by side. Neukölln is proud of the fact that citizens from 165 nations live together within its borders. At 50 percent—70 percent in northern Neukölln—Turks comprise by far the largest share of the district's population, with affiliated Arab nations making up the second-largest group. Racially motivated assaults of the kind seen in the new federal states, where foreigners were rare, were almost unheard of in Neukölln. On the contrary, locals there spoke fondly of "our Turks." They spoke less fondly, however, of the Arabs who had arrived in Germany decades after the Turks—often illegally.

For a prolonged moment of shock the mixture of tolerance and turning a blind eye that characterized the Germans' basic attitude toward immigrants gave way to an irksome question: How did they tick anyway, these fellow citizens of Muslim faith whom you knew from the U-Bahn and vegetable stand but rarely invited to your kids' birthday parties? Did they ultimately have a completely different value system? Were some of them—and how many of them, anyway?—happy about the murders that inspired revulsion in the native German population?

The social worker Haroun Sweis, whom I knew from the

Courage against Xenophobia initiative, gave me a pragmatic answer: in the eyes of many Muslims in Berlin, everything that was happening to the United States was simply "a good thing, to begin with. At last the arrogant West feels compelled to take any interest at all in its fellow Muslim citizens!" In fact, Germans had recently started to read the Quran, he said; it was sold out in the months after the terrorist attack.

Reading Necla Kelek yields a very different answer. In recent years, her books and public statements have caused a furor both in German mainstream society and Muslim associations.

Necla Kelek didn't choose this role. She grew up in a secular Turkish family from Istanbul, which immigrated to Germany in the 1960s. She was a good student, learned German quickly, and soaked up the culture of the west. As a young girl, she read *Gone with the Wind*, identified with Scarlett, and waited for her Rhett Butler. Since she earned her PhD in Germany, she easily could have followed the path of other academics of Turkish origin who have gained a foothold in the German university world. But since the ruling consensus in the relevant faculties was that immigrants were the victims of German society, Kelek and her very different story and viewpoint wouldn't have been welcome there. For it was her own family, and not her German environment, that had caused the first bump in her initially smooth acclimatization.

When Kelek reached puberty, her father took away her sports bag—from then on, she was no longer allowed to participate in gym class or school trips, even though gym and swimming had been her favorite subjects. Unlike her brother, she also wasn't allowed to ride her bicycle to school anymore since she might "injure" her virginity on the way. Her brother was still allowed to roller- and ice-skate and meet up with his German friends—all of which Necla was suddenly forbidden to do. She wasn't allowed to have German friends, wasn't allowed to go over to their houses or invite them to hers. And, when she was home, her brother's Turkish and German friends weren't allowed in the house either.

Necla felt that her parents were excluding her from the world in which she was growing up. She participated less and less in class, lost herself in daydreams, and sat apathetically at her desk. At the time, Necla Kelek recounts in hindsight, she went into "internal emigration." Once, she fell from her chair during class. When she regained consciousness, the teacher sent her home. Necla got into bed and decided not to go back to school. "I'm not going there anymore," she told her mother. "School is making me sick." Neither her mother nor father contacted the school; they also never attended parent-teacher meetings. As far as her mother was concerned, at this point Necla should have only one goal anyway: to find a husband as soon as possible. Her parents' failure was in perfect harmony with the school's faux tolerance, or indifference. No one at school seemed to miss Necla when she didn't show up. Even though her parents still received a children's allowance from the state, nobody came by to enforce compulsory attendance. In parting, her teacher had told her, "Read a nice book! After all, we don't want to upset your father."

From then on, Necla Kelek recounts in her autobiographical book *Die fremde Braut: Ein Bericht aus dem Inneren des türkischen Lebens in Deutschland* (The Foreign Bride: An Inside Report of Turkish Life in Germany), she lived like a prisoner in her parents' home. Sometimes she would hide the salt or sugar in the kitchen so she'd have an excuse to go into the city. Her father, who had initially brought his family to Germany out of enthusiasm for the western ideals of freedom and self-determination, attended to his business. He rarely came home and didn't concern himself with his daughter's fate. At the end of each month, he would go to the payroll office of the ceramics factory where Necla's mother and sister worked to pick up their paychecks. Otherwise he rarely showed his face at home. The head of the ceramics factory was the only one who finally intervened when Necla's mother tried to get the adolescent girl a job there as well: "What are you doing here? You're not even fourteen yet! Why aren't you in school?" He wrote to the school administration, finally setting the wheels of the German bureaucracy in motion. The school informed Necla's father of his daughter's truancy and threatened to penalize him. Necla's favorite teacher came by and urged her mother to send the child back to school immediately.

The final break with Necla's father came about later. When Necla refused to greet him and locked herself in her room, he smashed the door with an ax and lunged at his daughter. A tussle between father and daughter ensued. Necla fled to a neighbor. Her father left his home and family and, soon afterward, Germany. He never came back. For years, Necla Kelek was plagued with guilt. She blamed herself for the fact that her father had left her family—until, after years of therapy, a psychoanalyst finally set her free with one sentence: her father had been completely irresponsible.

Necla Kelek's book became a sensational success. Before it was published, the situation of Turkish immigrants had mostly come up in relation to the keyword "guest worker"—an expression that referred almost as a matter of course to male immigrants. Never before had the German public concerned itself with the situation of Turkish girls and women in Germany, never before had their suffering been described so poignantly. I, too, was shocked when I read the book. How was it possible, I asked myself, that we, pioneers and enthusiasts of a multicultural society, had never noticed that many Muslim girls and women are living like prisoners in our midst right here in Germany? Why had we never taken an interest in the fate of women who could watch our "multiculti" celebrations only from behind closed windows?

It wasn't just the German media, but the country's political parties as well that took up the book's theme and celebrated its author for bringing the issue to light. In addition to Kelek, two other rebellious authors also provided insight into the lives of Muslim women living in Germany: Seyran Ateş (*Große Reise ins Feuer,* or Journey into the Fire) and Serap Çileli (*Wir sind eure*

Töchter, nicht eure Ehre, or We Are Your Daughters, Not Your
Honor). Their books told of a nightmarish life in the heart of Germany, dictated by archaic, centuries-old tribal customs that were
a thing of the past in major Turkish cities like Istanbul, Izmir, and
Ankara—of involuntary isolation, forced marriages, abduction,
rape, and a wholesale oppression of women that can only go by
the name of slavery.

A murder that occurred in Berlin the year Kelek's book was
published broadened the discussion. A young Kurdish woman by
the name of Hatun Sürücü was shot to death by her youngest
brother—a minor—because she refused to return to her family
after escaping from a forced marriage and, flying in the face of
her family's threats, insisted on leading "the life of a German
woman." She used makeup, wore her hair down, went to clubs,
sported rings and necklaces. In the minds of her parents and brothers, she had sullied "the family's honor" with her western lifestyle.
Just a few short days before she would have received her certificate of apprenticeship as an electrician, deadly shots fired by her
little brother put an end to her life. The family's choice of her
brother as the assassin was the result of a cynical calculation: underage murderers in Germany are given a maximum of ten years
in prison and have a good chance of being set free after serving
just two-thirds of their sentence if they show good conduct.

In the decade prior to Hatun Sürücü's murder, at least thirteen other such "honor killings" had occurred in Berlin—and dozens throughout Germany—but never before had they caused such
an outcry.

Public attention focused on two practices in particular
that Muslim girls are subjected to in Germany to this day: "forced
marriage"—every year, several thousand girls were and are
forced to marry men their parents have chosen for them; and the
custom of flying in "import brides" from Turkey—year after year,
their pockets filled with money, Turkish mothers living in Berlin
travel back to their native towns to choose wives for their sons.

Without any proficiency in German or cultural preparation to speak of, these bought brides are flown into Germany, where, in keeping with old tribal customs, they lead isolated lives in the families of their in-laws, deprived of all rights. In short, explains the Turkish lawyer Seyran Ateş, Turkish men who want to marry and live according to sharia can do so much more easily in Berlin than in Istanbul.

For a long time, advocates for a multicultural society brushed off such warnings, believing that cultural "dissonances" like these would disappear by themselves by the third or fourth generation. It was a false hope. A study published in 2012 by the Ministry of the Interior on the willingness of non-German Muslim youths between the ages of fourteen and thirty-two years to assimilate found that the problem had intensified. Roughly a fourth of the respondents rejected the western lifestyle and showed no willingness to integrate.

As had been the case for earlier surveys, it wasn't the message itself but the messenger—in this case, the German minister of the interior—that aroused indignation. Arm in arm with Islamic associations and female scholars of Islam, spokespersons for the Social Democratic Party and Greens deplored the "discrimination" and "categorical suspicion of Muslims." It once again became clear that the mere mention of disturbing facts automatically raises the suspicion of discrimination.

The fact that a parallel Muslim society was able to emerge in Germany—unlike in the United States, for example—requires some explanation. For four decades, Germany's conservative governments refused to acknowledge that Germany had become a country of immigrants. One consequence of this denial was a complete lack of language courses and constructive policy of assimilation. For Germany's leftists, guilt further stood in the way of requiring immigrants to learn German: after all, we can't force the poor immigrants to learn our "language of murderers." When I moved to the United States with my family and enrolled my children in public schools there, they were required to take a daily course in English as a second language. It is only very recently that kindergartens and schools in Germany have begun to offer similar courses. Another factor also comes into play. Since the recruitment ban on Turkish guest workers in 1973, roughly 2.5 million Turkish family members have entered Germany through the country's family reunification policies. The great majority of them—mostly women and children—land in Germany's social nets the day they arrive and remain tangled up in them. Germany lacks the most important tool for integrating new arrivals into society: participation through work. The same is true for asylum-seekers—Kurds, in the case of emigrants from Turkey. Until a decision is reached on their applications, which often takes years, asylum-seekers aren't allowed to work in Germany. Consequently, here, too, the crucial prerequisite for successful assimilation is missing.

Apart from that, the different geographic locations and images of the two immigrant nations also influences newcomers' willingness to assimilate. As a rule, Muslims who leave Turkey or the Arabic nations to go to the United States want to leave behind their old lives and become American citizens. This is not the case for immigrants to Germany. First of all, for a long time, Germany didn't offer them the possibility of citizenship; secondly, the country didn't present itself to immigrants as a desirable homeland. Who would want to become a citizen of a nation whose inhabitants—for good reasons—aren't even proud of it? Besides: it's just a two-hour flight back to Istanbul.

Finally, it's important to remember that the percentage of Muslim immigrants in Germany is far higher than in the United States. Compared to Germany's at least 4 million Muslim immigrants—about 5 percent of the population—the United States has only about 2.4 million—about 0.6 percent of the population.

As long as Necla Kelek limited herself to the topic of the oppression of Muslim girls and women, she was a media darling and the recipient of countless prizes. That changed abruptly when she expanded her research to include the causes of this oppression. Why, Kelek and the public asked, had women in the Islamic world not even begun to achieve the kind of gender equality commonly seen in the democratic West today? Why did Islam play such a determining role in the everyday lives of Muslims? Why, unlike Christianity, had it never achieved separation of church and state? It was above all Kelek's assertion that Islam—after a period of liberalization during the Middle Ages, which benefitted the entire Occident—had insulated itself against attempts to historicize the Quran, thereby closing the door to scientific thinking and modernity, that made passions run high. Islamic associations and a group whose members referred to themselves as "liberal Muslims" rang the discrimination alarm; in petitions, open letters, and articles, German women scholars of Islam and female adherents of the notion of "multiculti" accused Kelek of poor scholarship and of demonizing Islam. Suddenly she was decried as a critic—an enemy, even—of Islam; she gave Muslims a bad name, they said, she threw open the gates to Islamophobia and reactionary prejudices; indeed, she herself was reactionary. Kelek was denounced for claims she had never made—for example, that Muslims needed to break away from Islam before they could access the realms of science and enlightenment. She was denigrated as a fundamentalist and women's libber gone wild in the context of every debate regarding Muslims in Germany: during the discussions concerning the building of new mosques, the caricatures of Muhammad in the Danish press, and Thilo Sarrazin's controversial bestselling diatribe against Muslims, *Deutschland schafft sich ab: Wie wir unser Land aufs Spiel setzen* (Germany Is Abolishing Itself: How We Are Putting Our Country at Risk).

These arguments revealed a shortcoming: secular Muslims—about half of all Muslims in Germany—aren't organized, don't have an association, and have only a few spokespersons. Instead, German Muslims are represented by the three major Islamic associations, which receive a significant portion of the money they use to build their mosques from Turkey and Saudi Arabia. Yet at most a fifth of all Muslims living in Germany regularly attend a mosque.

Kelek doesn't consider herself a revolutionary. Nevertheless, she didn't content herself with writing down the story of little Necla, destined for a life of captivity and archaic structures in the middle of Germany. Her research and studies brought her face-to-face with the fact that her personal story is anything but unique. In examining the causes of the scandalous conditions she had uncovered, she came across two guarantors of these conditions: the upholders of traditional Islam, and the German cultural relativists who believe that an immigrant group's cultural traditions deserve protection even if they infringe upon human rights. She has taken on representatives of both of these groups. By leading this war on two fronts, Necla Kelek hasn't exactly made life easy for herself in her declared homeland of Germany. Yet she is only demanding what should be a given: that Muslim women in Europe should have the same rights as their local female counterparts.

Despite all the hostilities, Kelek and her fellow fighters have accomplished a great deal. They have contributed significantly to the fact that forced marriage is now forbidden by law in Germany. Importing underage brides from Turkey—under the pretext of family reunification—is also a punishable offense. Any Turkish woman immigrating to Germany in order to marry must be at least eighteen years old and is required to learn basic German. Obligatory assimilation courses now exist that require all foreigners seeking naturalization—not just young Turkish women wishing to get married—to learn certain basic German language skills and the rules of a democratic society. There's no doubt that these belated initiatives are still in need of funding and appropriate locations. Teachers are paid as much as unskilled laborers, and the ministers of the interior of the federal states still balk at the expense of compulsory German-language courses like the English as a second language classes that have been obligatory in the United States for decades.

Nevertheless, Necla Kelek and her fellow female campaigners have established a new basis for the coexistence of Turkish immigrants and local residents. In the future, no democratic party or group will be able to turn a blind eye to her arguments. All the same, it remains remarkable that, at the beginning of the third millennium, it should have taken a few brave Muslim women— following in the footsteps of Gotthold Ephraim Lessing and Immanuel Kant—to remind Germans of the universality of human rights and the basic tenets of democracy.

Another result is also apparent. In June 2013, in the wake of the protests on Taksim Square in Istanbul, relatively large groups of cheerfully demonstrating Turks gathered on the streets of Berlin. They carried signs that said TAKSIM IS EVERYWHERE and expressed solidarity with their compatriots on the Bosporus who feel that their civil rights are being curbed by Erdoğan's government. Turks in Berlin spontaneously closed ranks with those in Istanbul. Germans of Turkish origin who had gone back to their old homeland to try their luck in the wake of the economic recovery there in recent years doubtless also played an important role; the German media had no trouble finding local witnesses to the protest movements in Istanbul or Ankara who explained the events to them in fluent German. Many Berliners suddenly felt at home in Istanbul, even if they had never been there: Aren't those our Turks taking to the streets there? Indeed, what was and is at issue are nothing but the very same human and civil rights that Necla Kelek had so fiercely demanded in her first book.

A MAYOR FLOUTS
POLITICAL CORRECTNESS

The longtime mayor of the Neukölln district of Berlin, Heinz Buschkowsky, has never had it easy within his own party, the Social Democratic Party of Germany (SPD). With remarks as funny as they are caustic, he regularly defies the consensus of the other members, who turn a blind eye to the emergence of a parallel Muslim society. If anyone in Berlin has a "Berliner Schnauze"—literally "Berlin snout," a slang term for the brusque and coarse attitude attributed to Berliners—it's Heinz Buschkowsky. His flippant, utterly un-PC remarks are legendary. "Here in Neukölln, people who don't use their welfare payments to cover the rent seem like gentrifiers to us." Or: "If all we do is just keep watching, ten to fifteen years from now Neukölln-North won't be very different from Whitechapel anymore. Today, 75 percent of children here under the age of fifteen already live off welfare benefits. We have schools where 95 percent of the students' parents are unemployed. Gainful employment isn't something that exists in the world these kids live in." It was above all his claim that the "multiculti" concept had failed that earned him the hostility of his party's left wing and of the Greens.

But Buschkowsky has never let his party "rehabilitate," let alone silence, him. His approach to Germany's Muslim immigrants can be described as a risky mixture of empathy and prodding. He supports strict compliance with and monitoring of compulsory school attendance and penalizing parents who don't send their children to school: "If a child doesn't show up at school, the federal children's allowance doesn't show up in the parents' account." He supports employing guards in at-risk schools, to keep out non-school-related individuals and to intervene in schoolyard fights. At the same time, he favors the individual supervision of problem students by coaches and social workers, who help give these students self-esteem and convince them that they can do it, that the world can be their oyster—if they want it to be. He is famous and infamous for having his hand on the pulse of his district and for not feeling tied to the party line. Everything he knows, he explains, comes from conversations with people from his district. "What I know, I don't learn here at the office. I learn it when I go to schools and speak with the teachers, when I go to a daycare center and talk to the instructors—after all, that's where life happens!" When he then tells the educated bourgeoisie about his experiences, he continues, he finds that people stare at him with eyes as wide as saucers, as if he were from another planet, as if he were some sort of alien. "They can't imagine there's a world where first-graders are still brought to school in strollers because they can't walk properly yet—and that they can't walk because they're always being pushed around in their strollers. That children are breast-fed until the age of five. That teachers tell me about kids who can't drink from a cup because they spend all day sucking on 'Spanish drinking bags.' When I tell educated middle-class people about this, they ask themselves if I've already hit the bottle this morning. They can't imagine that there are kids who have never held a marker, who don't know how to hold a pair of scissors, who don't know what clay is. If you tell them that our fourth-graders don't know how to read—normally, a first-grader knows how to read by the end of the first school year—they say, no way, that's impossible!"

When he calls up the schools once the academic year is under way to ask how many of the German students registered in Neukölln have enrolled in their local schools, he always finds out that they've registered in other, more affluent neighborhoods—having established false residencies there using an uncle or aunt's address. "After all," Buschkowsky sums up, "German parents are extremely resourceful when it comes to avoiding their zoned schools. There's the kid who may not even be able to run straight without hurting himself, but needs to attend a specialized sports school at all costs; or the little Paganini who doesn't know with which hand he's supposed to hold his violin bow, but absolutely *must* go to a school with a strong music program, et cetera."

Buschkowsky tells the story of a group of new Neukölln residents—"gentrifiers, of course!"—who founded a daycare center on their own initiative. They set the fees so high that they could rest assured that no child from a family receiving Hartz IV welfare benefits would enroll. While they prided themselves on their "international solidarity," their love did not extend so far as to want to see kids from the Turkish underclass in their swanky daycare center. Their maxim was: my child is not an "assimilation pioneer" or a subject for social experiments with uncertain outcomes, thank you very much. The problem came to a head for the parents after kindergarten: in which school in Neukölln should they enroll these privileged children, who had been pampered with special programs? Together, they decided to enroll all of their children in one and the same class in one of Neukölln's better schools. But now the other parents protested: the class makeup no longer reflected the school's social and ethnic mix. There was talk of "racism," "the creation of an elite," and "favoritism"; the story made the rounds in the Berlin media. The group resorted to a predictable alternative: the parents took their children out of the school, rented a VW van, and had them shuttled from Neukölln to a school in Rudow every day.

One of the kickers of this story is that an extremely indignant journalist from the left-leaning daily paper *taz* was forced to admit that she had done the same thing with her own child: though she lived in the immigrant-heavy Kreuzberg, she sent her child to school in bourgeois Charlottenburg.

Right at the outset of our interview, Buschkowsky dismisses my conjecture that things have improved significantly in his jurisdiction. If I'd been hoping to get on his good side by using this opening, I had miscalculated. "I really don't know what this claim that Neukölln is experiencing an upswing is based on. I have no idea what gives you that idea. It certainly isn't reflected in our daycare centers and schools." I understand Buschkowsky's exasperation, of course. Right from the start of our conversation, he has presented himself as a mayor fighting like a lion for his high-risk district. Just admitting that the situation has improved would weaken his existential cries of alarm in the eyes of the public and of Berlin's senator of finance, who keeps putting off tackling the city's enormous debt. Yet this master of dramatization also has compelling arguments. Reluctantly Buschkowsky admits that the beginnings of an artists' enclave can be seen in a section of northern Neukölln: "Galleries, small bars, a few scattered electric guitar or luthier shops, and even large coworking spaces with multiple desks and Internet access for rent—yes, yes, that's very in right now!—and trailers parked in an old factory space that an entrepreneur with a punk hairstyle rents out as hotel rooms." "Sleeping in trailers in a factory space?" I ask with disbelief. "Of course," the mayor replies, "that's what young people are doing these days!"

This was Buschkowsky at his best: with his on-the-ground knowledge, he manages in next to no time to astonish any journalist who only knows the lay of the land based on previous media coverage. "These good beginnings," Buschkowsky continues, "reveal next to nothing about Neukölln's development. I always say that until the ground floors grow all the way up to the fifth floor everything is just an episode." "Why should the ground floors grow up to the fifth floor?" I ask. "Well, it's obvious: the studios, galleries, and boutiques are on the ground floor. But as long as the new tenants don't establish roots upstairs, start families, settle down, it's all just a fireworks display, a passing episode. In the lives of these young settlers, those of us here in Neukölln are just an episode. A few years down the line, they'll be sitting across from the head of human resources during a job interview and they'll say: 'Did you know that I lived in Berlin-Neukölln for two years? And I survived—I'm a tough cookie!'"

It may be true, Buschkowsky admits, that one hears many more languages in Neukölln than one used to—not just Turkish and Arabic, but also French, Italian, and a great deal of Spanish. But the new residents, he points out, haven't changed the structure of the district. Sure, there's an organic Bio Company supermarket on Sonnenallee, which targets customers willing to pay sixty cents for a roll every now and then. But the new boutiques and bars aren't popular among the neighborhood's long-standing jobless and militant leftist *Autonome*. Many small entrepreneurs keep the doors to their businesses locked during the day because they're worried about attacks and demonstrations; you have to knock if you want to buy something in these shops. The entrenched Hartz IV recipients consider the young professionals who get up in the morning to go do something a provocation. "Yes, there are new bohemians," Buschkowsky concludes, "but these people are neither in a position nor mood to create a new Neukölln. If you ask them, you'll find that most of them have been here for only five to eight months. They'll leave again in five years, at the very latest—many after just two."

The conditions in many schools in Neukölln, the mayor explains, are still catastrophic: the student body is 80 to 90 percent Muslim, with only a fraction of native German students; the kids in these schools speak Turkish or Arabic among themselves. Yet, in Buschkowsky's view, the problem isn't the students' ethnic background, but the Muslim students' home life. As an example of a successful "turnaround," he mentions the Albert Schweitzer High School and its recovery. To begin with, a new principal was

appointed: the Czech head teacher Georg Krapp, who had succeeded in getting students in Prague to complete the German
academic high school curriculum. In consultation with this new
principal, Turkish was introduced as a subject, along with a reme-
dial course in German—to the annoyance of the German Association of Philologists. In the minds of the philologists, obsessed
with Wilhelm von Humboldt's model of the ideal school, anyone
who attends a German high school should already speak German, period! This ideal obviously has little to do with the reality
in Neukölln. Coaches were sent to the school, and it was transformed into an all-day school, with students remaining in class
until four or five in the afternoon. In four years, the number of
students doubled, the number of graduates even quadrupled, and
the average GPA at graduation was 2.5 (roughly the equivalent of
a 3.1 in the United States)—and this despite the fact that the
school's ethnic makeup hadn't changed at all! Today, the school is
one of the most popular and successful in Neukölln.

Buschkowsky tells me the farcical story of the building of
a new gym for the school. The Berlin architects had designed it
with one wall made entirely of glass. Buschkowsky asked them if
they really thought that Muslim girls would do sports behind this
glass wall—exposed to the gaze of the male students in the schoolyard. Regarding him with pursed lips, the architects had retorted
that it worked just fine in their neighborhood, Mahlow—an ex-
clusive residential suburb of Berlin.

I ask Buschkowsky how the Albert Schweitzer High School
managed to attain the same level of academic achievement usually seen in Berlin's bourgeois districts without changing the
makeup of its student body. What was the recipe of its success?

Buschkowsky laughs. "Well," he replies, sizing me up to
gauge whether his choice of words makes me cringe, "the fact is
there are also Turks and Arabs who aren't stupid. It's these kids
that we need to help against their parents. The kids here are kept
dumb—made dumb—by their home environments. They aren't
born dumb here. Just as many dumb Turks and Arabs are born

here as dumb Germans are born elsewhere." Their home life was preventing these children from taking advantage of the country's educational opportunities and from climbing the social ladder—the way that he, the son of proletarian parents, had moved up thanks to his parents' constant pushing and encouragement. "These days, parents here simply don't tell their kids: Read this book! Turn the damn TV off! Shut down that damn computer!" These children are prisoners in their parents' homes, with television sets running 24/7—"only Turkish programs, mind you!"

If a TV set gets that much use, I point out, at least it will break down a bit faster.

"You're wrong about that!" Buschkowsky immediately retorts. The manually skilled son of a metalworker, he explains to me that turning a television set on and off—the cooling down and warming up—is what causes the most wear and tear. If a TV is always on, it lasts forever. "The kids have a TV in their rooms when they're five or six. I always ask them. They all have a TV and two-to-four-hundred-euro cell phones—five-, six-year-old kids. But when I then ask them who's a member of a sports team, nobody raises their hand."

Achieving success in a neighborhood like this, Buschkowsky explains, means taking the students' entire social environment into account. It means chipping away at the system of the parallel society, day after day, hour by hour. It means supervising children's after-school lives—in other words, helping them do their homework in school after school. Girls shouldn't even make it home in time to do the dishes. One kindergarten teacher had told him, "'We're on the east side of Sonnenallee'"—a major, four-lane thoroughfare—"'My kids are never going to cross Sonnenallee to the west! So now we've started practicing taking trips to the other side of the street with the kids!'" Things, in other words, remarks Buschkowsky, that German children take for granted.

I ask if it isn't possible to involve the parents in exercises like this.

The mayor reacts skeptically. Sure, you could get a Muslim

mother to accompany her child on a class trip to the zoo, or to attend a daycare party or parents' meeting. But it wouldn't suddenly turn an Anatolian mother into a liberal Euro-Muslim. The cultural rituals they carry with them are simply too powerful. He tells me about a daycare center in Neukölln. A father goes to pick up his daughter, who tells him that they ate gummy bears at school that day. The father knows gummy bears are made with gelatin and that gelatin is made from pigs' bones. He goes to the kitchen, douses a sponge in powerful abrasive cleaner, and uses it to wipe the inside of his daughter's mouth, to clean her oral cavity of the piggish filth. In the process, he chemically burns his "defiled" daughter's mouth so badly that she has to be taken to the hospital. "You deal with crazies like this every day here!"

Buschkowsky tells me another story. The director of a daycare center in Neukölln had confessed to him that she just couldn't do it anymore, that she wanted to quit her job, which she had been doing for thirty years, because she found herself growing more severe and impatient every day. And she didn't want to turn into the harsh, angry woman she saw herself becoming in the future. Six months later, he saw her again. "Hey, Ms. Singer," he greeted her. "What ended up happening, did you quit? Can you stand being away from Neukölln?" She told him that she was working in the neighboring district of Friedrichshain now—a completely new experience for her. For the first time in thirty years, kids came into her office who spoke in complete sentences.

"So," Buschkowsky concludes, looking at his watch, "we have the Albert Schweitzer High School and the Rütli School—two bits of evidence that this district has potential that we just have to leverage. But is that what we're doing? Nope—at least I don't see it. We have schools here that, I'll tell you quite honestly, I'm ashamed that they're in Neukölln. Schools with totally burned-out teachers who are completely over it. Who tell the kids: You're nothing but another one of those camel drivers. You'll never be German—don't even bother learning anything here! We have teachers here who hit the kids. All that blather started by Berlin's mayor Klaus Wowereit—'This problem district really ought to have the best schools and teachers!'—it's really just stupid blah-blah. Sure, you can write that down, I don't have a problem with it—I'll say it again: It's all just stupid blah-blah! The truth is, these are the reject districts. Anywhere there are teachers no one wants anymore—the boneheads among teachers, the losers—they send them to us. And that's why they can't hack it!"

You can criticize Heinz Buschkowsky for his tendency to exaggerate, accuse him of vanity—even call him a preacher of hate, as some do. But no one can deny that this natural-born tribune of the people's provocations burst the false reassurances of the "multiculti" enthusiasts, bringing them back down to earth. I, for one, don't doubt for a second that this effusive and gifted speaker loves his district with all his heart—and its Muslim majority, which is either unable or unwilling to assimilate since it can live off the poisoned benefits of the welfare state. Buschkowsky is an exception, a two-armed bandit who could motivate even a young anarchist to consider a career as a civil servant.

YES, YOU CAN: THE RÜTLI SCHOOL

In the summer of 2008, a cry of alarm from the teaching staff of one school in Neukölln caught the world's attention. The teachers informed the responsible school inspector in Neukölln that the conditions in their school had got so out of hand that it had become impossible to teach a lesson with any real semblance of order. The teachers were spit at and insulted, violence and anarchy ruled in the schoolyard—things couldn't go on like this for one more day. "That's why any help our school receives can only mean making the current situation more bearable . . . In the long term, the school in its current form needs to be closed and replaced by a new kind of school with a completely different structure."

The school in question belonged to a group of secondary schools known as *Hauptschulen*. It had 270 students, roughly 85 percent of whom were of Muslim origin. A large number of these Muslim students came from Arab countries and differed from the Turkish students in their even higher rate of absenteeism and propensity toward violence.

The *Hauptschule* is a form of lower secondary school that doesn't offer students the option of earning a high school degree. It has long been highly controversial. At the end of ninth or tenth grade, students—provided they haven't dropped out earlier—

graduate with a *Hauptschule* diploma, which allows them to apply for apprenticeship positions. However, many students never graduate, but drop out sooner, generally ending up unemployed or in unskilled jobs. Indeed, before reforms to these schools were introduced in Berlin, only 6 percent of all elementary school students subsequently enrolled in *Hauptschulen*; the vast majority attended high schools that offered a complete secondary-school curriculum. *Hauptschulen* became the catch basins for the two or three most difficult students from any given elementary school—a situation that more or less guaranteed academic failure. Until recently, approximately ten thousand students attended Berlin's fifty *Hauptschulen*. By seventh grade, at most a thousand students were still registered.

Many experts consider this type of school one of the main reasons why Germany's education system is particularly impermeable to children from socially disadvantaged backgrounds. Compared with the European average, children from working-class and immigrant families in Europe's economic powerhouse have vastly lower chances of graduating from high school.

But the cry of alarm from the Rütli School never would have caught the attention of the national press, and then of the world media, if it hadn't been for an erroneous—or, let's say, overblown—headline in the Berlin paper *Der Tagesspiegel*. It read, FIRST BERLIN HAUPTSCHULE GIVES UP AND DEMANDS TO BE CLOSED DOWN. In reality, the teachers had said nothing about "giving up" or "closing down." Apparently one of the cosignatories had leaked the internal letter addressed to the school inspector to the public; there was no way he or she could have foreseen the misleading headline, or the uproar that ensued. In any event, overnight and for several weeks, the small Rütli School in Neukölln and its 270 students became the pet project of a suddenly extremely concerned public and the subject of countless comments.

The official in charge of the Department for Education, Youth, and Science of the Berlin Senate, Siegfried Arnz, had been in the position for only two years at the time. He was a man of practical experience, who, before going into school administration, had worked as a teacher and principal for thirty years, most recently at one of Berlin's most difficult *Hauptschulen* in the Nord-Tempelhof district. Arnz had taken over the school at a point when it didn't have a single voluntary enrollment. The student body was 98 percent immigrant, and all newly assigned students had been rejected by other schools.

In four years, Arnz had succeeded in turning the school into one of the most sought-after *Hauptschulen* in the district. Suddenly the school was inundated with requests for available spots. Arnz's recipe, as simple as it was successful, was participation: you have to convince the students to do something for themselves. The teachers alone don't determine what should happen in the school; the students have a say as well. The teachers don't ensure that the bathrooms are kept clean; the students are responsible for overseeing the toilets. It's not up to the teachers to enforce the ban on smoking; the students themselves designate a smoking area and make sure that the rest of the school building is a no-smoking zone.

The night before the incendiary *Tagesspiegel* article appeared in print, Siegfried Arnz spent hours in front of his computer. He read the online version and watched how, in next to no time, a tsunami of public indignation bore down on him. With the tabloid press leading the pack, the entire German media jumped on the *Tagesspiegel* headline. Arnz, who by this point was in charge of education in the Senate, decided not to waste a single second trying to discover the whistleblower. Instead, he saw the indiscretion and misleading headline as a chance to push for fundamental school reforms he had long sought. He had always opposed the *Hauptschule* as a type of school. The uproar over the Rütli School, he decided, was an excuse to make a change. He referred to it—initially just to himself, later publicly as well—as the "Rütli momentum."

It was clear to Arnz that he had to find someone to save the school that very night. Not a typical civil servant, but a charismatic figure and—since he or she would be a civil servant entitled to a pension in any event—why not a hero, capable of turning around the negative energy at the Rütli School? From his years as a principal, he remembered a successful colleague from a *Hauptschule* in the Reinickendorf district, Helmut Hochschild, with whom he had occasionally exchanged ideas at the time. Before the end of the night, Arnz had convinced Hochschild to take on the Rütli School challenge. He felt weak in the knees when he introduced the new man to the Berlin media—not just the entire German press, but the international press as well. Dozens of journalists and camera teams jostled for position in the small room, filled well beyond capacity.

That same day, Arnz, Helmut Hochschild, and the school senator at the time, Klaus Böger, reported to the Rütli School. The senator and Arnz began by introducing the new interim principal to his teaching staff. The introduction was met with polite silence. The next, more important, meeting was with the student council.

Arnz and the new principal didn't hold any long speeches. They said: You know what the situation is here at your school; you know what your teachers are saying. We don't even want to know what's true and what isn't. What we want to know is: What're we going to do now? What do you want? What's next?

By getting the faculty and students to work together on every problem, Hochschild succeeded in making a new spirit of personal responsibility popular at the Rütli School. One of the first things they agreed on was keeping the press out of the school—because, now that the issue had made the headlines, an army of reporters was hunting for new stories every day. *Bild* had published pictures of a fight in front of the Rütli School; it later turned out that the paper's reporters had incited several students to act out the scenes in question. But the excessive public attention also had a positive side, Arnz reports. Civil society offered to help the school in various ways, lending a hand by volunteering and donating money. The introduction of so-called student companies was also a big success. Hochschild, who had experience teaching *Arbeitslehre*—a subject encompassing theoretical and practical lessons to prepare students for employment—encouraged students taking this class to found student companies and produce sellable products. "Rütliwear" was the motto. Rütli students made T-shirts and other items, which they sold at weekly markets.

One problem Hochschild encountered was the composition of his teaching staff. As part of reunification, teachers with civil servant status from the East had been redistributed more or less at random across the entire Berlin region. The senate hadn't given much thought to the makeup of the teaching staff in the respective schools. Without the slightest preparation or special training, teachers from East Germany, who had never dealt with the children of immigrants, let alone those of the Muslim faith, had been transferred to schools where such students made up 80 to 90 percent of the total student body. It just so happened that the majority of the Rütli School's teaching staff was from former East Germany. That said, the teachers from the West who taught there hadn't exactly distinguished themselves as pioneers of their profession either. Arnz remembers a teacher from his years as the principal of another school, a "lazy" instructor who had been shown to neglect his teaching duties and whom Arnz had wanted to get rid of at the time. Sparing herself the arduous and usually futile process of suspending the teacher, the school inspector in charge of the matter had simply transferred the teacher to another school. And who should be the first person Arnz saw on the morning he introduced Helmut Hochschild to the Rütli School's faculty? None other than the teacher he had once hoped to fire.

In analyzing the Rütli School's resources, Arnz and Hochschild discovered to their surprise that this school of all schools had above-average facilities. In particular, it had many language-teaching resources at its disposal. But what good are resources if no one avails themselves of them? Every school was required to present its own concept for language instruction. The Rütli School had barely made use of its resources, which were considerable compared with those of other schools in Neukölln, and its students' language skills were correspondingly abysmal. The notoriously high rate of sick leave among teachers, which functioned according to a revolving door principle—when one teacher came back from sick leave, the next one called in sick—exacerbated this deficiency.

An entertainment group from the United States, which had heard about the Rütli School from the endless hubbub in the media, came to the new principal's aid. With financial support from, among others, a European Union cultural fund, the Young Americans and their school tours initiative had been traveling through Europe for some time. Time and again they had succeeded in reviving the community spirit in problem schools and in schools people had basically given up on by putting on musical performances with their students and staff. The first prerequisite for their work was that any school that agreed to the experiment had to suspend regular classes for a week, and all students and teachers had to support the project. The second prerequisite was that the students' parents had to contribute financially to covering the costs of the project and had to put up the roughly twenty-five artists in their homes.

In the case of the Rütli School, satisfying this second requirement was out of the question. The students' Muslim parents were neither willing to accommodate the artists nor to contribute financially. But the Americans didn't let that dissuade them. They agreed to waive a significant chunk of their usual remuneration and slept in cheap hotels. The Rütli School struck them as the ideal candidate for their project: "Rütli tanzt—wir können auch anders" ("Rütli dances—there *is* another way").

Hochschild, the new principal, did what he could to make

the most of this unexpected hand from abroad. Getting the teaching staff excited about the project proved to be much more difficult than doing the same with the students. But there was no time for drawn-out efforts at persuasion. The show had to go up in a week. The American group's principle was as simple as it was uncompromising: any student or teacher who wanted to participate was expected to get up onstage and do his or her thing.

The performance, which hundreds of other *Hauptschule* students attended, was a resounding success. Dressed in yellow, red, and orange T-shirts, the students sent the audience into raptures with their solos and dance numbers. Some did hip-hop routines, others stole the show with a song; whenever the students struggled, the American pros sang along with them or covered their slipups with improvisations of their own. A surprising number of teachers participated, performing standout renditions with the students of songs including "Let It Be," "I Believe I Can Fly," and "We Are Family." The Ghetto Jokers—all the bands and solo numbers had been created just days before the premiere—sang: "We sit alone here in our mess / And everyone else couldn't care less." One fifteen-year-old strutted his stuff with an original rap: "I'm from Neukölln and I'm ready as can be / I live on my own terms here, it's plain to see."

Arnz remembers watching adolescent Arabs from the Rütli School standing next to West Coast Americans and singing their hearts out as if they'd never done anything else in their lives. It had given him goose bumps.

Hochschild gradually managed to change the composition of his teaching staff. He had gotten the Senate to agree to allow him to let reluctant teachers go. "Whoever can't stay, can leave," he told the astounded faculty. Far fewer teachers than expected ended up taking him up on his offer. And those who did agree to transfers were replaced by new teachers, provided that Hochschild gave his approval. This was a first: even though the education act of 2004 guaranteed principals a voice in hiring new teachers, in practice this rule had hardly ever been applied. Hochschild was able to hire young and enthusiastic teachers capable of keeping the new momentum going at the school. Unlike in the United States, where teachers at comparable schools may earn more but have only five-to-eight-year contracts, every teacher in Germany enjoys lifetime tenure.

After the performance, media coverage of the Rütli School also changed. Headlines like VOM SCHIMPFWORT ZUR MARKE—FROM CURSE WORD TO BRAND NAME—replaced the earlier negative captions. The once ridiculed Rütli T-shirts became trendy and started showing up in clubs. After the *Hauptschule* merged with the neighboring Heinrich-Heine-Realschule (another form of secondary school), the once notorious compound became a community school and celebrated model: Campus Rütli.

For the students, probably the most important part of the experience was that they were seen for their preferences and talents rather than their weaknesses. It was only in the process of preparing their musical numbers that they had come to know and respect themselves—and some of their teachers. Principal Hochschild did what he could to ensure that the musical experiment didn't end after this one performance. In fact, the musical groups, as well as the teams that had designed the costumes and sets, continued their work and soon put on shows of their own.

With the help of Neukölln's mayor Heinz Buschkowsky, a 540,000-square-foot "social space" for five thousand residents was built on the compound, along Rütlistraße. It includes two kindergartens, a music school, and an adult education center that offers language courses for parents; sports fields are being renovated, and a job center is planned for the future. The main idea behind the project goes back to the concept known as "district management," which is based on the premise that individual aid measures such as language instruction, replacing teachers, et cetera, don't work on their own. For a turnaround to be successful, the entire environment—parents, recreational activities, supervision of children and adolescents, criminal context—needs to be taken into account. In the case of the Campus Rütli, the scheme seems to have worked.

Above all—to Siegfried Arnz's great satisfaction—the plan to establish *Gemeinschaftsschulen* (literally "community schools," a new type of secondary school) is now being implemented throughout Berlin. From now on, the city will no longer have any secondary schools that don't offer students the possibility of earning the kind of diploma that will give them the option of pursuing university studies. As part of education reforms made in 2010, 150 *Hauptschulen*, *Realschulen* (secondary schools that are ranked higher than *Hauptschulen* but lower than the academically oriented *Gymnasien*), and *Gesamtschulen* (comprehensive high schools that have replaced the traditional three-tiered secondary school system of *Hauptschule*, *Realschule*, and *Gymnasium* in many parts of Germany) in Berlin's twelve districts have been transformed into 120 integrated secondary schools.

The unexpected success of the Rütli School has many supporters and sponsors, who are keeping the Rütli momentum going with money, private initiatives, and sponsorship. Neukölln's other problem schools enviously eye the generous resources that have poured into Campus Rütli.

"What we have to achieve," according to Arnz, "is to win the children of immigrants over to the values of our democratic society as early as possible. In twenty years, 85 percent of newborns in Neukölln will be Muslim. If we let them slip through our grasp, we're going to have an enormous problem on our hands."

HELP, THE SWABIANS ARE COMING!

I knew the eastern Berlin district of Prenzlauer Berg from before the fall of the Wall. Among the friends I used to visit there at the time were Klaus Schlesinger, and Gerd and Ulrike Poppe. Heiner Müller and his Bulgarian wife, Ginka, lived in a one-bedroom apartment on Kissingenplatz. I often asked myself when Heiner Müller actually found the time to write his impressive body of work. He always had friends visiting from the East and West, and most of them brought along the obligatory gift of a good bottle of whiskey. The bottle was usually opened in the afternoon and never lasted until the end of the evening, when guests from the West would have to set out to make the trip back across the border crossing point. The omnipresent Volkspolizei ensured that I saw virtually nothing of the streets and buildings I passed on my way to Kissingenplatz. East Berlin was nothing but one big tunnel to me, into which light only penetrated once I had parked my car on Kissingenplatz.

After the fall of the Wall, I drove back to Kissingenplatz once out of curiosity, even though Heiner and Ginka no longer lived there. I was stunned by the extent of the deterioration. All the façades that caught my eye hadn't been repaired since the end of World War II. The support brackets under Müller's small balcony were eaten up by rust; instinctively, I took a few steps back out of fear the balcony might come crashing down that very moment and crush me. How had I never noticed this decay in all my years of visiting Heiner? The state of the buildings alone would have made it clear to any impartial observer that East Germany was on its last legs. But I wasn't an impartial observer. Under no circumstances had I wanted to act the part of the arrogant "Wessi," who forces his hosts in East Berlin to see that they live in a condemned state. Any such impulses were reliably held in check by the bottle of whiskey we always immediately broke open.

Living in Prenzlauer Berg in the 1980s was a credo of sorts. Prenzlauer Berg was one of the few neighborhoods that had barely been damaged in the war. Eighty percent of its buildings—mostly six-story residential structures with apartments without individual bathrooms and a communal toilet on the landing—had survived largely unscathed. The communist regime had dispossessed the vast majority of private owners. Only a few avoided this fate; the Kommunale Wohnungsverwaltung (KWV)—Communal Housing Administration—managed most of the apartments. Those owners who did manage to hold on to their property titles were punished through rent control, which kept their income from tenants so low that it didn't even cover the cost of repairs. The buildings deteriorated so rapidly that the authorities lost track of which apartments were even still habitable.

Young families and tenants who believed in the "real socialism" were drawn to the newly erected *Plattenbauten* in Hellersdorf, Marzahn, and Hohenschönhausen. There they found apartments that, even though they had lower ceilings, featured bathrooms, toilets, central heating, and television outlets. Those who stayed behind in Prenzlauer Berg were people who didn't particularly care about the living standards in the *Plattenbauten*—or rather, who didn't mind the shortcomings of the old apartments: writers, artists, intellectuals, contrarians, adventurers—people leading every kind of precarious existence. And that was how Prenzlauer Berg turned into a sort of habitat for nonconformists, whom Mielke's "company" suspected of being dissidents. Indeed, almost all protests in East Berlin—against the escalation of the arms race, the militarization of kindergartens, and the East German Communist Party's election fraud, which finally led to the great rally of November 4, 1989—began at the Gethsemane Church in Prenzlauer Berg.

One of the last holdouts in Prenzlauer Berg today is the literary historian Wolfgang Thierse, a former member of the civil rights movement and of the New Forum. In January 1990, he joined the SPD and became the first chairman of the East SPD. In 1998, he became president of the German Bundestag and, in 2005, its vice president—an office he holds to this day. In the years after reunification, Thierse stood out for his full beard—typical of many civil rights activists. At the time, beards like his had become the subject of profound debate. The culture supplements of West German newspapers wondered whether the beards sported by the dissidents perpetuated a primal male pride that had fallen victim to westernization in former West Germany and was now deserving of protection, like an endangered species. Others saw it as a vestige of a type of male who hadn't yet broken free of his old German—or Germanic—heritage. In the end, it was the female sex that decided the fate of the East German beard. Men with full beards, it turned out, enjoyed significantly less favor among women. As a result, most full beards succumbed to this noiseless yet efficient process of selection, making way for significantly pared-down variations: the original big, bushy beard was replaced by a wide palette of carefully pruned goatees and mustaches. Incidentally, this also led to the rediscovery of facial hair among West German representatives of the sex. Wolfgang Thierse resisted this evolutionary pressure for a long time before finally settling on a compromise. Today, his chin sports only the elegantly trimmed remains of the full beard that for so long prevented women from following the movements of his lips as he brought forth polished sentences in the finest High German.

For forty years, the Thierses have been living in an apartment located at one of the most coveted addresses on today's international real estate market: Kollwitzplatz. They still rent the apartment. Thierse turned down the official residence in the western district of Dahlem that he was entitled to as president of the Bundestag. The only reason he can still afford his Prenzlauer Berg apartment, he explains with a laugh, is because he still has the old rental agreement from the East German days. In fact, over the course of decades, with the help of relatives in the West, he personally paid for every improvement made—central heating, a tile bathroom, private toilet, built-in kitchen. The floor-to-ceiling bookshelves in the living room and hallways reveal the mark of creative chaos of a learned literary historian and voracious reader who has imposed his own order onto his library. The kitchen and back of the apartment look out onto the wall of Berlin's largest inner-city Jewish cemetery. Thierse has always felt drawn to this cemetery. Back in the East German years, wanting a view of it, he obtained permission to break two windows into the rear wall of his apartment. He also managed to get ahold of a key to one of the side entrances from the cemetery caretaker. On countless solitary walks between the graves, he explored the names, dynasties, and histories of the Jewish families that had once risen to prominence and wealth in this city and had found their final resting place here. From the dates on the gravestones, Thierse could trace the rise of Berlin's Jewry in the eighteenth and nineteenth centuries, and its abrupt end. One of the most recent graves in the cemetery belongs to little Vera Frankenberg. Thierse would sometimes see an older man standing by this grave. Striking up a conversation with him, Thierse learned that the girl had been killed during one of the last bombardments of Berlin; because of her Jewish background, she hadn't been allowed into the bunker and hadn't survived the air raid. For a long time, Thierse was haunted by a memorial plaque at the entrance to a gated shaft, which allowed a glimpse into a narrow pit. The inscription reads:

NOT WANTING
THE DEATHS OF OTHERS
WAS THEIR DEATH.
IT WAS HERE THAT PACIFISTS
HID AT THE END OF 1944.
DISCOVERED BY THE SS
THEY WERE HANGED FROM THE TREES
AND BURIED IN THE GROUND HERE.

Thierse soon knew more about the genealogy of Berlin's Jewish families than the members of East Berlin's small Jewish community did. When he took Avi Primor, the ambassador of Israel to Germany from 1993 to 1999, on a tour of the cemetery, Primor was unable to hide his astonishment at the former East German's extensive knowledge.

Already before the fall of the Wall, Prenzlauer Berg had cultivated a unique mixture of poor bohemians. The East German authorities had been quick to shut down the first "Kinderladen," a kind of antiauthoritarian alternative kindergarten, on Husemannstraße. After reunification, an idiosyncratic arts scene exploded in the dilapidated backyards: painters without galleries and poets without publishers invited the public to free exhibitions and slam poetry festivals. At the time, the neighborhood wasn't on the radar of any West German or Swedish investors. During the run-up to the first postreunification elections, the grizzled writer Stefan Heym had canvassed for the Party of Democratic Socialism (PDS), which replaced the former Socialist Unity Party of Germany (SED), by claiming that Prenzlauer Berg was going to turn into the biggest poorhouse in Berlin—nay, in Europe. Thierse, his social-democratic challenger, declared that, to the contrary, this barely damaged and relatively central district with its young, partly university-educated population had a great future. Heyms's apocalyptic prognosis, dovetailing as it did with the electorate's worldview, won out. But though Thierse lost the elections, his prediction proved to be right.

It wasn't long before an international run on the neighborhood began. The complicated name Prenzlauer Berg, explains Thierse, "soon fell from the lips of European and overseas investors, who barely knew where the neighborhood was located, more easily than the names Frankfurt and Munich." Apartments in new buildings financed by major real estate funds were snatched up before ground was even broken. Lawyers, managers, and accountants bought condominiums for themselves and their children; today, newcomers make up 80 percent of the neighborhood's population—90 percent at the southern end, near Kollwitzplatz. The new arrivals are predominantly young families with children; most are academics with good jobs in administrative bodies or businesses. The streetscape is dominated by stroller-pushing mothers and fathers, crosswalks, and one-way streets that exasperate drivers unfamiliar with the area. The proportion of foreigners remains lower than in the rest of Berlin and hasn't reduced the preponderance of white complexions—it is mostly other Europeans and Americans, and rarely Turks, who have taken up residence in Prenzlauer Berg.

Today, Prenzlauer Berg is considered the district in Europe with the most children—not necessarily to the delight of the "digital bohemians" with their iPhones and tablets, who try to maintain the greatest distance possible between themselves and child-toting patrons in the cafés. Yet the single and the childless already seem to have lost the battle against total domination by tots, who thunder across the cobblestones in their chunky plastic cars and have never heard a single word of admonishment from their parents' lips.

In late 2012, a harmless remark by Wolfgang Thierse set off a media storm that lasted for weeks. Half seriously, Thierse complained about the fact that the saleswoman at the corner bakery had looked at him blankly when he had asked for a *Schrippe*—the Berlin term for a "roll." In order to be served, he was obliged to replace the Berlin expression with the Swabian word *Wecken*.

Lately, he had also found himself having to utter the Swabian idiom *Pflaumendatschi* instead of *Pflaumenkuchen* when he wanted a piece of plum cake. Thierse crowned his criticism with a mocking remark about the Swabian mania for cleanliness: "They come here because everything's so colorful and adventurous and lively, but once they've been here for a while they want things to be the way they are back home—you can't have it both ways . . . My hope is that the Swabians will realize that they're in Berlin now and no longer in their small towns with *Kehrwoche*"—literally "sweeping week," a tradition of making households responsible, in rotation, for cleaning shared sidewalks and public spaces.

Without suspecting it, with his appeal for Swabian assimilation, Thierse had struck at the very heart of German-German sensitivities in Prenzlauer Berg—except that this time it wasn't about the well-known differences in mentality between East and West, but between North and South. A significant number of Berliners consider newcomers from the southern German state of Swabia the epitome of the wealthy, order-obsessed gentrifiers they resent. Thierse received three thousand e-mails. "Asshole" and "pig" were among the kinder names he was called; he was reviled as a Nazi and racist. Swabian political VIPs laid into him. One Swabian EU commissioner in Brussels piped up, reminding Thierse that Berlin depended to a significant extent on the equalization payments Swabians made for the indebted capital, as part of the federal financial equalization system—in Germany, the wealthy southern states, including Bavaria, Baden-Württemberg, and Hessen, are required to surrender a portion of their surpluses to households in the poorer northern states. It was only thanks to the billions from the south that Berlin could afford its "racy lifestyle," he argued. Writing in Berlin's most popular tabloid, one critic asked what problem the vice president of the Bundestag had with cleaning and clean streets anyway—after all, dilapidation was the capital's biggest problem; did Thierse feel at home only in a "dilapidated Berlin"? An aged cabaret performer from Munich tried to defuse the argument by remarking that the smell of urine and mildew in Berlin's U-Bahn stations always filled him with joy: as a Luftwaffe (German air force) assistant during the last years of the war, he had always associated the smell of going down the stairs into a U-Bahn station with "vacation." The cabaret performer's remark promptly led one polemic commentator to snidely recommend that a central U-Bahn station pumped full of every imaginable odor be reserved for the generation of Luftwaffe assistants.

The feud said more about how cut off from the wider world Germany's better circles are than about the reality in Berlin. Because, the fact is, the second most common compliment foreign tourists to Berlin report back to their compatriots is how clean Berlin's streets, train stations, and public transportation are. Italians, Spaniards, and Greeks have been known to go into veritable raptures on this issue. The impression made on visitors from the German south, on the other hand, is an entirely different matter. There's no doubt that, compared with the standard of cleanliness of the Swabian capital, Stuttgart, reunified Berlin retains traces of its old grubbiness. But a global metropolis that tried to live up to the ideals of Stuttgart or Zurich wouldn't *be* a global metropolis. A certain vestige of disorder and laxer attitudes regarding building rules, business closing times, and nighttime noise limits stand for something that, if anything, is more important than cleanliness: tolerance and open-mindedness. In reality, the influx of Swabians to Prenzlauer Berg was already causing a fair amount of resentment, along with slurs like "Swabians—out!," long before Thierse uttered his remarks. Swabians in Prenzlauer Berg are accused of wanting to introduce not just *Wecken* and *Pflaumendatschi*, but also other aspects of their lifestyle into their new habitat: all restaurant tables should be cleared from the sidewalks by 10:00 p.m. sharp, excessively lively parties reported to the police, and nighttime quiet and cleanliness treated as holy. How are the poor Swabians supposed to know that even though most of these rules also apply in Berlin, the police enforce them only if one neighbor reports another for violating them? As rumor happens to have it, the number of report-happy neighbors has risen noticeably since the invasion of the Swabians.

The truth is, the dispute about the Swabians in Prenzlauer Berg merely brought to light a point of contention that now affects all the city's coveted residential areas. The Swabians represent a wealthy minority that is infusing money into a formerly neglected district, pushing out the "natives" who sustained and breathed life into it. As it happens, Berlin's new well-heeled residents are by no means thronging to its traditionally bourgeois neighborhoods. They also aren't eager to eat out at three-star restaurants every day. What they want is to breathe in the air and adventure of the alternative lifestyle that developed in formerly or still poor areas such as Prenzlauer Berg and Kreuzberg. But by buying and renovating apartments and buildings in these neighborhoods, they're driving out the very untamed life that drew them there in the first place. Prices in the trendy bars are rising, as are rents; no longer able to afford living in their old neighborhoods, artists and other creative types are being forced to move out. At the end of this process, the new owners of the formerly trendy areas will find themselves alone with themselves and their ilk, and, in quiet moments, will ask themselves why they even moved here in the first place.

So far, this process of displacement has been facilitated not only by Berlin's various mayors but by all the mayors of the western world—who, indeed, have basically declared it a law of nature that no city can escape. According to their gospel, there simply is no such thing as a human right according to which tenants may stay in a neighborhood whose rents they can no longer afford—an argument that sounds so logical that objecting to it immediately elicits suspicions of communist sympathies.

Lately, there are signs that this principle is cautiously being abandoned in Berlin—a compromise model. Recently, the municipal government introduced several measures against a wholesale selling out of the city, prompted not least by the campaigns of so-called antigentrification activists. Historically, "gentrification" simply means expulsion—the displacement of an area's traditional inhabitants by more well-off nonlocals with deep pockets. As used by Berlin's militants, the combat term has degenerated to rowdy cries like "No more trolleys!," "Burn the tourists!," and "Fist the tourists!" For a while, Berlin's *Autonome* scene, with its absurd attacks on organic grocery stores, so-called luxury cars, and cafés selling latte macchiato, trivialized the matter, which certainly deserves to be taken seriously.

In fact, the city is now tentatively tackling the problem that the wildly raging actions of the antigentrification activists did more to discredit than illuminate. More and more voices are being raised loudly against the logic of blindly accepting the highest bid for urban construction areas, demanding that money not be the last word. We've already seen the extraordinary success of the KaterHolzig club. Its bid for a property it never could have acquired in an open competition was accepted thanks to a new restrictive covenant, according to which the cultural value of certain construction areas are to be given priority over their market value.

Independently of the Berlin Senate, several district city councils have also opted to take into account criteria other than market value. Jens-Holger Kirchner, the city councilman for construction in the eastern Berlin district of Pankow, decided to prohibit luxury renovations—and associated rent hikes—in several residential areas. In these areas, owners are no longer allowed to install parquet floors, floor-heating systems, or fireplaces. Needless to say, the heralds of the free market economy are up in arms about these limits. Have we somehow ended up, via a detour that took us through the revolution and reunification, back in the world of dictatorship and central planning? they ask. They're not entirely wrong to allude to the political origins of this sort of interference. Because of course it isn't coincidental that, to date, it has affected only the left-governed districts of the former East German capital: Pankow, Prenzlauer Berg, and Weißensee. On the other hand, so far the indignant market fundamentalists have failed to come up with any alternative suggestions as to what might be done to curb the market-driven logic of displacement.

A BELATED CEMETERY VISIT

Just months after visiting Wolfgang Thierse, I made a trip to the Jewish cemetery on Schönhauser Allee. The dense canopy of leaves overarching the cemetery offered me shelter from the incipient rain. Many of the headstones and tree trunks are overgrown with ivy. Hebrew names and inscriptions predominate on the oldest gravestones. The dates of birth and death are indicated according to the Jewish calendar; the Christian calendar dates and corresponding inscriptions are recorded, if at all, on the backs of the headstones. On more recent graves, the Christian calendar dates and standard phrases like PEACE ON HIS ASHES and HERE RESTS IN PEACE jump to the front. On the occasion of the cemetery's inauguration in 1827, Jacob Joseph Oettinger, the first rabbi buried here, gave his speech in German, for which he was reprimanded by the Prussian government for "imitating Christian customs." The orthodox members of the Jewish community voiced similar criticisms. Yet the process of assimilation was inexorable. Soon, only the Star of David on the gravestones still attested to the deceased's Jewish identity. Many of the men buried here bear first names like Carl, Ludwig, Gustav, Herrmann, Max, Hartwig, Heinrich, Herbert, Otto—there's even a Siegfried and an Adolph among them—and last names like Schneider, Müller, Meyer, Beer, and Lessing; names like Abel, David, Moses, Israel, Goldstein, Lilienthal, and Friedländer are in the minority.

But, as I see it, the most important message the gravestones convey is about the deceased's professions and the mark they left on the city's history.

Take, for example, the neobaroque tomb of the banker Gerson von Bleichröder, whose bank took a leading role in financing the German railway and industry. Even though he was granted hereditary nobility and gave a great deal of money to charitable causes, he remained an outsider in Germany's upper class.

A simple gravestone in the shape of an obelisk pays tribute to the publisher Bernhard Wolff, the founder of the first German news agency and a cofounder of the liberal *National-Zeitung*, which became one of Berlin's highest-circulation newspapers.

For sixty years, the tomb of the politician and banker Ludwig Bamberger stood in the cemetery without a name or inscription. Sentenced to death for his participation in the Revolution of 1848, Bamberger had fled to Switzerland. Thanks to an amnesty granted in 1866, he was able to return to Berlin, where he became a cofounder of Deutsche Bank, which he left again two years later. The Nazis removed his name from his grave, as they also did in the case of his political companion Eduard Lasker. It was only in 2001 that, with the support of the cultural foundation of Deutsche Bank, which was very slow to remember its Jewish founders, the original name and dates were restored.

An orientalized tomb—a circular granite pavilion with columns—honors the memory of Georg Haberland, who was the director of the real estate development company Berlinische Boden-Gesellschaft. Under his direction the incorporated companies Schmargendorfer Boden AG and Tempelhofer Feld AG—on whose grounds the Tempelhof Airport was later built—were created. Haberland's son Kurt, who joined the board of managers in 1929, was forced to sell his shares as part of the Aryanization of Jewish businesses. In 1942, he was murdered in the Mauthausen concentration camp. A family mausoleum made of marble became the final resting place of another branch of the Haberland family. The textile manufacturer and *Kommerzienrat*—councilor of commerce, an honorary title—Salomon Haberland, together with his son Georg, implemented development plans elaborated with the help of a first-class advisory group. The Haberlands' most well-known projects include the Bavarian Quarter and Wagner Quarter in Berlin-Friedenau.

A sober black funerary stele memorializes one of the greatest physicians of his day: James Israel, who volunteered in the Franco-Prussian War and, in 1875, was entrusted to manage Berlin's Jewish Hospital. Globally renowned as a surgeon and diagnostician, he declined the offer of a chairmanship—on condition that he be baptized—at the University of Berlin. Nevertheless, he was the first doctor to receive the title of professor without first having qualified formally for a professorship.

Three truncated obelisks honor the memory of the family of the publisher Leopold Ullstein, whose publishing empire was Aryanized and confiscated in 1934 and reverted back to the family in 1945. In the 1950s, in financial straits, the empire was gradually taken over by Axel Springer Verlag.

An inconspicuous, extremely weather-beaten tomb made of shell limestone is the final resting place of the women's rights campaigner Josephine Levy-Rathenau, a niece of the foreign minister Walther Rathenau. She founded an information office for women's issues, which specialized in educational and income-related questions regarding the professions that were open to women. In 1918, she and her husband joined the newly founded liberal-left German Democratic Party, and she became the Tiergarten district city councilwoman.

The composer Giacomo Meyerbeer is also buried in the Jewish cemetery on Schönhauser Allee, even though he died in Paris in 1864. In the early nineteenth century, his father Jacob Judah Herz Beer was considered Berlin's wealthiest citizen; his mother's father Liepmann Meyer Wulff was called the "Croesus of Berlin." Even though Giacomo Meyerbeer became the Prussian general music director in Berlin, he lived primarily in his countries of choice, France and Italy. It wasn't until the twentieth century that his role in nineteenth-century opera music was recognized. The state of Berlin granted him an honorary tomb.

Another honorary tomb memorializes the *Märzgefallene*, or "March dead," who took a stand for a free and united Germany and lost their lives in the street fighting that broke out in Berlin on March 18 and 19, 1848. The dead included "twenty-one Israelites, which—considering the population ratio of 8,000 to 400,000—is a very large number," the *Allgemeine Zeitung des Judentums* wrote at the time. Two of them were given a place of honor in the Jewish cemetery on Schönhauser Allee.

Probably the most famous figure in the cemetery is the painter Max Liebermann, who is interred here with his wife, Martha, and his brother Georg. Martha committed suicide by taking an overdose of barbital after the death of her husband and before her imminent deportation. Her mortal remains could be transferred from the Jewish cemetery in Weißensee to the honorary Liebermann family tomb only in 1954.

It wasn't until after my visit to the Jewish cemetery on Schönhauser Allee that I discovered the importance of one grave so unassuming I had barely noticed it—a black gravestone with the sober inscription JAMES SIMON, BORN SEPTEMBER 17, 1851, DIED MAY 23, 1932. I was almost done writing this book before I realized that Berlin's most important and generous philanthropist and patron of the arts was buried here.

I found myself alone in this vast field of graves under the rain, the chorus of all these voices, fallen silent so long ago, swirling around me like a powerful music. All of them, everyone who was buried here, had once belonged to this city—had wanted to belong to it—had shaped, influenced, and improved it through their work as doctors, publishers, lawyers, civil servants, workers, artists, scientists, bankers, and entrepreneurs. Attesting to the lives and activities of Berlin's Jews as it does, the cemetery struck me as a wonderful memorial site that inspires awe and gratitude above all—in contrast to the guilt that memorials to the murdered Jews inevitably elicit in Germans of my generation, which easily stifles empathy and admiration for their accomplishments, for what they left behind in their lives, and in the life of the city.

THE MAN WHO GAVE NEFERTITI AWAY

Until the fall of 2012, the name James Simon had all but disappeared from the city's memory. Only experts still knew about him—despite the fact that Berlin's Museum Island probably never would have reached its international standing without this philanthropist's generous gifts. The present-day Pergamon Museum owes him the Ishtar Gate and the Procession Street of Babylon, which probably never would have been recovered from the depths of Mesopotamia and been shipped to Berlin without the excavations Simon financed. He enriched the Gemäldegalerie with important pieces from the Middle Ages, a major Renaissance collection, and priceless paintings and etchings by Rembrandt, Bellini, and Mantegna; gave the present-day Bode Museum (known as the Kaiser Friedrich Museum in Simon's day) his collection of Italian paintings, along with valuable fifteenth-to-seventeenth-century medals and sculptures; and bequeathed all of the spectacular finds—including the bust of Nefertiti—from the excavations at Tell el-Amarna, which he funded, to the Neues Museum.

A few isolated historians and connoisseurs, including Cella-Margarethe Girardet, Olaf Matthes, and Bernd Schultz, kept Simon's memory alive but received far too little recognition for their pioneering work. Credit for most recently bringing this unusual man to wider public attention goes to the journalist and director Carola Wedel, whose many books and television programs documented the renovations of Museum Island after the fall of the Wall. The figure and fate of the forgotten philanthropist James Simon became her passion. After prolonged research and trips that took her halfway around the world, she managed to track down the few surviving photographic and written documents by and about Simon. She discovered that the Pergamon Museum's entire Near East Museum—or twenty-six of its twenty-eight rooms—can be traced back to this one man and his commitment. In December 2012, Wedel presented her moving film about Simon's work to German television audiences: *Der Mann, der Nofretete verschenkte: James Simon, der vergessene Mäzen* (The Man Who Gave Nefertiti Away: James Simon, the Forgotten Philanthropist).

James's father, Isaac, a skilled tailor from the Uckermark region of Germany, had made his fortune together with his brother Louis with a cotton and linen factory in Berlin. Amassing large stores of cotton, the Simon brothers were able to satisfy rising demand when the Civil War in the United States caused shipments from America to dry up. Isaac Simon, who considered himself a Prussian Jew, sent his son James to the Berlinisches Gymnasium zum Grauen Kloster (Berlin Gray Cloister High School), already then a famous elite Protestant institution. It was probably here that James's early love of the sciences of antiquity—archaeology in particular—was born. For his father's sake, however, he forwent studying the classics, instead joining the family business when he was twenty-five. Under his leadership the Simons' cotton business became the biggest in the sector on the European continent. In boom years, annual turnover reached 50 million reichsmark, with 6 million in net profits. Simon became one of the richest men in Berlin. He belonged to a small group of Jewish bankers and entrepreneurs who were invited to the kaiser's "gentlemen's evenings"— Chaim Weizmann, the first president of the State of Israel, mocked them as "Kaiser Jews." No doubt the infatuation with "the Orient" that took hold of the aristocracy and vast swaths of Germany's bourgeoisie around the turn of the century also infected James Simon. Watching the archaeological triumphs of the colonial powers France and England with envy, Kaiser Wilhelm II, who himself had gone digging in Corfu, wanted to compete with them. With the kaiser's blessing, James Simon and other like-minded individuals founded and financed the Deutsche Orient-Gesellschaft (DOG; German Orient Society), which present-day historians consider the "archaeological spearhead of Germany's imperial cultural ambitions in the Orient." But, unlike the other German Orient enthusiasts, James Simon was driven by his thirst for knowledge and artistic sensibility: he wanted to investigate the roots of Judaism and walk in the footsteps of Abraham. As the director of the society, he singlehandedly funded the excavations of its chief archaeologist, Ludwig Borchardt. He sought the advice of the greatest experts of his day for his art acquisitions and for the excavation campaigns he financed. When Wilhelm von Bode, who later became the general director of Berlin's museums, would visit Simon in his stately villa by the Tiergarten, his host would often let him choose whatever he liked for his museum: the present-day Bode Museum.

In Tell el-Amarna, two hundred miles south of Cairo, Borchardt discovered an entire ancient archive of sculptures, which included numerous portrait heads of the Pharaoh Akhenaten and his family, and a bust of his wife, Nefertiti. On December 6, 1912, in his journal, Borchardt remarked laconically on this find: "Colors as though just applied, very excellent work. Describing is useless; to be seen." Borchardt's clumsy sketch of the find below this entry looks like a cartoon drawing by a six-year-old.

Discovered in 1912, the Queen of the Nile was only displayed publicly in Berlin for the first time in 1924. James Simon, who immediately recognized the beauty and value of the find, initially didn't understand why Borchardt warned him about showing it publicly. Apparently the archaeologist worried that exhibiting the bust might disrupt future excavations in Egypt. Simon followed his advice. Indeed, he invited only the kaiser to view the bust in his villa, even though His Majesty's visits always gave Simon and his wife a slight case of the jitters: after all, if the emperor's eye happened to fall on an art object that inspired him to particular praise, Simon hardly had any choice but to make a gift of it to him. On this occasion, Simon precluded any such impulses by giving the kaiser a copy of the Nefertiti bust that he had commissioned.

For the time being, Simon kept Nefertiti for himself. In her film, Carola Wedel "re-created" a scene that isn't captured in any surviving photograph: James Simon sitting at his desk in his villa, the original bust of Nefertiti on the desktop diagonally across from him. In fact, the bust apparently stood there for two years. We can only speculate how the magic of this three-thousand-year-old beauty from Egypt influenced Simon's dreams and work. Yet, as far as he was concerned, it was a given that he wouldn't keep this treasure for himself. In 1920, Simon donated the bust—which is now insured for 390 million euros—along with other gems from Tell el-Amarna to the Egyptian Museum of Berlin. He did so despite the fact that his company was in dire straits at that point—rayon and viscose were conquering the market. Yet it never would have occurred to Simon to consider his artistic treasures as an investment he could fall back on in case of an emergency.

To mention only Simon's contribution as a patron of the arts would be to tell only half of this unusual philanthropist's story. Following an old Jewish tradition, to which Simon's grandmother had introduced him, Jews were expected to give roughly 10 percent of their earnings to charitable causes. Simon didn't stick to this share. Year after year, he spent at least a quarter of his income on social initiatives and his art collections, which he then almost invariably gave away. And while, today, this only just rediscovered patron is renowned for the artworks and collections he bequeathed, Simon actually dedicated the vast majority of his donations to social projects: he organized and funded special concerts by the Berlin Philharmonic for members of the working class, with tickets priced between thirty and eighty pfennigs; built a holiday camp for the children of workers on the Baltic Sea at his own expense; founded the Association to Protect Children from Abuse and Exploitation and financed the Haus Kinderschutz (Children's Welfare Home), a large residence in Zehlendorf for child workers; and established public bathhouses—a total of more than half a dozen in Berlin—for the poor, who couldn't afford regular personal hygiene. He established kindergartens, schools, teachers' seminaries, and the Haifa Technical College in Palestine. Watching the anti-Semitic pogroms in Eastern Europe with increasing anxiety, he financed and organized the emigration of Eastern European Jews from Romania, Russia, and Galicia as the president of the Aid Association of German Jews. Sealed westbound trains crossed Germany, their passengers allowed to get off only once they reached the port of Hamburg, where they boarded boats to the United States and Palestine. Ten years later, scaled freight trains crammed with Jews would make their way out of Nazi Germany and the occupied territories in the opposite direction.

After the demise of his cotton business, Simon sold the two most valuable pieces in his collection—a painting each by Franz Hals and Jan Vermeer—to the United States, where they now hang in the Frick Collection. He deposited the proceeds and a large part of his private fortune into his employees' pension fund. He didn't expect any gratitude for it, in keeping with his motto "Gratitude is a burden one shouldn't impose on anyone." He was forced to sell his stately Tiergarten villa, where he then stayed on as a tenant in his own house. After the death of his wife, Agnes, he continued to live there alone on the ground floor for a few years before finally moving to an apartment on Kaiserallee (now Bundesallee) in the Wilmersdorf district. A photo shows the living room of his last apartment, filled with paintings, books, and furniture—far too small to accommodate even the remains of the villa's furnishings. Simon died in 1932, half a year before Hitler seized power.

One rumor has it that James Simon's closest family members were spared deportation only because of Hitler's passion for Nefertiti. But while Simon's son, Heinrich, managed to flee to the United States with his family just in time, his daughter Helene had to beg and plead for her life. Irene Bader, a great-granddaughter of James Simon, spoke about her mother's—James Simon's granddaughter's—fate in a radio interview on the German public broadcasting station Deutschlandfunk: "She was 96.5—or 97.5—percent Jewish according to the 'Race Laws,' after all. So in January 1945, she received an order to proceed to Theresienstadt. Leaving behind a suicide note saying that she was going to drown herself, she managed to find a hiding place with a peasant family, where she worked as a farm girl."

But the Nazis didn't stop at threatening James Simon's relatives with annihilation. They attempted to wipe out every last trace of this patron and philanthropist: the commemorative plaque in the Amarna room of the Neues Museum; all references to his donations and related correspondence. It was unacceptable that a Jewish German should have made such an exceptional contribution to Berlin's museum culture. East Germany, under whose authority Museum Island fell after the war, also didn't have much interest in resurrecting the memory of this Jewish "upper-class bourgeois"; in 1982, the director of the Gemäldegalerie made a laudable exception when she organized a commemoration for James Simon. Even after reunification, it took the city another ten years to rediscover its greatest patron.

The bust of Nefertiti has been a bone of contention ever since it was first exhibited publicly in 1924. The dispute continues to this day, and the legal arguments of the parties involved are as complicated as the jurisdictions in Egypt during the colonial era.

The year of the bust's excavation, Egypt was under British administration, but French officials were responsible for the supervision
of antiquities. James Simon had negotiated a valid license agreement with the Egyptian state for the excavations he funded in
Tell al-Amarna. Among other things, the agreement stipulated
that half of the finds—based on a division to be made under supervision of the French officials—would become the property of
the finders; the other half would stay in Egypt.

In the case of the finds from Tell el-Amarna, the French antiques inspector in charge, Gustave Lefebvre, had chosen an unusual antique folding altar. The colorful stele showed Akhenaten
and Nefertiti with their four daughters; in exchange for this altar,
Lefebvre was willing to leave the bust of Nefertiti to the Germans.
Without a doubt, Lefebvre's decision was one of those mistakes
that can rob a person of a good night's sleep for the rest of his
life, and his historical misstep was inevitably followed by a series
of accusations, speculations, and allegations, which resurface
regularly every few years and include the claims that Lefebvre
hadn't been able to get a good idea of the singularity of the find
based on the "unfavorable black-and-white photos" of Nefertiti;
that Nefertiti's face had been smeared with clay when the bust
was transported away; that the Egyptian folding altar that had so
captivated Lefebvre, causing him to overlook Nefertiti, was actually a fake.

It was Lefebvre's successor Pierre Lacau, a veteran of World
War I and a noted anti-German partisan, who set in motion the
chain of restitution claims that continues to this day. In the summer of 1925, Lacau had conceded that, based on his research, the
finds had been properly presented with "complete and accurate
lists" and "good photographs": "So it is a question of our own mistake . . . I think we are defenseless, legally speaking." Yet, despite
this admission, that same year Lacau imposed the very moratorium on excavations by the German Orient Society that James
Simon had feared.

And so the discussions regarding Nefertiti's restitution continued under the Nazis. On October 4, 1933, Hermann Göring, the
prime minister of Prussia at the time, decided to give the bust to
the Egyptian king Fuad I. It was Adolf Hitler who put an end to
the dispute at the time. In the führer's opinion, Nefertiti belonged
to the Reich. He resolved to build a new museum for her.

The restitution demands were taken up again most recently
in January 2011 by the Minister of State of Antiquities Affairs under Mubarak, Zahi Hawass. He alleged that Nefertiti had been
deliberately defaced with clay and smuggled out of the country
illegally. Moreover, according to him, only the German Orient
Society and the French antiquities administration had been involved in the division of the finds in 1912—the Egyptians had
never been consulted.

Zahi Hawass lost his position in the course of the Arab Spring
in Egypt. But, even though the scholarship largely agrees that
James Simon was the rightful owner of the Nefertiti bust, it wasn't
long before an antiques administrator appointed by the Morsi administration took up the old accusations and demands again—
possibly with more convincing arguments this time. For, as it
happens, a present-day dispute between Egyptologists has provided new fodder for the old rumors. Apparently the most recent
UV-light analysis of the folding altar, carried out in a laboratory in
Cairo, has shown the "find" to be a forgery. The German Egyp-
tologist Dietrich Wildung dismissed this conclusion as "a load
of bull," while his colleague Christian Loeben insisted that, to
the contrary, it provided "absolute proof of forgery." In addition,
other recently discovered documents have cast doubt on the exca-
vator Ludwig Borchardt. There are claims that he had contacts
with forgers and copyists. Should the suspicion of forgery be confirmed, Borchardt's name is likely to appear at the very top of the
list of suspects. Whatever the final outcome, it's clear that the dispute over Nefertiti's ownership is the stuff of enduring conspiracy
theories.

After everything that has happened, isn't it time "to generously give the Egyptians back their cultural heritage?" *Der Spiegel* asked the director of the National Museums in Berlin, Hermann Parzinger. Biting the bullet, Parzinger replied, "Nefertiti is part of humanity's cultural heritage. I fundamentally do not think that restituting the bust simply for generosity's sake is justifiable."

Parzinger points to the fate of major artistic monuments in the most recent wars in Iraq and Afghanistan. If all the museums of the former colonial powers decided to give the art treasures they acquired or robbed back to their countries of origin, this might benefit the respective governments of these countries, but not necessarily the artistic treasures themselves.

Yet the conflict persists. For Parzinger knows, of course, that James Simon himself was ready to exchange Nefertiti for other "pieces of equal rank" in the museum in Cairo. In fact, Simon feared that restituting the bust was the only way to ensure that further excavations would be possible. In her film, Carola Wedel shows a letter from Simon to the director of the Egyptian Museum in Berlin. In this open letter, Simon reminds the director that he has already agreed to return Nefertiti; in keeping with proper business etiquette, a promise made must be kept. Simon even threatens to take back his gift. As it happens, the director of the Egyptian Museum, too, had been ready to make the trade. But the restitution of the by now world-famous bust was prevented by a public storm of indignation kindled by the press. Deeply wounded, Simon accepted the decision of the museum he had so generously endowed. But he sent back the two invitations he had received to the opening of the Pergamon Museum.

The fact that James Simon, the rightful owner of this icon— which is the undisputed star of Museum Island today—advocated returning it to the Egyptians still inflames passions to this day. The *Tagesspiegel* culture editor Bernhard Schulz stresses the fact that "the era of dividing the finds in archaeology had come to an end with World War I." Possibly Simon didn't realize that there was no future for the excavations that he financed in the Middle East. In any case, Simon's willingness reveals an attitude that is foreign to today's art industry. Evidently this art lover didn't particularly vaunt himself on having landed the most spectacular and valuable art object in the world. What he cared about when it came to his collections and donations was that an art epoch be represented in a coherent manner. To him, Nefertiti was without a doubt an exceptional—an adored—unique piece of the culture of Amarna. But more important to him than Nefertiti was the future of the excavations and of Berlin's museums, which he wanted to continue to fill with works of art that would bring them to international renown.

It was only on the hundredth anniversary of Nefertiti's discovery, eighty years after Simon's death, that his work was finally given the recognition it deserves. Simon will now be remembered as a humble giant of philanthropy and art patronage. Since 2006, the James Simon Foundation, created by Peter Raue and Bernd Schultz, has been working to ensure that this bighearted patron's work is given a place in the city's memory. A bronze bust and commemorative plaque at the Stadtbad Mitte on Gartenstraße, a public swimming pool built by Simon, evoke his memory. The future entrance to the main hall of the Neues Museum by David Chipperfield, who has already added a wonderful staircase to the museum, will bear Simon's name. On the other hand, for now, the only tribute to him in the Bode Museum is the tiny James Simon cabinet, which holds just two small Italian Renaissance porcelain reliefs he donated. The cabinet makes reference to hundreds of works of art donated by Simon, but fails to provide any information whatsoever about what became of these objects or where they are today.

The attempt to name a street in central Berlin after James Simon failed due to an idée fixe—or, more precisely, a resolution—of the members of the municipal council of Berlin Mitte. According to this resolution, no more streets in the city's Mitte district may be named after men until an equal number of streets bear the names of deserving women.

But this story has another hero too. If Berlin is finally honoring the Jewish patron who originally brought Nefertiti to Germany, it owes a little-known American officer for the fact that the bust remained there after 1945. At the time, the then thirty-year-old architect Walter I. Farmer was assigned by the U.S. Army to oversee the safekeeping of art and to head the Central Collection Point (CCP) in Wiesbaden. It was here that, after the war, hundreds of boxes of paintings, sculptures, relics, and copperplate engravings were brought, which the U.S. Army had unearthed from the bunkers, mine shafts, and tunnels where the Nazi authorities had kept them stashed. A medium-size box marked "The colorful queen" was among them.

On November 6, 1945, the White House ordered Farmer to prepare two hundred valuable paintings from the Gemäldegalerie and the Nationalgalerie to be shipped to Washington, D.C. Farmer was outraged by this order. For, unlike the Soviet Union, the American occupying forces followed the principle that all art treasures collected during the war were to be returned to their rightful owners. The next day, Farmer succeeded in rounding up almost all of the army's thirty-two officers in charge of the safekeeping of art at the Wiesbaden CCP. Together, they wrote a letter of protest dated November 7, 1945, whose key sentence read: "We wish to state that, from our own knowledge, no historical grievance will rankle so long or be the cause of so much justified bitterness as the removal for any reason of a part of the heritage of any nation even if that heritage may be interpreted as a prize of war."

The letter of protest was too late to prevent the shipment from leaving for the United States, though Farmer did make sure that Nefertiti wasn't included. There is a commendable coda to this story. After *The New York Times* and other American papers published the officers' letter, public opinion in the States succeeded in changing the mind of the newly elected American president Harry S. Truman. In 1949, all of the paintings were returned to Germany.

Shortly before his death in 1997, during a visit to Germany, Farmer reported that he had often spent hours gazing at the beautiful Egyptian at night. Nothing in his life had ever moved him more deeply than his time alone with Nefertiti.

JEWISH LIFE IN BERLIN

An acquaintance of mine from the United States, who visited Berlin for the first time shortly after the Wall came down, surprised me when he told me that, though he was impressed by the atmosphere of renewal in the city, he worried about the "future of the past." In his walks around town, he hadn't come across a single memorial in a central location that commemorated the Holocaust. I told him that there probably wasn't another city in the world that had created as many and different kinds of places of remembrance as Berlin—there must be well over a hundred in all. And a central memorial near the Reichstag was also still being debated at the time (it has since gone up). Yet, in showing him some of the sites, I discovered that their messages weren't accessible to foreign visitors, since the texts were usually provided only in German.

Since then, like almost everything else in the city, Berlin's culture of remembrance has also undergone a radical transformation. I remember a memorable dispute in the city's cultural bureaucracy in 1993. The Schöneberg district wanted to set up a new form of memorial to honor the roughly sixteen thousand Jews who had lived there. Katharina Kaiser, the woman in charge of organizing the exhibition, wanted the poster for it to feature not one of the typically used documents of horror, but the face of a young woman instead. The exhibition would then show this young woman's progression through all the stages of disenfranchisement and discrimination, through to her deportation. If possible, it would also show the same for hundreds of other Jewish families that had been residents of Schöneberg. The exhibition would focus on the living rather than the dead; its aim was to individualize the victims to prevent them from being swallowed up by the vast anonymous number of the murdered and exiled.

I interviewed Katharina Kaiser at the time. She told me that the new concept had caused fierce disputes in the team—tears had been shed, cruel words spoken, friendships broken. The approach seemed to cast doubt on the holiest tenet of the existing culture of remembrance: namely, the conviction that the only way to elicit the necessary shock among future generations was by representing the full extent of the crimes committed. Some of Kaiser's colleagues felt somehow betrayed by her claim that showing the fate of a single person and his or her family is more likely to inspire empathy than citing the total number of victims. After all, in the first three decades after the end of the war, Germany's culture of remembrance had been dominated almost exclusively by images of horror: freight trains in motion, nameless emaciated concentration camp survivors, piles of hair, shoes, or corpses plowed by bulldozers. One only ever thought—when one thought of them at all—about the murdered Jews, not about the fact that they had been living people. It was only the U.S. television series *Holocaust*, broadcast in Germany in the late 1970s, that finally broke this death-fixated tradition of remembrance. The show was about the fate of the German-Jewish Weisses, among them a woman, played by Meryl Streep, who had married into the family, though she was not herself Jewish. After an extended period of persecution and disenfranchisement, most of the family end up in the gas chambers of Auschwitz. The series was seen as a tremendous provocation in Germany. Depicting the Holocaust using the "methods of the American family saga"—so went the typical objection—didn't do justice to this crime. Yet the enormous success of the series attested to the effectiveness of this approach. The show generated the first wide-scale discussion about the Holocaust in Germany.

Katharina Kaiser's Schöneberg exhibition drew visitors in droves and changed people's idea about this kind of exhibition in the city. The original 1993 exhibit *Formen der Erinnerung* (Forms of Remembrance) has now become a permanent installation in the Schöneberg town hall titled *Wir waren Nachbarn: Biografien jüdischer Zeitzeugen* (We Were Neighbors: Biographies of Jewish Contemporaries)—and the accompanying texts are also available in English:

> Apart from the 131 biographical albums, the display includes a further five elements: On the wall there are filing cards with the names of more than 6,000 former inhabitants of Schöneberg and Tempelhof who were deported and murdered, with street names in alphabetical order. Apart from the names, these cards bear the last address as well as date and destination of the transports. Visitors of the exhibition are surrounded by the filing cards and thus get an impression of the vastitude of these campaigns. Last but not least the filing cards mark the first stage of the project.

Unfortunately, Katharina Kaiser's concept has barely made any inroads in German schools. I was born in 1940 and learned next to nothing in school about the Third Reich and the crimes perpetuated against the Jews. But the way students today are overwhelmed with facts and data about the Nazi terror is not necessarily a recipe for success. It's not rare for them to be confronted with images of horror from Auschwitz as early as the age of ten. In junior high and high school, the Holocaust is addressed in no less than three subjects: biology, history, and German. As I see it, the oft-lamented ignorance of German students about the Holocaust has little to do with a lack of information, but rather with the kind of information they are given: even though teachers claim to have the opposite intention, inundating students with horrifying data elicits feelings of guilt and defensiveness more than anything else. Students are confronted with the workings of a murder machine that was operated by criminals, obsessive racists, and subordinates willing to blindly follow orders, and that nipped any attempt at resistance in the bud. They are far more familiar with the names of the prominent criminals than with the civilian heroes who hid away some thirteen hundred Jews in Berlin. Yet why did Spielberg choose to make his film *Schindler's List* about a tarnished hero of all people, who, despite his involvement with the Nazis, saved more than a thousand Jews? After all, Schindler is hardly representative of the Nazi Party. Apparently Spielberg wanted to show his audience that even in a perfect regime of terror people retain some measure of choice—and that there were people who exercised this choice.

Today, Berlin's culture of remembrance has adopted the principle of "less is more." There are now a multitude of memorials in Berlin that counterbalance the weight of the enormous, unfathomable numbers with a more regional and local approach. One of the most successful examples is the memorial by Renata Stih and Frieder Schnock. In Berlin's Bayrisches Viertel (Bavarian Quarter), Stih and Schnock have attached signposts to eighty streetlamps. On one side of these signs, pictograms of simple objects and goods—bread, a bag, a thermometer—describe the commercial environment of the time. On the other side, there are short quotations from the German anti-Jewish laws of the 1930s and 1940s, including: "Only respectable national comrades of German or congeneric blood may become garden plot holders. 22.3.1938." The first signs provoked a wave of phone calls to the police—residents thought that neo-Nazis had blanketed the neighborhood with anti-Semitic slogans—and they had to be removed. The signs were later put up again, now accompanied by explanatory texts.

Stolpersteine—literally, "stumbling stones"—is the name of another initiative that had its beginnings in Berlin and has since spread across Europe. It began as an illegal campaign by the conceptual artist Gunter Demnig in 1996. In front of the entrances to buildings in Berlin, Demnig laid down gold-colored metallic stones the size of cobblestones, onto which he had engraved the names of former Jewish tenants of these buildings. He had to win some peculiar battles before his idea managed to prevail: Charlotte Knobloch of the Jewish Community pointed out that stepping on "gravestones" is against Jewish tradition; the fiscal authorities initially refused to grant him the reduced value-added tax that generally applies to creative works. In 2000, Demnig's project was finally recognized and given the legal green light. Since then, he has laid down 3,000 *Stolpersteine* in Berlin, and well over 35,000 have been placed throughout Europe. Volunteers now research the biographies of the Nazi victims and handle the financing: each *Stolperstein* costs 120 euros.

In 2005, a central Holocaust memorial opened near the Reichstag. The debate over this memorial had lasted for seventeen years. It was passionate, wild, ambitious, banal, highly philosophical, grotesque, and magnificent. There was no argument that wasn't made during the course of this debate, and none that wasn't just as quickly refuted; there was no left or right front that lasted, no Jewish or non-Jewish bastion that didn't have defectors. Jewish intellectuals explained that they didn't need the memorial and considered it completely superfluous or even harmful; others claimed it was long overdue. Some non-Jewish spokespeople agreed with the former group, others with the latter. Opponents of the memorial changed their minds overnight, emerging as vehement advocates the next day—and vice versa.

Essentially, there were three groups of questions at issue. (1) Do we even need a central Holocaust memorial—and who is "we"? Won't a central memorial also "centralize" memory and detract attention from the fact that the concentration camps are Germany's, and Europe's, real memorials? (2) How big should the memorial be? Is it really necessary for the size of the crime to be reflected by a memorial that would cover the entire extensive area set aside for it south of the Brandenburg Gate? Is it even possible to come to grips with the Holocaust through aesthetic means? (3) Should the memorial be dedicated exclusively to the Jewish victims of the Holocaust, or should it also include other groups, such as the Sinti and Roma, homosexuals, Jehovah's Witnesses, and Polish and Russian prisoners of war, who were murdered in the concentration camps and other camps? And if it were going to be the former, wouldn't it be necessary to immediately start looking for other suitable places in the city for these other groups of victims? This last issue in particular unleashed a dispute of incomparable acrimony. The Jewish journalist Henryk Broder asked Senator Peter Radunski, who was trying to justify the memorial's exclusivity, why, according to his scale of values, "Jewish Nobel Prize winners rank higher than Romanian gypsy fiddlers"—since, if that weren't the case, there would be "no reason to once again select and hierarchize the victims of the Nazis."

The attitude of Berlin's Jüdische Gemeinde, or Jewish Community, toward the question was contradictory. Dating to 1671, the Jewish Community of Berlin represents the religious, social, and legal interests of its members. It is considered the official, and to a large extent respected, voice of Berlin's Jews. After being dissolved and destroyed by the Nazis, it regained recognition in 1946. On October 3, 1990, the day of German reunification, the respective Jewish communities of East and West Berlin also merged. When it came to the Holocaust memorial in Berlin, the speakers of Berlin's Jewish Community emphasized on the one hand that it was a German, and by no means Jewish, project. On the other hand, they left no doubt about the fact that they wanted the memorial to be exclusively for the Jewish victims of the Holocaust.

Yet it was the proposals submitted for the Holocaust memorial that posed the greatest difficulties. An unlikely mixture of naïve symbolism, guilty conscience, megalomania, and a county-fair aesthetic seemed to muddle the minds of many of the participants in the competition. One presented a model for an enormous carousel on which freight cars of the sort used for the transports to Auschwitz would circle through the air. One day, a friend of mine who was participating in one of the many committees told me that he and a small group had finally hit upon the solution to the Holocaust memorial. It was simple, honest, no-frills: put up a brick smokestack in the city, more than 330 feet tall, from which smoke would pour incessantly. "And how will you produce the smoke, what are you going to burn there?" I asked. He looked at me, at a loss. Another proposal imagined a grave slab the size of a soccer field rising diagonally from the ground, onto which the names of all of the victims of the Holocaust would be carved. The German artist Jochen Gerz wanted to populate the available terrain with thirty-nine tall lampposts. Neon letters on each post would inscribe the question "Why?" into the sky in the thirty-nine languages spoken by the persecuted Jews. Over the course of the years and decades, answers provided by visitors to the memorial would then be engraved into the ground plate beneath the artwork, which would supposedly have room for 145,000 answers.

The "nonmonument" proposed by the previously mentioned artist duo Renata Stih and Frieder Schnock stood out from this aesthetic and moral mishmash. Instead of turning the space near the Brandenburg Gate into a memorial, they wanted to build a bus station there, from which buses would leave regularly for concentration camps and other sites in Europe associated with the German extermination machinery.

The design of the New York duo Peter Eisenman and Richard

Serra ultimately emerged victorious from the final round of the competition. Reminiscent of tombstones, dark gray concrete steles of various heights, arranged in narrow, parallel rows, cover a slightly undulating surface of some 4.7 acres. Thanks to the initiative of the state minister of culture Michael Naumann, an urgently needed museum, the so-called Place of Information, was added to their design for the memorial; the originally planned number of steles of various heights was reduced from 4,000 to 2,711. Richard Serra, who refused to accept these and other changes, pulled out of the project. On June 25, 1999, the Bundestag voted to build the Memorial to the Murdered Jews of Europe, which was then ceremoniously inaugurated on May 10, 2005.

Anyone who visits the memorial, which has already become a Berlin landmark, can only conclude that, after all the quarreling, warnings, and adjurations, after the passionate and cutting statements for and against it, something great has been accomplished here. Amazingly, the sheer essence of the memorial nullifies virtually every objection that was raised against it. You can't, nor would you want to, imagine that any other memorial could have stood here. Despite its size, it blends into the cityscape virtually seamlessly. It doesn't overwhelm visitors with any sort of symbolism, nor does it force a sense of guilt on them. "The place isn't suited for state ceremonies and also balks at the meaning people are likely to attribute to it of being a sort of *ex negativo* national memorial," the authors Claus Leggewie and Erik Meyer conclude. Walking on the uneven ground, which seems to sway slightly, through the forest of steles, which from the outside looks like a wind-tossed sea of dark gray stone, you may and can think about anything: partying at Berghain last night, your impending wedding or divorce, or the genocide of the Jews—and of all the other victims of the Holocaust.

According to data from the Central Council of Jews in Germany, 220,000 Jews have immigrated to Germany since reunification. The Jewish Community in Berlin is considered the fastest growing of its kind in the world. The program and executive director of the Jewish Museum in Berlin, Cilly Kugelmann, cites twelve thousand Jewish Community members; add to this the thousands of Jewish residents who, like Kugelmann herself, *aren't* members. The German press speaks of some seventeen thousand Israelis living in Berlin. As Israelis, they are entitled to a German passport if their parents or grandparents were Jews expelled from Germany. Kugelmann's explanation for this development is very practical: "Just as today's Germans aren't as German as they once were, today's Jews in Germany also no longer live a typically Jewish everyday life—and in that respect of course they have a shared future." What's new in Germany, Kugelmann continues, is the fact that even secular Jews openly profess their Jewish identity and experience this identity as positive.

After reunification, Kugelmann explains, there was a growing influx of Central and Eastern European and Russian Jews to Berlin. The Russian Jews had been cut off from practicing their religion since the October Revolution, and many of them didn't even know what Jewish customs, religion, and identity meant anymore. The Soviet Union didn't allow people to practice the Jewish religion—or any other. In the Soviet Union, Judaism was considered an ethnicity and a nationality, for which the autonomous oblast of Birobidzhan was created near the Chinese border, where naturally no one wanted to live. As a result, the *Yevrey* were Russian citizens of Jewish nationality. Religion was beside the point.

According to an arrangement between Germany and the Soviet Union, a Jewish family was allowed to immigrate to Germany if one of its members was Jewish according either to the halacha, the Jewish religious laws, or to Russian citizenship laws. In Germany, the local organized Jewish communities were then responsible for assimilating these *Yevrey*. However, only about half of all

Russian-speaking Jews actually became members of these communities. First, they had to—and wanted to—find out what membership would mean for them in concrete terms; ultimately, many of them weren't interested in establishing a long-term connection to a Jewish institution.

Cilly Kugelmann distinguishes between various phases of Jewish immigration to Germany. The Jews who came to Germany from the East right after World War II were survivors of the Holocaust; they were mostly traditional and religiously oriented, and most had survived the camps or returned from the Soviet Union to Poland, from where they had then flown further westward. Every major political crisis—from the Polish October in 1956 under Gomulka and the Hungarian Revolution that same year, to the last wave of anti-Semitism in Poland and the Prague Spring in 1968, to the victory of the Islamic Revolution in Iran in 1979—brought new Jewish refugees to Germany who shared a similar outlook. Until the 1990s, Jewish life revolved almost exclusively around the idea of Zionism: many supported the fledgling Israeli state emotionally and ideationally, some contributed financially, some even immigrated there.

But now, the newest arrivals, children of Russian-speaking immigrants, are no longer primarily interested in Zionism or the State of Israel. They learn German quickly and want to succeed and build careers for themselves in the new world in which they are growing up. The postwar Jewish community's profound coming-to-terms with Zionism and with the history of persecution in Germany has been replaced by an increased return to its own religious roots, which, interestingly, coincides with a fundamentalization of religions around the world. Powerful religious trends can be seen in Berlin today. The Hasidic Chabad-Lubavitch group is very visible in the city and has a growing following; on the other hand, communities with more liberal congregations influenced by modern American Judaism are also increasing their numbers.

In Berlin, newcomers from the former Eastern Bloc have out-numbered the long-established Jews of West Berlin for some time now—by a ratio of eight to two in the city's Jewish Community. The result is enormous tension between these two very different groups. Russian seems to be the main language spoken in the city's Jewish Community today. The old leadership accuses the new "Russian regime," under executive chairman Gideon Joffe, who was elected with a large majority by the "Russian faction" in 2012, of having used electoral fraud to seize power in a putschlike manner. One of the points of contention regards the pensions of the community's staff. Already under Heinz Galinski, the now long deceased former chairman, employees of the Jewish Community enjoyed higher supplementary pensions than those received by any other city employees. In recent years, the number of community employees has grown explosively—and, with it, the cost of their pensions, which the Berlin Senate is expected to pay. There is talk of 20 million to 40 million euros of debt, which the Berlin Senate is now reminding the Community that it owes. Insurmountable differences regarding other issues have also arisen between the old West Berlin leadership around Lala Süsskind, who became chair in 2008, and her successor, Joffe. The main point of contention has been the Jewish Community's new budget. The new leadership ignored the suggestion of Sergey Lagodinsky, a member of the opposition, to try to compromise and "reconcile." Violence broke out at a meeting; someone lunged at the throat of a member of the opposition—six cases of bodily harm were reported to the police. When Lagodinsky recorded the altercation with his cell phone, Joffe took it from him and deleted the file. Members of the opposition threatened to—and in some cases actually did—resign. The journalist Claudia Keller was reminded of the 1920s, when the "assimilated Jews from genteel Charlottenburg didn't want anything to do with the 'Eastern European Jews' from East Berlin's barn quarters."

In the meantime, according to Kugelmann, the Jewish Community is shrinking again. After all, she explains, its enormous expansion wasn't the result of natural growth but of the mass migration of sorts that began after the fall of the Wall. Moreover, Jewish communities throughout the country are registering many more deaths than births. Since 2005, Germany has insisted that only "halachic Jews"—people of Jewish origin on both their mother's and father's sides—have the right to immigrate to Germany. Kugelmann is convinced that Germany's Jews are about to enter into a new chapter. She believes that the concept of a "shared fate" has been "used up," that the Jewish community's symbolic role as the victim of the Holocaust is "finished"; young Jews no longer define themselves according to their parents' example. German society's interest in the Jews, so typical of the "old" Federal Republic, is also dwindling. Today's heterogeneous German society of 80 million people faces a completely different set of problems. "Jews in Germany," says Kugelmann, "now need to find their place as a minority among many other and larger minorities, or risk becoming marginalized as a *quantité négligeable*."

When I ask Cilly Kugelmann about anti-Semitism in Berlin, she tells me that she herself has only rarely experienced it. The last time was at a dinner where she ran into someone from a large Berlin publishing house, whose administration she had contacted to request a donation for a project. She didn't even know who had written the declining response, but its author now introduced himself to her of his own volition. He made no attempt to explain his reasons for turning down the request. Instead, he said, "Oh, you know, you have that little button under your desk, after all. All you have to do is push it and say, 'It's for something Jewish,' and you've got the money!"

In late August 2012, the German rabbi Daniel Alter was attacked by a group of Arab youths in the western district of Friedenau. "Are you a Jew?" they asked before beating him to a pulp in front of his six-year-old daughter. That same day, hundreds protested against the act of violence. At a demonstration in which more than a thousand Berliners took part, Daniel Alter addressed the participants with a bandage on his cheek. "I had my cheekbone broken," he said. "But those guys didn't break my determination to take a stand for interreligious dialogue." Alter also expressed his gratitude for the "wonderful wave of moral support" he had received in the days since the assault.

This perhaps is the most important thing to have changed in Germany since the attacks in the years immediately after reunification: anti-Semitic and racist incidents still occur, and they will continue to occur in the future. But, today, the public at large immediately rises up in force to respond to and condemn these acts.

The most surprising and unexpected phenomenon in the development of German-Jewish relations remains the influx of Israeli immigrants to Berlin. Not long ago, the United States and Canada were considered the destination of choice for Israelis looking to emigrate. In the last few years, however, Berlin has risen toward the top of this wish list. It is mostly young people who are drawn to the German capital: high tech experts, engineers, scientists, artists, creative types—and no small number of them are homosexual. The German public has become aware of this phenomenon only very recently—an awareness prompted in part through a Facebook post by the Israeli minister of finance, Yair Lapid, about a speech he gave to the Hungarian parliament in Budapest:

I came here [to Budapest] to speak before parliament about anti-Semitism and remind them how they tried to murder my father here, just because the Jews didn't have a country of their own; how they killed my grandfather in the concentration camp; how they starved my uncles; how my grandmother was saved at the last moment from the death march. I have little patience for people who are willing to throw into the garbage the only country the Jews have, because it's more comfortable in Berlin.

Instead of sympathetic agreement, a flood of comments from young Israelis, ranging from mildly critical to outright indignant, rained down on Lapid. An op-ed piece in the newspaper *Haaretz* reminded the minister that it was only thanks to the swelling wave of protest in Israel over the high cost of living and unaffordable housing and tuitions that he had been swept into the Knesset:

Rather than denouncing those who choose to leave Israel, Lapid would do better to take action about improving the situation. He is the finance minister and the party he heads has 19 Knesset seats. That empowers him to take steps to change the economic reality, not only complain about it in social networks.

Lish Lee Avner, a twenty-seven-year-old Israeli high-tech expert living in Berlin, also contested Lapid's view, writing:

I didn't leave Israel because of the three shekels separating one type of cheese from another or because of the rent. I lived in Tel Aviv, but I got a fantastic job offer from a Berlin-based international company, and in life one must know how to take advantage of opportunities, especially it [sic] involves great business development and a corresponding salary.

Yet Avner went even further, calling into question the core rationale of the official Israeli position on emigration to Germany:

Shouldn't we support the desire of Israeli citizens, whose family history includes Germany as well, to experience their family's past in this country when they have an employment opportunity allowing them to do so? Or should we beg them to stay in Israel because of the Holocaust?

And in general, the Holocaust is mentioned and Berlin immediately becomes a taboo. Anyone who ever visited Berlin knows that this city is like one big monument commemorating the Holocaust. Like high school students' visit to Poland to experience the horror, life in memory-filled Berlin creates a strong national experience among Israelis. Being in Berlin educates Israelis about the Holocaust and reminds them what Jewish identity is all about. [. . .]

Jewishness and Israeliness, therefore, are alive in Berlin too, and that's a good thing. Berlin offers not only the memory of the Holocaust but also a modern life: Restaurants and institutions established by Israelis, a Facebook group with 7,000 members who help each other work out the German bureaucracy, and the creation of friendships and important future relationships between Israelis and Germans.

The Israelis in Berlin are our ambassadors abroad.

It should be noted that the newfound enthusiasm and openness toward Germany among young Israelis concerns primarily Berlin. In no other German city has the attempt to confront the monstrous history of the crimes against the Jews resulted in so many memorials and places of remembrance. Yet it is also the city's turbulent present, with its nightlife and all that it offers the creatively inclined, that makes Berlin attractive to young Israelis. Those arriving from Tel Aviv feel at home in the unfinished German capital, which, unlike Frankfurt, Munich, and Hamburg, is not yet ruled by money. I remember a discussion in which I participated in Washington, D.C., in the 1980s. The renowned Israeli historian Moshe Zimmermann argued that the Holocaust had settled the question of the future coexistence of Jews and Germans once and for all. While I respected Zimmermann's position, I cautiously disagreed with him. But I never would have imagined that Berlin would become a city of dreams for the grandchildren and great-grandchildren of victims of the Holocaust. Of course it would be premature and misguided to speak of a new *convivenza* between young Jews and Germans in Berlin. After all, what motivates many Israelis to move here isn't just the destination, Berlin, but conditions back home as well. Many of these young émigrés have absolutely no intention of settling permanently in Berlin; they are more interested in putting some distance—temporarily, perhaps for a few years—between themselves and the tense and precarious situation in their native land: they are interested in taking a break from Israel. Whatever their reasons, the influx of seventeen thousand young Israelis to Berlin still strikes me and many of my generation as a miracle.

SPRING IN BERLIN

Some consider the period from November to March in Berlin a season for suicide—and even the fall of the Wall hasn't been able to change that. Often, weeks go by before a solitary ray of sunshine finally finds a crack in the leaden sky to peek through. What was the sentence that escaped Napoleon after his march into the city in 1806? "Six months of rain, six months of snow—and this is what these fellows call Fatherland?!" During the dark months, the city's forty-eight-hour-long parties and cultural goings-on seem to serve the sole purpose of consoling Berliners for this lack of light. But just when you've forgotten that seasons even exist, the first blackbirds in the city's courtyards pipe up to announce the end of the siege. At the sidewalk cafés, the first patrons sit at the tables outside—bundled in scarves and coats—with a glass of white wine, turning their winter visages to the afternoon sun. Though they can still see their breath floating skyward in little white puffs, that doesn't stop them from testing out their rusty voices and celebrating the end of the darkness. Bicycle messengers speed by, zipping past drivers flaunting their convertibles with the roof down and traces of snow on the hood. Motorcyclists in dark leather gear, in turn, overtake these maniacal cyclists and convertible show-offs, revving their machines to sixty miles per hour only to have to come to a stop seconds later at the next traffic light. During the first warm days of the year, Berlin's otherwise rather environmentally pious population acts out a Mediterranean ritual: anyone with an engine under his rear feels compelled to burn rubber and seems to think that only first and second gear exist.

I don't know of any other city that has changed as much—and for the better—as Berlin in the last five decades. The fall of the Wall and the reunification of Berlin's two halves have sped up the city's pulse, injecting new life energy into it. It's as if the city had won back a temporal dimension that, during the years of the Wall, seemed to have disappeared from West Berlin and was merely alleged to exist in East Berlin: the future.

In the summer of 2013, many beaming faces from Berlin's municipal government could be seen on television. The reason? For the first time in living memory, the city had generated a surplus of 750 million euros and was able to put forward a budget that would reduce the debt burden from 63 billion to 61.8 billion euros by 2016. Hurray! Only 61.8 billion euros of debt left! Sober viewers like me asked ourselves why a city like Detroit with a debt of $17 billion has to declare bankruptcy, while Berlin considers a debt burden four times as large a reason to celebrate!

This much is true: The world has tremendous faith in the city. Berlin is second only to the state of North Rhine–Westphalia in foreign direct investments in Germany. In response to the question of which three cities in the world were most likely to develop a company like Google, Berlin was the only German city named—albeit in tenth place, after cities like Beijing, San Francisco, and Shanghai. The city's information technology sector ranks fourth in the world—after those of Silicon Valley, Tel Aviv, and Singapore. Prophets claim that Berlin's expenditure of 3.5 percent of gross domestic product on research and development despite its enormous debts will pay off in the long term. And, today, entrepreneurs from around the world gleefully factor into their strategic considerations the fact that Berlin has two prestigious universities and 160,000 students.

Yet for all these future prospects, the city faces just as many challenges. In 2012 alone, Berlin grew by some 45,000 inhabitants. Assuming continued growth of this magnitude, by 2030 the city will have roughly 250,000 more inhabitants—the equivalent of a whole new district. There's no lack of space. Since Berlin—with or without the development of the Tempelhof field—has more vacant inner-city areas than virtually any other major city, it could easily accommodate even a million more inhabitants. But the city is already short some 100,000 apartments and has only hesitantly begun to tackle the construction of affordable new housing. Then there are the social problems associated with this growth. For, the number of persons aged eighty years and over is set to grow the most. By 2030, Berlin will have 120,000 more seniors than it does today—the equivalent of almost half of the total projected population growth. The anticipated growth at the other end of the demographic spectrum is much weaker: the number of children under the age of six years will remain roughly constant, at 200,000. The number of schoolchildren will increase only by roughly 64,000 to 400,000—as many schoolchildren as were last registered in the city in the years immediately after the fall of the Wall.

There's no doubt that what Berlin needs more than anything else are qualified immigrants who are willing to assimilate. In the last few years, the city has created some of the necessary prerequisites for this in the school and childcare sector. But Berlin needs the cooperation and involvement of immigrants at all levels. It needs more social workers, teachers, policemen, district mayors, and senators of Turkish, Polish, and Russian origins—and why not a mayor of immigrant background someday soon? Happily, the basic level of tolerance necessary for this has gradually begun to take hold in the city.

Berlin has also mastered a very different problem of integration better than most of the rest of Germany: overcoming the "Wall in the mind." Until the fall of the Wall, Berlin was the only city in Germany where people were confronted constantly with an unfinished chapter in their postwar history: the division of their country. Today, Berlin is the city in Germany where reunification has made the greatest progress. And that doesn't mean that the differences between the two German cultures have simply been leveled. It was always an illusion to believe that reunifying the two German states would leave behind nothing of East Germany but its green arrow turn signs and the now iconic little traffic-light men at intersections. In reality, the westernization of the East has long since been matched by the easternization of the West. For years, this trend has been confirmed by a triumphal procession of "Ossis" in literature and art. The Leipzig art scene, headed by Neo Rauch, succeeded in the New York art market with the help of pseudo-profundity-stammering gallery owners. Today, almost all the major literary awards go to writers from Germany's East—to the considerable annoyance of their West German colleagues—and hardworking officials from the new federal states have gained a foothold in all the important juries, commissions, and academies of the reunited republic. For all the resentment over the "Ossis" clientelism, who can deny that artists forced to overcome an existential break in their living conditions and to reassess all their values are going to have more to say than their western counterparts, who are mere observers of these enormous changes? In recent years, almost all of the major novels and movies about the division of Germany have been the work of writers and directors who grew up in East Germany.

In politics as well, the historical "losers" from the East have achieved astounding success. The fairy tale–like career of "Angie" (Angela Merkel) was an early indication. Here was a woman from the East who had managed to rise through the ranks of a male-dominated West German party, which had never shown any interest in the topic of "female emancipation" before, to become

Germany's first woman chancellor. Merkel ensured this success by confidently poaching in the garden of the Social Democratic Party (SPD), repotting virtually every viable seedling and relabeling each with the mark of the Christian Democratic Union (CDU). Thanks to this unscrupulous gardener, the value system of the reunified Germans has also shifted eastward, in the direction of "social values." The conservative wing of the CDU watches Merkel's machinations, nonplussed—after all, the protean chancellor guarantees majorities—while, on the other hand, many SPD voters no longer know why they should even vote for their party anymore. In the meantime, a second "Ossi" has also risen to the top ranks to become federal president—not necessarily to the delight of Angela Merkel, since Joachim Gauck comes from very different East German traditions, namely, the circle of dissidents. In short, things are getting mixed up in the Berlin republic; the old political lines no longer offer any certainty. Anyone seeking handy proof of this quiet yet nonetheless radical cultural shift in Germany has to look only as far as its current political representatives. For the past eight years, a former East German citizen has been governing the country; the federal president, also from the East, lives out of wedlock with his partner in Berlin's Bellevue Palace; the former secretary of state and the current mayor of Berlin are both cheerfully out of the closet.

Small but sustained miracles can be seen in Berlin's everyday life as well. While you still encounter the occasional self-righteous Berliner rudely yelling admonishments through an open car window, his is a dying breed—and he knows it. The long-absent expression "Excuse me!" and vanished acts of courtesy such as "Please, after you!" are finding their way back into the vernacular— which probably has as much as anything to do with the city's many newcomers, including the Swabians. Increasingly, visitors to Berlin tell me how friendly and polite Berliners are—and I catch myself thinking that they must be talking about a different city. Apparently some part of me is still living in pre-1989 Berlin.

Suddenly there are dog owners, their fingers sheathed in plastic, bravely gathering up their four-legged companions' offerings and disposing of them properly. A dog-owning friend of mine attributes this great leap forward in civilization to a new product offered online: it was only after dark plastic baggies specially designed for this purpose became available for sale that people adopted this habit. Others suspect that the change is due to the cleanliness-obsessed Swabians in Prenzlauer Berg. Whatever the reason, a pedestrian scraping the sole of his shoe against the curb has become a rare sight in the city.

And what has become of the pigeon plague? The hordes of pigeons I encountered when I arrived in Berlin have disappeared. Initially, I suspected that the city, behind the backs of animal-rights activists, had carried out a mass extermination campaign. But my research revealed that the decimation of Berlin's pigeon population is actually due to a process as complicated as it is gruesome. Over the course of years of small, cumulative efforts, the birds were fed contraceptives, the eggs in their nests replaced with plaster eggs, nets spread, and even the smallest ledges covered with metal spikes to prevent the pigeons from landing on them. In 2000, the authorities in Berlin estimated that there were 40,000 breeding pairs in the city. By 2012, according to the response of the undersecretary of the environment to a question by the CDU, the pigeon population had shrunk to just 4,827. Yet their natural predators—the hawks in Berlin—have proven to be the pigeon's deadliest foe. Apparently Berlin's hawks, which have increased dramatically in number since the fall of the Wall, devour some 19,000 pigeons a year. How anyone arrives at these figures is a mystery to me. Then again, in Berlin even the trees are counted.

What has survived the tumultuous changes are Berlin's landmark preservationists. After decades of watching helplessly or approvingly as entire layers of Berlin's history were torn down in the city's center, some of the members of this guild have suddenly turned radical. Of all things, they want to preserve the structural monstrosities that the architects of the communist dictatorship erected behind Alexanderplatz. In the eyes of these preservationists, the high-rise *Plattenbauten* from the East German years are simply part of the city's architectural history and should be preserved as landmarks. The preservationists don't claim that these atrocities are beautiful or even in good shape—their only reason for defending them is that they happen to have been built.

Berlin is facing a new battle between the defenders of long-standing eyesores and the advocates of a new architecture, which so often in Berlin has merely resulted in the creation of new eyesores. No one would deny that the *Plattenbau* towers near Alexanderplatz deserve several illustrated pages in a scholarly piece on Berlin's building history. But do they really need to stand there full-size and in full view of future generations—as a historical lesson and punishment for the construction sins of their forefathers? Imagining a future flaneur's stroll through the city, the Berlin journalist and city expert Peter von Becker muses, "What begins as the center of the capital at Unter den Linden would thus end in Pyongyang for all eternity."

Berlin lives on its ruptures. But that doesn't mean you want to wish the capital a central square—really *the* central square—that remains neither beautiful nor lively.

In the end, what has also survived all the turmoil are the city's natives with their quick-wittedness, tolerance, and will to survive. Perhaps no one has captured the current state of the city and its inhabitants' defiant attitude toward life better than the social worker Anneliese Bödecker. "Berliners," she casually remarked, "are unfriendly and inconsiderate, gruff and self-righteous; Berlin is off-putting, loud, dirty, and gray, with construction sites and congested streets wherever you happen to be or go. But I feel sorry for anyone who can't live here."

NOTES

CLASH OF THE ARCHITECTS

19 *"echoes of fascist architecture"*: Heinrich Klotz quoted in "'Bloß nicht diese Hauptstadt!' Heinrich Klotz im Gespräch mit Nikolaus Kuhnert und Angelika Schnell," *Arch+* 122, June 1994: 24.

19 *"I reject the idea that"*: Daniel Libeskind, "Berlin Alexanderplatz: Ideologies of Design and Planning and the Fate of Public Space," *The Journal of the International Institute* 3, no. 1, Fall 1995.

POTSDAMER PLATZ

29 *"one of the last examples of modern commercial architecture"*: Wolf Thieme, *Das letzte Haus am Potsdamer Platz: Eine Berliner Chronik* (Hamburg: Rasch und Röhring, 1988), 207.

30 *"the most hated construction project in Berlin"*: Manfred Gentz, interview with the author, November 2012.

38 *Wilder kept his celluloid dickey*: Hellmuth Karasek, *Billy Wilder: Eine Nahaufnahme* (Hamburg: Hoffmann und Kampe, 1992), 59.

BERLIN SCHLOSS VERSUS PALACE OF THE REPUBLIC

49 *"Once the Schloss is gone"*: *Berliner Extrablatt*, newsletter of the Association for the Berlin Schloss, September 2011.

53 *Goerd Peschken's study*: Goerd Peschken, Hans-Werner Klünner, Fritz-Eugen Keller, and Thilo Eggeling, *Das Berliner Schloss: Das klassische Berlin*, 4th edition (Berlin: Propyläen, 1998).

54 *Siedler pointed out that, unlike other European cities*: Wolf Jobst Siedler, *Abschied von Preußen* (Berlin: Siedler Verlag, 1991), 122.

61 *"I would not rebuild it"*: Helmut Schmidt in "Was soll das eigentlich?," an interview by Louisa Hutton, *Die Zeit*, February 7, 2013.

WEST BERLIN
81 *political leaders from dueling fraternities*: Members of dueling fraternities traditionally engaged in fencing duels with rival fraternities.

A "WESSI" ATTEMPTS TO FIND BERLIN'S SOUL
84 *the Gendarmenmarkt, which Karl Friedrich Schinkel enlivened*: More than any other architect, Karl Friedrich Schinkel, a multitalented contemporary of Johann Wolfgang von Goethe and Wilhelm von Humboldt, shaped the neoclassic center of Berlin in the first half of the nineteenth century.

BERLIN: EMERGENCE OF A NEW METROPOLIS
90 *"Four times as much space would hardly be"*: James Hobrecht quoted in Ulrich Zawatka-Gerlach, "Magistralen und Mietskasernen," *Der Tagesspiegel*, August 2, 2012.
90 *"In the center of the city"*: Peter Schneider, *The Wall Jumper*, translated by Leigh Hafrey (Chicago: University of Chicago Press, 1998), 4.
90 *"I found the house without difficulty"*: Christopher Isherwood, *The Berlin Stories* (New York: New Directions, 2008), 81.
93 *"Under socialism the client"*: Tom Wolfe, *From Bauhaus to Our House* (New York: Farrar, Straus and Giroux, 1981), 26.
94 *"It has been my wish for a long time now"*: Heinrich Himmler quoted in *Waldsiedlung Krumme Lanke* (Essen: GAGFAH Group in association with Landesdenkmalamt Berlin and Untere Denkmalschutzbehörde Steglitz-Zehlendorf, 2012), 12.
94 *Of the old street signs, carved out of wood*: Ibid., 17.

CITY WEST VERSUS CAPITAL CITY (EAST) AND VICE VERSA
98 *"Trepidation and veneration of the old"*: Quoted by Jörn Düwel in "Die Sehnsucht nach Weite und Ordnung: Vom Verlust der Altstadt im 20. Jahrhundert," *Berliner Altstadt: Von der DDR-Staatsmitte zur Stadtmitte*, edited by Hans Stimmann (Berlin: DOM Publishers, 2012), 49.

LOVE (AND SEX) IN BERLIN
106 *"The largest room in the villa"*: Christopher Isherwood, *The Berlin Novels* (London: Minerva, 1993), 52–53.

107 *"the most liberal place in the world"*: Dagmar Herzog, personal communication with the author, December 27, 2013. See also Herzog, *Paradoxien der sexuellen Liberalisierung* (Göttingen: Wallstein, 2013), 26: "To put it plainly, at the beginning of the twentieth century, Germany had the most liberal sexual culture in the world."

113 *A photograph shows him*: Jochen Brunow (ed.), *Scenario 3: Film- und Drehbuch-Almanach* (Berlin: Bertz und Fischer, 2009), 180.

LOVE IN DIVIDED BERLIN
119 *"We regularly drove to the East"*: Quoted in Deniz Yücel, "Türkdeutsche und Ostdeutsche: 'Diese verfluchte Einheit,'" *taz*, October 1, 2010.

LOVE AFTER THE FALL OF THE WALL
124 *"The number of women who never"*: Judith Fritz, "An der Schnittstelle von Konsum und Sexualität" (master's thesis, University of Vienna, 2011), 27.

THE GHOST OF BER INTERNATIONAL AIRPORT
173 *A raft carrying opponents*: Alexander Fröhlich, "Lärmbelästigung beim Flughafenchef," *Der Tagesspiegel*, August 20, 2012.

THE STASI LEGACY
185 *"The available records of the Ministry of State Security"*: Jochen Staadt quoted in Uwe Müller, "Die verlorene Ehre des Ulrich Mühe," *Die Welt*, January 14, 2008.

191 *"I find your attempt to romanticize"*: Claus Jürgen Pfeiffer's letter to Florian Henckel von Donnersmarck is published here for the first time, with the author's permission.

THE NEW RACISM
210 *In November 2012, a representative investigation*: Oliver Decker, Johannes Kiess, and Elmar Brähler, *Die Mitte im Umbruch: Rechtsextreme Einstellungen in Deutschland 2012*, edited by Ralf Melzer for Friedrich-Ebert-Stiftung (Bonn: J.H.W. Dietz Nachf., 2012).

ANETTA KAHANE AND THE AMADEU ANTONIO FOUNDATION
222 *"why I completely forgot about it"*: "Geständnis: Wolf von IM-Akte geschockt," *Berliner Zeitung*, March 3, 2009.

THE NEW BARBARISM

226 *"fun carrying out gratuitous violence"*: "U-Bahn-Schläger zu mehrjährigen Haftstrafen verurteilt," *Süddeutsche Zeitung*, December 21, 2011.

227 *On February 11, 2011*: Various Berlin newspapers.

227 *On April 23, 2011*: Julia Jüttner, "U-Bahn-Schläger Torben P.: Hartes Urteil, milde Strafe," *Spiegel-Online*, September 19, 2011.

227 *Early on the morning of September 17, 2011*: Kerstin Gehrke, "U-Bahn-schläger streitet Hetzjagd ab," *Der Tagesspiegel*, February 21, 2012.

228 *In the early morning hours of Sunday, October 14, 2012*: Sabine Rennefanz, "Gewalt in Berlin: Wem gehört Jonny K.?," *Berliner Zeitung*, November 18, 2012; and various Berlin newspapers.

229 *"The reason for these acts"*: Kirsten Heisig, *Das Ende der Geduld: Konsequent gegen jugendliche Gewalttäter* (Freiburg: Herder, 2010), 26.

TURKS IN BERLIN

235 *"I still remember November 11, 1992, perfectly"*: Necla Kelek, *Chaos der Kulturen: Die Debatte um Islam und Integration* (Cologne: Kiepenheuer und Witsch, 2012), 216.

235 *"But who is 'the people'?"*: Ibid., 217.

235 *"They were the people who were free now"*: Ibid., 234.

238 *from then on, she was no longer allowed*: Necla Kelek, *Die fremde Braut: Ein Bericht aus dem Inneren des türkischen Lebens in Deutschland* (Cologne: Kiepenheuer und Witsch, 2005).

YES, YOU CAN: THE RÜTLI SCHOOL

263 *Headlines like* VOM SCHIMPFWORT ZUR MARKE: Mechthild Küpper, "Berliner Rütli-Schule: Vom Schimpfwort zur Marke," *Frankfurter Allgemeine Zeitung*, September 2, 2008.

HELP, THE SWABIANS ARE COMING!

267 *and of the New Forum*: The New Forum was an alliance involved in the East German citizens' movement. A proclamation titled "Die Zeit ist reif—Aufbruch 89" (The Time Is Ripe—New Start '89) paved the way for the group's founding on September 19, 1989. Initially signed by thirty individuals, by the end of 1989 it had garnered the signatures of hundreds of thousands of East German citizens. After reunification, part of the New Forum joined the Green Party as Alliance 90, while other members affiliated themselves with the SPD and the CDU.

269 *"Not wanting / the deaths of others"*: Jörg Kuhn und Fiona Laudamus (eds.), *Der jüdische Friedhof Schönhauser Allee, Berlin: Ein Rundgang zu ausgewählten Grabstätten* (Berlin: Jüdische Gemeinde zu Berlin, 2011), 14.

271 *"They come here because everything's so colorful"*: Wolfgang Thierse quoted in "'Schrippen—nicht Wecken': SPD-Abgeordneter Thierse kritisiert Schwaben in Berlin," *Focus Online*, December 30, 2012.

A BELATED CEMETERY VISIT

277 *Take, for example, the neobaroque tomb*: The information about the graves and those buried there is taken from Jörg Kuhn und Fiona Laudamus (eds.), *Der jüdische Friedhof Schönhauser Allee, Berlin: Ein Rundgang zu ausgewählten Grabstätten* (Berlin: Jüdische Gemeinde zu Berlin, 2011).

THE MAN WHO GAVE NEFERTITI AWAY

281 *A few isolated historians and connoisseurs*: Cella-Margarethe Girardet, "James Simon, 1851–1932: Größter Mäzen der Berliner Museen," in *Jahrbuch Preußischer Kulturbesitz*, vol. 19 (Berlin: Gebr. Mann, 1982); Olaf Matthes, *James Simon: Mäzen im Wilhelminischen Zeitalter* (Berlin: Bostelmann und Siebenhaar, 2000); Bernd Schultz (ed.), *James Simon: Philanthrop und Kunstmäzen / Philanthropist and Patron of the Arts* (Munich/London/New York: Prestel, 2006).

283 *With the kaiser's blessing, James Simon*: Olaf Matthes, *James Simon: Die Kunst des sinnvollen Gebens* (Berlin: Hentrich und Hentrich, 2011), 72.

284 *To mention only Simon's contribution*: Michael Zajonz, "Mäzen James Simon: Ein selbstloser Wohltater," *Der Tagesspiegel*, December 2, 2012.

286 *"She was 96.5—or 97.5—percent Jewish"*: David Dambitsch, "'Aus jüdischer Tradition gehandelt': Der Kunstmäzen James Simon und seine Nachfahren," *Schalom: Jüdisches Leben heute* (radio program), Deutschlandfunk, May 31, 2013.

287 *"complete and accurate lists"*: Julia Emmrich, "Neue Argumente im Streit um die Büste der Königin Nofretete," *Westdeutsche Allgemeine Zeitung*, November 24, 2012.

289 *"to generously give the Egyptians back"*: Marco Evers and Ulrike Knöfel, "Wir verschweigen nichts," *Spiegel* 49, 2012: 133.

289 *"the era of dividing the finds"*: Bernhard Schulz, "100 Jahre Entdeckung der Nofretete: 'Die bunte Königin,'" *Der Tagesspiegel*, December 3, 2012.

292 *Shortly before his death in 1997*: Kurt Buchholz, "Die Bunte, die da lag," *Berliner Zeitung*, August 6, 2005.

JEWISH LIFE IN BERLIN

295 *"Apart from the 131 biographical albums"*: "Wir waren Nachbarn: Biografien jüdischer Zeitzeugen," exhibition brochure (English edition), Berlin-Schöneberg town hall.

296 *One of the most successful examples*: Henning Tilp, "Orte des Erinnerns im Bayerischen Viertel, Berlin und Bus Stop—The Non-Monument, Projekt für das Denkmal für die ermordeten Juden Europas, Berlin von Renata Stih und Frieder Schnock" (contribution to an online project initiated by Dieter Daniels and Inga Schwede as part of their course "Mahnmale in Berlin" at the Hochschule für Grafik und Buchkunst Leipzig, 2004, available at www.hgb-leipzig.de/mahnmal/sischno.html).

298 *"Jewish Nobel Prize winners rank"*: Henryk M. Broder, "Wer ein Menschenleben rettet, rettet die Welt," *Der Tagesspiegel*, August 22, 1997, reprinted in *Das Holocaust-Mahnmal: Dokumentation einer Debatte*, edited by Michael S. Cullen (Zurich: Pendo, 1999), 167.

300 *"The place isn't suited for state ceremonies"*: Claus Leggewie and Erik Meyer, *"Ein Ort, an den man gerne geht": Das Holocaust-Mahnmal und die deutsche Geschichtspolitik nach 1989* (Munich: Hanser, 2005), 309.

301 *According to data from the Central Council of Jews*: The Central Council of Jews in Germany, "Twenty Years of Jewish Immigration to Germany," press release, September 22, 2009, available at www.zentralratdjuden.de /en/article/2693.twenty-years-of-jewish-immigration-to-germany.html.

303 *Violence broke out at a meeting*: Claudia Keller, "Wüster Tumult in Berlin: Schlägerei im Parlament der Jüdischen Gemeinde," *Der Tagesspiegel*, May 24, 2013.

303 *"assimilated Jews from genteel Charlottenburg"*: Claudia Keller, "Nach der Schlägerei in Berlin: Tiefe Konflikte in der Jüdischen Gemeinde," *Der Tagesspiegel*, May 24, 2013.

305 *"I had my cheekbone broken"*: "Rabbiner Alter: 'Berlin bleibt eine tolerante Stadt,'" *Die Welt*, September 2, 2012.

305 *"I came here [to Budapest] to speak"*: Yair Lapid quoted in "Yair Lapid's Short-term Memory," *Haaretz*, October 3, 2013.

306 *"Rather than denouncing those who choose to leave"*: Ibid.

306 *"I didn't leave Israel because of the three shekels"*: Lish Lee Avner, "Israeliness Alive in Berlin," ynetnews.com, October 17, 2013, available at www .ynetnews.com/articles/0,7340,L-4441984,00.html.

306 *"Shouldn't we support the desire"*: Ibid.

SPRING IN BERLIN

310 *In response to the question*: "Die Zahl der Tauben in Berlin ist drastisch gesunken," *Der Tagesspiegel*, October 22, 2012.

310 *The city's information technology sector*: Moritz Döbler, "IHK-Präsident Eric Schweitzer: 'Arm und sexy – das ist vorbei,'" *Der Tagesspiegel*, September 16, 2012.

311 *The anticipated growth at the other end*: Anja Kühne et al., "Die Zukunft der Hauptstadt: Berlins Agenda 2030," *Der Tagesspiegel*, December 30, 2012.

314 *In 2000, the authorities in Berlin estimated*: "Die Zahl der Tauben in Berlin ist drastisch gesunken."

314 *Apparently Berlin's hawks*: Sebastian Leber, "Tauben in der Stadt: Sie wollen nur turteln," *Der Tagesspiegel*, May 27, 2012.

315 *"What begins as the center of the capital"*: Peter von Becker, "Denkmalschutz in Berlin: Schrecken statt Schönheit," *Der Tagesspiegel*, August 14, 2013.

315 *"Berliners," she casually remarked*: Anneliese Bödecker quoted in Carmen Schucker, "Fernes Heimweh—Heimliches Fernweh: 20 Gründe (zurück) nach Berlin zu ziehen," *Der Tagesspiegel*, February 7, 2013.

ACKNOWLEDGMENTS

I would like to thank everyone who helped me write this book by providing inspiration, information, and corrections. They include, in the order in which they appear in these pages: Renzo Piano, Volker Hassemer, Manfred Gentz, Inka Bach, Wilhelm von Boddien, Wolfgang Thierse, Danka and Anatol Gotfryd, Hans Stimmann, Christoph Klenzendorf, Claus Jürgen Pfeiffer, Roland Jahn, Anetta Kahane, Necla Kelek, Heinz Buschkowsky, Siegfried Arnz, Carola Wedcl, Katharina Kaiser, and Cilly Kugelmann.

I'm grateful to my children, Lena and Marek, for giving me insight into the city from the point of view of twentysomethings. I owe Christa Schmidt a favor for spending several nights partying till all hours with me in Berlin's clubs. I also owe Christine Becker one for joining me on a long walk to conquer Museum Island—deserted due to the onset of winter—and Sabine Damm for enriching my observations with her own during a mutual visit to Tempelhof Airport.

My thanks go to my agent, Steve Wasserman, and my editor, Jonathan Galassi, for encouraging me to write this book, and to Ike Williams for carrying forward Steve Wasserman's efforts. I'm grateful to Miranda Popkey for her tireless interjections, endearingly detailed requests for clarification, and meticulous review of the manuscript, and to Will Hammond for his valuable stylistic suggestions. My greatest thanks go to Sophie Schlondorff, who not only transposed my text with wit and rigor but also improved it with her suggestions and research.

Finally, I'd like to thank the residents of Berlin for always being there and for being who they are. They served as my models, bringing my views, prejudices, and love of the city up to date—without being asked and without so much as saying a word to me.

He just wanted a decent book to read ...

Not too much to ask, is it? It was in 1935 when Allen Lane, Managing Director of Bodley Head Publishers, stood on a platform at Exeter railway station looking for something good to read on his journey back to London. His choice was limited to popular magazines and poor-quality paperbacks – the same choice faced every day by the vast majority of readers, few of whom could afford hardbacks. Lane's disappointment and subsequent anger at the range of books generally available led him to found a company – and change the world.

'We believed in the existence in this country of a vast reading public for intelligent books at a low price, and staked everything on it'
Sir Allen Lane, 1902–1970, founder of Penguin Books

The quality paperback had arrived – and not just in bookshops. Lane was adamant that his Penguins should appear in chain stores and tobacconists, and should cost no more than a packet of cigarettes.

Reading habits (and cigarette prices) have changed since 1935, but Penguin still believes in publishing the best books for everybody to enjoy. We still believe that good design costs no more than bad design, and we still believe that quality books published passionately and responsibly make the world a better place.

So wherever you see the little bird – whether it's on a piece of prize-winning literary fiction or a celebrity autobiography, political tour de force or historical masterpiece, a serial-killer thriller, reference book, ...ld classic or a piece of pure escapism – you can bet that it represents the very best that the genre has to offer.

...... **you like to read – trust Penguin.**